Barbara Müller

The Balkan Peace Team 1994-2001

Non-violent Intervention in Crisis Areas
with the Deployment of Volunteer Teams

Translated by

Dr. Paul Foster

Barbara Müller

THE BALKAN PEACE TEAM
1994-2001

Non-violent Intervention in Crisis Areas
with the Deployment of Volunteer Teams

ibidem-Verlag
Stuttgart

Bibliografische Information Der Deutschen Bibliothek
Die Deutsche Bibliothek verzeichnet diese Publikation in der Deutschen Nationalbibliografie; detaillierte bibliografische Daten sind im Internet über <http://dnb.ddb.de> abrufbar.

A CIP catalogue record for this book is available from:
Die Deutsche Bibliothek
http://dnb.ddb.de

All rights reserved. No part of this publication may be reproduced, stored in or introduced into a retrieval system, or transmitted, in any form, or by any means (electronical, mechanical, photocopying, recording or otherwise) without the prior written permission of the publisher. Any person who does any unauthorized act in relation to this publication may be liable to criminal prosecution and civil claims for damages.

∞

Gedruckt auf alterungsbeständigem, säurefreien Papier
Printed on acid-free paper

ISBN: 3-89821-615-2
© *ibidem*-Verlag
Stuttgart 2006
Alle Rechte vorbehalten

Das Werk einschließlich aller seiner Teile ist urheberrechtlich geschützt. Jede Verwertung außerhalb der engen Grenzen des Urheberrechtsgesetzes ist ohne Zustimmung des Verlages unzulässig und strafbar. Dies gilt insbesondere für Vervielfältigungen, Übersetzungen, Mikroverfilmungen und elektronische Speicherformen sowie die Einspeicherung und Verarbeitung in elektronischen Systemen.

Table of Contents

Introduction 7

Chapter 1 War in Yugoslavia: "Something must be done!" 11

(1) How the Balkan Peace Team came into Being: From the Idea
to the Plan 11

(2) From Plan to Performance: The Balkan Peace Team 24

Chapter 2 The 'Otvorene Oci' Teams: With "eyes open" in Croatia 35

(1) Team Start and the First Year 35

(2) Presence at Violent Evictions in Croatia, 1994/5 48

(3) Human Rights Monitoring after Military Attacks, Western
Slavonia and Krajina, 1995 60

(4) Encouraging and Networking with Local Activists Following
Military Attack: Croatia, 1995 75

(5) International Alert: Conscientious Objector is Assaulted:
Croatia, 1996 89

(6) Reporting Uncomfortable Truths about Refugees' Return:
Krajina, 1997/8 95

(7) A "dignified departure": The Process of Leaving Croatia 107

Chapter 3 "Balkan Peace Team FRY" in Serbia and in Kosovo 113

(1) A Start with Obstacles. The Long Process to Develop an Ef
fective Team in Kosovo and Serbia (1994-1996) 113

(2) Building Bridges: Dialogue projects (1997) 133

(3) Solidarity, Support and a Channel for Information: The
Team's Role during the Escalation of Violent Conflict until the
beginning of the War (1998-9) 146

(4) Are There Still Points of Connection? The Transition from
BPT-FRY to the Youth Centre in Dragash 163

(5) The End of the BPT: Passing the Legacy on to Équipes de
paix dans les Balkans 175

Chapter 4 Interaction in the Balkan Peace Team 191

(1) Lack of Money restricts Initiative: Fund-raising in the Balkan Peace Team 191

(2) Leadership and Orientation: Who will determine the Direction of the Balkan Peace Team? 201

(3) How is Co-operation Organised? Co-ordination and Task-sharing 213

(4) All About Volunteers 224

Chapter 5 The Balance of the Balkan Peace Team and Lessons Learned 239

(1) Looking Back: Decisive Moments in the Life of the Balkan Peace Team 239

(2) The Balkan Peace Team as a Non-violent Project and its Functions as a 'Third Party' 242

(3) The Effects ... Tracking Them Down in Croatia 246

(4) Effects ... Looking for Tracks in Serbian und Kosovo 254

(5) What Has the Balkan Peace Team Brought to Its Participants? 256

(6) How Has the Idea Progressed in the Meantime? 257

Chapter 6 Appendix 273

(1) Abbreviations 273

(2) Sources and Literature 274

Introduction

The Balkan Peace Team - A treasure trove of valuable experience

For seven years, from 1994 to 2001, the Balkan Peace Team employing small teams of volunteers, was active during conflicts taking place in Croatia, Serbia and Kosovo. It pursued new methods in order to respond to the pressing challenge: "Something must be done!"

Accordingly, up to thirteen peace organisations from western Europe and the USA formed an unprecedented coalition in order to find volunteers for operations of this kind, to train them and to accompany them during their activities. The project has opened up a way and, moreover, has become an example of how qualified foreigners operating in crisis areas can provide a meaningful contribution to resolving conflicts. than nine active volunteers operating at the same time in Croatia, Serbia and Kosovo. Its effect could always be seen in small matters such as at the evictions in Split in 1995, for example: *"... they were the first activists here in 1994, and when they arrived, this kind of eviction [the particularly brutal kind] came to an end"*, a Human Rights activist notes. Other effects can be found on the conceptual level: *"If reconciliation is going to happen, the work of the Balkan Peace Team must continue and be strengthened."* This was the considered view in 1999 of the "Council for the Defence of Human Rights and Freedoms", Prishtina, Kosovo. However, until this point has been reached, several years passed, years in which the Balkan Peace Team felt very insecure.

Indeed, insecurity is something which accompanies this pioneer project at every turn. There are open questions: What, precisely, can our volunteers actually achieve? Again and again, the dynamics of conflict breaks in upon their endeavours as happened, for example, in 1995 in Croatia and again in 1999 in Kosovo, throwing up new challenges to which there are no certain solutions. Those participating are obliged to measure their commitment by the last objective, namely, to avoid war and violence or to overcome them. This is what drives them, and that which does not allow them to be satisfied with what they actually achieve.

When, in 1999, the long prognosticated war with the Federal Republic of Yugoslavia finally broke out, there was a sense of personal failure, a feeling that no alternative could have been realized. *"We need to continue to work on the possibilities that peace teams offer"*, said one of the initiators of the project. Yes, certainly, the potential inherent in non-violent intervention as far as the Balkan Peace Team is concerned is by no means exhausted, but it is the step from talking to doing. From wanting to do something to actually doing the job, and carrying out a project purposefully, having thought seriously about it beforehand. Just this happens again and again.

This book regards the experiences of the Balkan Peace Team as valuable and desires to bring these inestimable contributions to light. To this end, it seeks to examine motivation, impulse and the structural connections and associations, which come together in this coalition. It follows the teams in their work and describes what lies behind such abstractions as 'Networking', Human Rights Work', 'information channel' or 'dialogue', and what is implied by subtle, sensitive, painstaking, detailed work. High points and low points become clear, uncertainty and certainty.

It also attempts to show how the compulsive escalations of armed conflict provide new options for the teams involved and new tasks for the Balkan Peace Team. The observation of human rights and support for the local peace activists who find themselves constantly under pressure, is tough work for volunteers. No less hard is the task of getting people living in a profoundly divided society to talk to each other. So it is that volunteers are obliged to go through a hard school: "*I think if you manage to survive Otoc or BPT, then you are a very much stronger person*", one volunteer has said.

Quite a number of volunteers remain in the region, and this is an advantage to their partners. One of them, a human rights activist, describes it as follows: "*It's not an end, it's not losing, because a lot of people from BPT are today in this area, because they have accepted these problems, they have understood them and they have entered into them. And at the same time these problems enter into them, into their hearts. And at the same time they know the language, after the period in BPT, after the school of BPT. Yes, it's true. And they are again with us, and we again cooperate with them, although they are a part of other organisations*".

In keeping with its characteristically self-critical manner, the Balkan Peace Team has made all files accessible for this book. This enables the reader to gain certain insights into matters, which are normally withheld. In such cases, for example, experiences that have to do with difficulties come to light. These are to be found at every level: in the insecurity of leadership and strategy and, equally, in the processes of preparing and accompanying the teams. The book shows what progress the Balkan Peace Team has made in developing appropriate standards and procedures and what questions still remain open, questions, which present themselves in connection with other projects, too. While the Balkan Peace Team as a coalition might well be unique, as a project organisation employing volunteers it is certainly nothing unusual.

Lack of money has kept the project within the tightest limits and hampered its natural development. A treasurer comments: *"The reason why we came as far as this on this project is that we would never allow ourselves to be stopped by a lack of material, computers, data, communication or anything else."* The book outlines the attempts to acquire money, the struggle to survive materially, and their consequences. It concludes with an attempt to recognize what has been achieved and also to classify the Balkan Peace Team. Looking ahead, it concerns the work of current initiatives active in further developing non-violent intervention who now see themselves faced with challenges which are very familiar after having acquainted themselves with the history of the Balkan Peace Team

Preliminary Note

Together with Christian Büttner, I investigated the Balkan Peace Team during the years 1997 and 1998. This was made possible by the research association, Peace and Conflict Research (Lower Saxony), supported by the Volkswagen Foundation. Member organisations and the Balkan Peace Team itself have facilitated access to internal documents. We have been able to conduct interviews with many organisers and activists in the region, with organisers of other bodies and with volunteers. This has enabled us to acquire a broad view of the most varied perspectives of the Balkan Peace Team both from within and without.

We have accorded fictitious names to participants in order to maintain the confidentiality promised to them and, wherever possible, to preclude invasion of their private lives. This, with one exception, is also true for individual cases which are cited here as examples. The one exception concerns that of a conscientious objector whose case was published by Amnesty International.

For many of those interviewed, anonymity was not an important issue. Since the organisations are specifically alluded to and those taking part in them already known at the scene, conclusions as to their individual identity can hardly to be avoided.

If nothing is noted to the contrary, then the judgements and evaluations of situations in Croatia, Serbia or Kosovo reflect contemporary views and perspectives as these are expressed in the team reports and discussions within the Balkan Peace Teams.

The views and assessments of other authors are made clear in the text as they appear. They are cited either to describe matters of a higher order or represent external, contemporary views so to compare these with those of the team actually working in the country. Especially during the escalation phase of the conflict in Kosovo, which came to a head in 1998, we will find an interesting counter to those recommendations and evaluations, which maintain what is possible and what not.

In order to avoid a large-scale body of footnotes and commentaries, the relevant documents and literature alluded to in the text are briefly cited at the end of the chapter. A detailed list of references and sources concludes this report.

Responsibility for all kinds of error, misunderstanding and misinterpretation is to be attributed to the author.

Wahlenau, December, 2003 Barbara Müller

Sources

Broken Rifle 2000; BPT June, 1999 Report; Interviews: Frances E. 1998; Raj S. 1997; Sebastian K. 1998; Müller, Büttner, Gleichmann 1999.

Chapter I War in Yugoslavia: "Something must be done!"
(1) How the Balkan Peace Team came into Being: From the Idea to the Plan

The Balkan Peace Team is inextricably bound up with the catastrophe which brought about the violent disintegration of Yugoslavia at the beginning of the 90's. This conflict with its appalling, apparently inexorable escalation, to which the international community reacted with total inadequacy, provided the essential impetus. There were three discernible strands of development which joined together to form the Balkan Peace Team.

The first impetus was the wish to support non-violent resistance in Kosovo which had developed since 1989. The second starting point was the call for non-violent escorts from threatened peace activists who had been working in Croatia since 1991, and the third inner imperative was the need to develop a civil alternative to UN troops and military intervention which had been a point of continued, intensive discussion in Western Europe since 1992. Various organisations respectively made it their job to tackle individual issues. In Kosovo, for example, the War Resisters' International were active, consisting of a worldwide network of anti-militarist groups with their headquarters in London. In 1992, the French organisation, Mouvement pour une Alternative Nonviolente (MAN) which comprised 300 persons organised into 22 groups throughout France, decided to support the non-violent struggle of the Kosovo Albanians after a short visit to Macedonia had provided the first contact.

The Federation for Social Defence in Germany is also showing a keen interest in non-violent alternatives to military intervention at this time. Questions with regard to escorts were directed to the International Peace Brigades, which have their headquarters in London who, in turn, concerned themselves with their organisation. What was finally decisive for the various components coming together were the varied personal interconnections affecting the organisations on the scene. The urgent demands from peace organisations within Yugoslavia not merely to look on at what was taking place, coupled with the intense, insistent reports on a war presented, so to speak, at our doorstep were seen as an obligation on our part to help, and, moreover, as a duty not to be shirked.

The idea that the presence of foreigners could have an effect on the warring parties motivated many people to risky undertakings. Examples of these are aid transports, marches, 'caravans' or delegations, but also the civilian observers of the European

Union and those belonging to the Organisation for Security and Co-operation in Europe – OSCE. Experiences in this area contributed later to considerations as to how things could be better managed. The Balkan Peace Team is the result of deliberations both regarding the conflict itself, and the possibilities of influencing it which were open to those who might be described as working 'from below.' The whole thing is a process which will take years and one which will have to take form within itself as it proceeds.

Escalation of the Conflict: The Beginnings, Kosovo, 1989

The beginnings of the escalation take place in Kosovo when, in February, 1989, a general strike is put down by the army. In March, the autonomy of the province is suspended. This is followed by non-violent resistance, led by the LDK (The Kosovo Democratic League) whose leader is Ibrahim Rugova. The members of the resistance are Kosovo Albanians who pursue a strategy of non-co-operation in that they contest the legitimacy of Yugoslavian institutions, boycott elections and set up their own parallel concept of state independence. Under the weight of continued repression, they independently organize a revised education and health system. The second arrow to their bow is to internationalise the conflict in the fervid hope that the USA will intervene to their advantage.

1990: The Disintegration of Yugoslavia is Inevitable

By 1990, the insistence on the part of individual republics to disassociate themselves from the union of Yugoslavia is quite clear. It seems less and less likely that the state can deal effectively with its difficult situation using the political means at its disposal. A plebiscite carried out in Slovenia underlines the seriousness of these efforts to detach themselves from the federation. However, despite this, the international community clings to the concept of Yugoslavia's unity. Croatia, too, clamours for independence, while Serbian nationalists in the country who are also aware of what is going on are for another solution. They want to see a union of their settlements with other Serbian areas, which would mean a further partitioning of the country.

In July 1990, a 'Serbian National Council' is founded in Knin, the capital of Krajina which is mainly inhabited by Serbs. An opinion poll is organized and circulated throughout the region, the result of which is that a majority is for autonomy in the area. This is a public affront to the authorities in Zagreb who are eager to establish their own state of Croatia.

All this takes place for the most part unnoticed by world opinion. In August 1990, Iraq occupies Kuwait. The attention of the international community as well as that of many activists for peace is directed to this area of the world for at least a year. Six years after this event, a young social scientist, MARIE-JANINE CALIC sums up the matter by saying: *"When in 1991 the Yugoslavian federation finally collapsed, political attention was still riveted on the consequences of the Gulf War...that one of the greatest diplomatic crises since 1945 could arise from the inner turmoil of Yugoslavia was something that hardly anyone could have seriously considered possible."*

In December, 1990, a congress assembled in Cologne to consider the theme of 'Europe without Armies'. At this assembly, Slovenia was cited as an example of a country where its independence was sought with peaceful means. What could organisations like the Association for Social Defence do which propagates the concept of non-violent defence against military aggression? At this conference contact was established between the Association for Social Defence and the Centre for a Culture of Peace and Non-violence in Ljubljana during which a plan for the peaceful defence of Slovenia was developed with feverish intensity. The War Resisters' International in London received the first enquiries from Kosovo about international observers in this year.

1991: New Frontiers Secured with Violence

Kuwait is liberated by armed force in February 1991. The war in the Gulf is a controversial issue. The opponents of war try to avoid the last escalation using dramatic methods. Some of them volunteer to proceed to Baghdad and there present themselves as living shields, and others want to form themselves into human barriers in the desert against advancing tanks. Gandhi's idea of the 'living wall' consisting of trained volunteers setting up deliberate resistance to brute force had been revived.

New challenges are presented to the peace movements in Western Europe, challenges which first have to be inwardly processed. During the Cold War at a time when millions of people were actively engaged in halting nuclear re-armament by steadfastly working in groups and organisations committed to peace, they were primarily concerned with their own safety, and with their personal survival. Now this threat has passed, other issues have pushed their way into the foreground. What is the attitude one should take with regard to conflicts in other societies and world regions? And what is our attitude in general to war and violence as a means of resolving conflicts? After the war in the Gulf came to an end in the spring of 1991, little by little the crisis in Yugoslavia gains more and more significance as a European trouble spot.

The first armed conflicts in Croatia at the beginning of 1991 create an atmosphere where *"fear is the dominant feeling. Self-organisation signifies, in most cases, militarisation, social mobilization, and the recruitment of males with guns. Thousands of small arms have been recently imported into the country. Everything is in place for a long conflict."* So writes MARKO HREN, social scientist and activist at Ljubljana's centre in April. After that, things follow thick and fast.

By the end of June 1991, Croatia and Slovenia have each decided for independence from Yugoslavia. The erection of frontiers in Slovenia provokes the Yugoslavian federal army to take action, which then exchanges fire with the newly recruited militia and also deploys its air force. The European Community sets up a negotiating committee, which in turn sets up a resolution to at least halt violence in the country.

When contacts had been established in the previous winter, a delegation formed by the Association for Social Defence departed for Ljubljana on 16th July, 1991. Once there, they were confronted with an extremely tense situation. *"The Centre for the Culture of Peace and Non-violence in Ljubljana requests support from the peace movement"*, the delegation reported.

Slovenia just manages to avoid catastrophe. While the Serbs can do without Slovenia, the other areas settled by Serbs in Croatia are important to Belgrade. The weekend of the 20th July is to be a 'Revolt for Peace' to which groups from all over Yugoslavia are called to be present in Sarajevo. Throughout the country, peace groups come together. However, the escalation of violence is quicker. Croatian and Serbian militia arm themselves and within Croatia itself the tendency to violent conflict now intensifies. The division of the country follows ethnic borders. For the first time, thousands of Serbs flee their villages in Croatia.

The Triennial of the War Resisters' International in 1991

Only a few days later, at the end of July 1991, a conference took place in Belgium at another place. The War Resisters' International gathers together every three years at a large conference, and on this occasion met at Namur in Belgium. The national groups of this worldwide organisation assembling at the conference concern themselves with the theme 'Peace on the Move'. The conflict in Yugoslavia is a new phenomenon for them at that moment. How are the 'ethnic' conflicts there arising within a crumbling block system to be understood? On Tuesday, 30th July, hardly a month after war had shattered Slovenia, Marko Hren, who is also on the executive committee of the War Resisters' International, reports on the situation in Yugoslavia to the whole assembly. In an accompanying essay, entitled Essay on Borders, he confronts idealists and activists as a whole who, for their part reject borders in general, with the question of how one can change borders. Is one at all at liberty to ask such a question or should one rather dismiss such an idea and talk about principles instead?

The War Resisters' International accepts the challenge. *"WRI was really willing to prioritise Yugoslavia,"* notes the secretary of the organisation at the time, looking back on this event. A theoretical concern with new conflicts and non-violent strategies is one thing, whereas actually managing them is quite another. And this is only possible when there are people in the affected country who wish to deal with conflict without using violence. To find such people, to understand their motives, to support them, to figure out solutions with them and in this way to activate the potential and knowledge of a worldwide network – that is what is meant by the practice of War Resisters' International.

"I think the subgroup on Yugoslavia that met outside the bounds of any schedule was extremely important. It actually was an important body of people in terms of later work."- this the reflection of a former WRI – secretary, Daniel M., and speaks of how many people were involved. Apart from Marko Hren, there are others from other organisations, notably Sabine M. of Germany who at this moment is working for the Association of Social Defence and who is also on the executive committee of the War Resisters' International along with Eugene D., who is the secretary of the International Fellowship of Reconciliation in Alkmaar, Netherlands.

An Appeal for Support

Marko Hren made use of the meeting in Namur to call for support for the newly formed peace groups in Yugoslavia. He offers the centre in Ljubljana as a meeting place and for making contacts. He says: *"Don't ask what is needed in Yugoslavia, because the answer will be - everything, since there are all kinds of problems, and they vary from village to village."*

This and other appeals did not fall on deaf ears, even when the war cannot be halted. The question of 'What can we do?' concerned the peace groups of many countries in Europe from that moment on. The history of civil commitment in this conflict remains to be written, but it is important because it is the history of mutually experienced solidarity. At the same time, it runs precisely counter to the idea of a barricaded fortress of Europe, against increasing hate for foreigners and the sealing off of national frontiers against refugees. The amount of activities cannot be assessed. If we were to really understand the European context even in part, then we would have add groups and organisations from France, Great Britain, Austria, Switzerland, Italy, Scandinavia and those belonging to the Low Countries to the list. The few described here represent the many, which have played a role in former Yugoslavia since 1991.

Training and 'Mr. e-Mail': The Communications- and Empowerment Approach of the Association for Social Defence 1991

The Federation for Social Defence has undertaken the work of training in Croatia since the summer of 1991: *"Conflict trainer from Minden soon to be working in Yugoslavia"*, the local newspaper reported. In Zagreb there is contact with the newly founded anti-war campaign whose newspaper is also to be financed and in the course of setting up an office there is also to be fitted with technical apparatus. In Germany, the Federation collects donations for the maintenance of the centre's office in Ljubljana. *"The centre in Ljubljana is urgently dependent on financial support. The telephone bill for July alone accounts for more than DM 2000."*

At the end of 1991, Oskar K., the Federation's trainer, travelled down to Yugoslavia on a special mission. There, he installed modems at the peace centres in Zagreb, Ljubljana and Belgrade, which then, via mailboxes, enabled them to communicate abroad. This is why he is referred to as 'Mr. E-Mail'. He set up independent communication possibilities for the activists working there by making use of the electronic media which were just coming into operation at the time. Meanwhile, the conflict continued to escalate.

In the autumn of the same year, the first reports of tension between various ethnic groups in Bosnia come in. However, for the moment, Croatia has remained the main theatre of conflict, a conflict which, in the meantime, had taken on military characteristics. During these spells of tension, the civilian population found itself crushed between two fronts. Ethnic 'cleansing' is not a by-product in this war, but a systematic strategy. In November, the east Slavonian town of Vukovar is conquered after a siege lasting several months. Seventy thousand Croatians flee.

The War Year of 1992

In January 1992, the armed conflict between Croatia and the rest of Yugoslavia can be stopped. After many abortive attempts on the part of negotiators from the international community to mediate between the warring parties, the fourteenth cease-fire is maintained. The so-called 'Vance Plan' places the controversial areas in Croatia under the protection of the United Nations' forces. More than 10,000 UN troops are employed in preventing further bloodshed along the crumbling demarcation lines. Croatia and Slovenia are recognized by the European Union as independent states, but almost a third of the Croatian state territory is not controlled by the central government in Zagreb. This is the interim result of military conflict. Just how the relationship between Serbs and Croatians in Croatia will develop is now one of the greatest challenges facing peace groups in Croatia.

After the beginning of April when the European Union had recognized Bosnia as an independent state, and the 'Serbian Democratic Party' (in Bosnia) had called a Serbian republic, that of Bosnia-Herzegovina into being, hostilities began. Armed conflict continues and these cast a shadow over the peace negotiations, which have been renewed in May. While all the warring parties are made responsible for this escalation, it is felt above all that Serbia is primarily at fault for this. The European Union and the UN Security Council together decide to levy sanctions, and EU observers and the UNO representative in Sarajevo leave Bosnia. Thereafter, heavy fighting breaks out, and the town of Sarajevo is the target of more and more intensive artillery fire, and shells are responsible for the first massacre among the civilian population.

In June, discussions arise for the first time between the Western European Union and NATO as to whether Serbian positions should be attacked by air. The European Union, too, threatens military action in order to secure a corridor for aid to Sarajevo. At the same time, there are mass demonstrations in Belgrade against the war and against Milosevic. In August, Bosnian refugees speak of Serbian concentration camps and torture. The Serbs for their part make serious accusations against Moslems to the effect that these had murdered 6000 Serbs. In October, Bosnian-Serbian troops take the town of Jajce. Thousands flee to the mountains. The first reports of systematic rapes are reported. At the beginning of December, Sarajevo is completely cut off.

In the attempts made by the international community to get to grips with the Yugoslavian crisis, many actors appear at various times with various mandates, but what is lacking is general agreement about how to tackle the problem in a concerted way. There is a mutual wish to end the violence in Yugoslavia. While, on the one hand, this is broadly proclaimed rhetorically, on the other it turns out to be, a matter which is only half-heartedly put into practice, and even when this is the case, it is anyway quite out of step with the dynamics of what is actually taking place. After the east-west confrontation, this new challenge finds precisely these European states unprepared.

The Debate on Humanitarian Intervention

In a situation where there are no simple answers at hand, violence at least appears to be a simple solution. The longer a war lasts and the more devastating the self-induced paralysis of the international community becomes, the more vehement the debate on military intervention. Peace groups working in the war areas demand this, too. A rift opens up. 'No to intervention in Bosnia-Herzegovina' say the War Resisters' International and the International Fellowship of Reconciliation in an open letter in June, 1992, to the anti-war groups in Yugoslavia. The peace group in Sarajevo in July 1992, contradicts this by saying that only military intervention can secure survival, and that now there is no intention of entering into a discussion about alternatives. In Western Europe, the feeling that something really must be done becomes more and more imperative. There is the growing conviction that military options should be abandoned, and that alternatives to military solutions must also be given room for consideration.

In the autumn of 1992, the Federation for Social Defence invited attendance at its conference entitled 'Crisis Intervention: Olive, Blue or Non-Violent'. From the title it is already clear that the question of 'whether' there shall be intervention or not is no longer a matter for debate. The experiences of observer missions in former Yugoslavia are reflected upon, and not only these, but also those of Peace Brigades International active in other continents. In talks taking place outside the conference itself there was a general consensus of opinion among members of the Federation that, *"we should go ahead ourselves and tackle the job of setting up a non-violent alternative to the UN forces."*

Peace activists are already on the way to war zones. The French organisation, Equilibre, for example, regularly travels to Yugoslavia in convoys, bringing humanitarian aid and it also tries to rescue children from acute situations by housing them with families in France. In Verona, in September, 1992, the 'Forum for Peace and Reconciliation' is founded which, as a permanent forum recruited from the civil society, will work out suggestions for a settlement of the conflict. A peace march to Sarajevo is to demonstrate solidarity with those under siege, and provide practical assistance for them. The Italian organisation, 'Beati i costruttori di Pace', organizes this initiative which meets with great enthusiasm in Italy especially.

As the ring around Sarajevo tightens in December, activists are able to enter the beleaguered city. *"Around 500 pacifists from Europe have been able to come to this capital under siege at the weekend. As the Federation for Social Defence reported on Monday in Minden, the group received a friendly and, to some extent, an enthusiastic welcome,"* the newspaper Frankfurter Rundschau reported in an article of 15th December, 1992, and spoke of a successful action. However, there is some doubt among the activists, who ask whether, where there is such a large number of people, these can't be active in more than a merely symbolic way. Kosovo again comes to mind. At the end of 1992, at an international conference, the Ljubljana Peace Institute concerns itself with the 'Albanian Question' and demands that the UNO intervene in time and in this case not with weapons, but by diplomatic means.

Intervening in Kosovo in time: The Preventive Approach of the War Resisters' International

At the beginning of 1992 at a meeting of the War Resisters' International, deliberations were made about holding a seminar in Kosovo which could support the Albanians in their non-violent struggle. To this end, international experts and consultants in social defence should come together with local resistance leaders to work out a strategy of non-violence. Even at the planning stage, there was talk about possible steps to be taken later such as sending observers into the region. However, this was later considered as too big a job for the current resources of the War Resisters International. Could the Peace Brigades International, which had had experience in this field help out here? The War Resisters' International, among other matters, spent the whole of 1992 on preparing this seminar. Notwithstanding, the security situation in Kosovo is still critical. The seminar has twice to be postponed and finally does not materialize at all.

Protective Escorts on Demand – the Hallmark of Peace Brigades International

The Peace Brigades International had already developed their concept in the crisis areas of Latin America in the 80's and, as unarmed escorts, they accompany threatened persons or are in attendance on the premises of threatened organisations.

The idea of deterrence is based on a simple if somewhat risky calculation. Peace Brigades International make sure that their presence in the host country is known to people enjoying high standing in that country, in the higher ranks of military personnel, for example, the police and political circles and even in the embassies of influential countries upon whose goodwill the host country is dependent. In Latin America, for example, this is the USA in particular. Infringement of human rights, for example, is most certainly a consideration that can tip the scales when it comes to decisions about military aid for certain countries. As long as the top level in political and military circles wish to avoid being exposed for the infringement of human rights, then such unarmed escorts provide real protection.

On the other hand, should the elimination of undesirable opposition elements be worthwhile, despite the loss of status and financial support, then the whole thing becomes a little hazardous. It becomes a particularly delicate issue, for example, when there is no certainty as to whether the gangs of killers who carry out the dirty work actually know about the tenuous immunity of unarmed escorts. The conditions for success of the peace brigades present an intricate analysis, a sophisticated information structure and an alarm system which functions very quickly. A host country dependent on goodwill from outside and on a functional system which relays orders both in the political and military sectors right up to the murderers themselves is one of the conditions for their effectiveness. Basis organisations in the host country can rely on these structures to widen their scope for action and strengthen their infrastructure.

It is small wonder, then, that the example of the Peace Brigades is an inspiration. At its London office there are many requests for escorts and accompanying protection of the Peace Brigades International. By the end of November, 1992, the point has been reached whereby one needs to know what possibilities there are for the members of the Peace Centre in Ossijek in Croatia to be protected from murderous attack, and to this end an investigation is organized to ascertain this. In December, 1992 and January, 1993, those commissioned to find out these facts are of the opinion that escort protection is no longer necessary.

1993: Methods and Means coalesce

In January, 1993, the executive committee of the International Fellowship of Reconciliation with its seat in Alkmaar, Netherlands runs through its scenario: the United Nations Organisation sends 10,000 troops to Kosovo; how do we react? The idea in the heads of those attending is that of an unarmed presence of foreigners. US Americans organized such a thing in the 80's on the borders of Nicaragua at a time when a US invasion of that country was feared. Here, too, the basic idea is that, *"typically, where there is the voluntary presence of outsiders, this will lead to a decline in violence."*

At the end of January, 1993, a co-ordination committee of the Peace Initiative for Ex-Yugoslavia met in Germany, and here, too, its immediate concern was not with the war going on in Bosnia: *"In view of the current situation which could make an extension of the war in Kosovo possible at any time, we feel that it is sensible to try to assemble all the ideas we have at hand to see what can be done to prevent such an escalation."* One of these ideas was the non-violent alternative to UN troops. Basically, this is the concept of the Balkan Peace Team which, during these talks, was being sounded out.

In February, 1993, Daniel M. for the War Resisters' International and Sabine M. for the Federation for Social Defence and the War Resisters' International drive to Kosovo to hold talks on the spot about what should be done next. During these, the idea is put forward of a possible continued presence there of international volunteers. Of the many impressions which they gain, one is dominant: the presence of foreigners seems to have the effect of checking the ever more brutal assaults of the police. In their debates, they ask: when the Kosovo-Albanian Committee for Human Rights drives into the villages in order to mitigate the harshness of the situation – is that not just the kind of work in which international volunteers can be supportive?

Like stone falling into water, this idea widens out to produce interest among more and more circles. It was introduced to the International Conference on Strategy for

Ex-Yugoslavia, which then organized the International Fellowship of Reconciliation. At the end of March in the same year, twenty-one organisations gather in Basle, Switzerland. Half of them are national branch organisations of the Fellowship of Reconciliation, and the other half consists of Christian and secular peace groups from the Netherlands, Germany, Switzerland, Croatia, Great Britain, Spain and Sweden. This exchange enables participants to express the incredible pressure which activists everywhere can sense. Oskar K. supplied the details on this occasion: *"One Kosovo Intervention Idea is to have 10-100 observers in different cities to bring out what they observe in order to build up public pressure. It will take a lot of energy."* The idea finds a positive echo among those assembled. Can tenable concepts be developed and turned into practical effect at last?

At the same time, the Anti-War Campaign from Zagreb and activists in Kosovo again request the presence of the Peace Brigade International. The circles close. Kosovo stands at the centre as an international presence and as the idea of prevention.

After a further two days of intensive work on formulation, Sabine M. has completed her project proposal on 'Non-violent Intervention in the Conflicts of former Yugoslavia: Sending teams of international volunteers' ready. What is the idea? Voluntary observers, first ten and then growing to a hundred, are to be present at various towns in Kosovo at events, in private schools and also in the offices of Albanian organisations. Their presence indicates a public body, since they are equipped with telephones, fax machines and vehicles, and can document possible infringements and publicize them. Where possible they are to mediate in conflict situations and supply threatened persons with unarmed escorts.

The plan, then, is a mixture of the Peace Brigade's idea of escorts, of experience gained from the presence of international volunteers in crisis areas, of dealing with conflict, of Human Rights and publicity work. It is also the result of experiences with symbolic operations against war from which it desires to disassociate itself. Looking back, Daniel M. describes the reasons, which speak for Kosovo and the chances available on the side of non-violent resistance for those committing themselves to the project: *"We saw as well that this was a classic case of there being a non-violent struggle appealing for international support. A key strategy of theirs was to internationalise their situation. And we, we needed to do what we could to help to speak with the voice of non-violence as well. I mean you don't want to be forever chasing a situation when it's too late and for once we seemed to be there in good time."* He also

stresses another aspect. *"When I first went to Kosovo in December 91, I managed to meet so many people in leading positions in the resistance, it was very short- and the next summer when we met Demaci in New York, in August, that got reported in the only paper the Albanians had at that time. You know people would say, we remember reading about that'. And so we were a much bigger deal in this relatively cut -off place that was just being ignored. And so it seemed more useful to us to apply our energies there than in Bosnia where we didn't have actual counterparts."*
However, things were going to turn out differently. The way to Kosovo was to become a detour.

Sources

Ages 1993; BSV 1991, 4; BPT 1.4.93; BSV, invitation 8.1.93; Bulletin 1992 No. 15, 2f.; Calic 1996, 1, 2, 90, 219, 157-185; Calic 1998, 2; Frankfurter Rundschau 15.12.92, 2; Der trügerische Frieden 1997, 84f.; friedenszeitung 1992, 10; Giersch 1998; IFOR, SC - Minutes 1993, 8-10, 18; Interviews Daniel M. 2/1998; Jens K. 1998; Hren, Yugoslavia, 1991, borders, 1991, Peace, 1991; Large 1997, 67; Mahony 1997,84-87, 93-99; Malmsten, 1993; Meder/ Reimann 1996, 3-6; Mindener Tageblatt, 18.9.1991; Information Sabine M. 5.1.03, Information Peter D. 22.4.97; PBI 28.11.92, 3; 5.12.94, 1; Peace News, August 92; Press releases of the Federation for Social Defence, Minden, 17.7.91, Ljubljana 19.7.91, 21.7.91, 27.9.1991, 6.92; Rußmann 1992; Schmitz 1998; Schweitzer 1991, 2. The Centre for the Culture of Peace in Ljubljana will be dissolved at the end of 1992 or the beginning of 1993. The research centre belonging to it will remain; Schweitzer 1996, 42f.; Preparation papers WRI Triennial 1991. Introduction to (some of) the Theme Groups; WRI 1993, 5; WRI Execmins 033, 7,5; 032, 3; 029, 8.

(2) From Plan to Performance: The Balkan Peace Team

From the time the first concept was committed to paper in the spring of 1993, it is almost a year before the first volunteers set off for the conflict area. One of the participants reviews this planning phase: *"We started to look at the whole naive way of thinking when we said to ourselves we could do it better than the army. You know, this sort of thing. However, when we tried to put it into practice, we discovered how hard it was. Of course, if we had had ten thousand, qualified, civilian, non-violent peace keepers in former Yugoslavia - wouldn't that have been a more effective use of money, than sending ten thousand soldiers in? That's all very well, but where are you going to find that sort of support? That was the kind of reality that overtook us."* Looking back, Eugene D. is astonished at how quickly the plan developed to become a negotiable project organisation. At the time, however, he felt that things were proceeding with painful slowness. This is not really surprising, since the war in Bosnia was drifting towards its gruesome climax.

The War Year, 1993

The theatre of military operations for this year is Bosnia. This year saw the United Nations engaging more and more fiercely in military activity. In October 1992, the UN Security Council empowered NATO to militarily enforce the imposed flight ban over Bosnia. In mid-April, NATO carried out its first combat mission in the region. Military advantage between the warring parties in Bosnia had shifted dramatically from the point where the formerly allied Croation and Moslem troops were now fighting against each other. Territorial gains secured by one or other of the armies were lost again shortly afterwards, and the armed struggle was atomised into small, diffused, sharply- focused areas.

Sarajevo remains in the memory as a besieged city. At considerable risk, private persons, aid organisations, international organisations and UN soldiers transport the millions of tons of provisions and medical supplies dropped from the air or transported overland into the streets of the city in an attempt at least to alleviate distress if they could not stop the murder.

The Security Council's flight ban over Bosnia was devised to put an end to constant attacks on the civilian population and on those who were trying to keep the city's people alive. However, this did not deter the warring parties in the least. In May

1993, the UN Security Council declared several beleaguered towns as 'protected zones'. The defiance of human rights continues. The negotiating tactics of the international community and the pressure exerted on the warring armies using coercion and offers in order to bring about a ceasefire now, at the end of the year, have to be recognized as having failed. The warring factions hold fast to their military advantages.

Under the influence of constantly increasing horror, the idea of 'Mir Sada' (Peace Now) was born. Where possible, a large group of people are to drive from Split in Croatia to Sarajevo in Bosnia-Herzegovina, there to remain for several days in order to contribute to reducing the fighting and perhaps even to bringing about a ceasefire as well as initiating the desire to find a peaceful settlement.

Beati i Costruttori di Pace, the Italian peace organisation and 'Equilibre', a French humanitarian organisation, were the main organizers of this action during which many European countries including the USA were mobilized. Two thousand people join in at the beginning of August and get as far as the edge of the war area. There, the journey comes to an end for almost all those taking part. When it becomes clear that none of the military leaders can guarantee a passage without being harmed, the organisations bring the action to an end. The great majority of the participants, after first taking part in a demonstration in Mostar, now return to Split. Small groups succeed in making their way through to Sarajevo where they are received by representatives of the city and make acquaintance with initiatives there and with its citizens.

Critical assessment of these actions turns out to be diametrically opposed. While some emphasize the motivation for the march as a sign of hope and an act of multiethical co-operation based on fraternal kinship, others are scathing in their condemnation of it: *"L'opération 'Mir-Sada' qui devait aller jusqu'à Sarajevo a été un échec"*, the news bulletin of the French International Association for Reconciliation asserts. *"This failure must be analysed in order to better organize actions in future."*

The lessons learned from failures such as these stimulate the organizers of the Balkan Peace Team Project to find forms which go beyond mere symbolic demonstration and from there to others which can achieve a more sustainable impact in the affected region. This is an impulse, which unites everyone in the next few months, stirs people to action. Former experience has taught us to be better prepared and has schooled us in better management.

The Kosovo-Peace-Team – Trying out New Partnerships

In April, 1993, the two organisations, War Resisters' International and the Federation for Social Defence, take up the project idea. Since that time, the kernel crew of the organisation, so to speak, the founders, Daniel M. and Sabine M. have sought to bring other organisations into their ranks. It is hoped that in this way time and energy will be saved, and that in working towards the realization of one project, the strengths of the various organisations can be put to good use.

In May 1993, representatives of the Peace Brigades International and the French organisation 'MAN' (Mouvemente pour une alternative nonviolente) come together in London. MAN has been active in Kosovo since 1992, accompanies convoys belonging to 'Equilibre' in crisis areas, and works together with teachers in the underground. In order to work more efficiently, they need a team there, but are unable to create one with their current resources. The Peace Brigades International has experience with escorts and with teams operating in war zones. The Federation for Social Defence brings a lot of energy, regional experience, the capacity to work and money into the project. The International Fellowship of Reconciliation has experience in organizing training and preparing people for their subsequent tasks.

For a project like the Kosovo Peace Team *"we are the ones who are responsible"*. Thus, the argument of the coordinator of the Peace Brigade International. The Peace Brigades, however, cannot testify to any expertise in the Balkans. This is something the WRI and the Federation (BSV) could bring into play, and so the Peace Brigades which, as a rule, go it alone would on this occasion 'only' be asked to co-operate as partners. There was agreement on a co-operative test phase. Now the plan had to be discussed with potential partners in Kosovo.

In May, Sabine M., Daniel M. and Ernst V., the director of the Federation for Social Defence, set off for Prishtina to obtain first-hand knowledge of the locality. There, the last publishing house has just closed, and since then ten of its editing personnel have gone on hunger strike. The atmosphere is tense. No one knows what will happen if one of the strikers dies. The exploration visit on the part of Western Europeans arouses great enthusiasm among those spoken to in the resistance groups. An international team is welcome and the sooner it is here the better, they say. However, just how the internationals will be able to get hold of a work permit is something no one really knows. Serbian authorities are known for their strict control and surveillance, and access to the country is something akin to passing through the eye of a needle.

After this trip, the concept is re-considered. The independence of the peace team must be a matter to push into the foreground, otherwise the Serbian authorities, who are responsible for issuing residence permits will automatically assume that foreigners are supporters of the resistance movements. The question remains as to how one can make the acceptance of teams attractive to the authorities. The tasks and objectives of the teams' work are formulated in neutral terms. The theme of escorts is kept in the background. There is no more talk of a hundred people, but only ten.

Paris in the Summer of 1993: The Balkan Peace Team Takes on Form

There has been enthusiasm for the plan for some time and the list of interested persons and organisation gets longer and longer. In June, this growing circle of interest comes together in the French capital. Their host is the French organisation, MAN (Mouvement pour une alternative nonviolente). The meeting in Paris becomes the cradle of the Balkan Peace Team. It receives its official title and acquires an effective system of co-ordination.

Those responsible for organizing the interested organisations change the name of the project into 'Balkan Peace Team', since it could be that it will have to work in other countries before a move into Kosovo is possible. They engage a coordinating group which keeps abreast of what is going on there. Like a magnifying glass, the Balkan Peace Team now begins to focus intensely on how to gain access to Kosovo, employing all the experience gathered in previous activities as separate working organisations and peace groups, a thankless job if ever there was one!

Gradually, matters boil down to what at first turns out to be a tactical variant, namely, that of making the first approach via Croatia. Why Croatia? Having at one time gained access to Croatia, this might well serve as an argument for the Serbian authorities to allow the teams a work permit in Kosovo. In Croatia, too, the presence of foreigners for local activists can be advantageous as repeated requests show. It is easier to work in Croatia. One does not require a visa; there is greater dependence on pressure from outside as far as the Croatian government is concerned, and there is only one new language to learn. It is possible to build up an infrastructure, gather experience and after that one will be immediately fit for action as soon as the doors to Kosovo are open.

In addition to this, there is also the 'Antiwar-Campaign Zagreb' in Zagreb itself, which would support us as partners, and in any case and would, of its own accord, be interested in the presence of international activists. In 1993, activists in Croatia had come to realize again and again that the police were not particularly impressed when they, as local inhabitants, tried to proceed against them for discriminating against minority groups. With this in mind, Anna D. entered into what she called 'negotiations' on the Balkan Peace Team, negotiations which, for her, took an incredibly long time. Finally, in the summer of 1993, Jacques B. of the Peace Brigades, took over the initiative and discussed with her what the essential expectations of a team could be. From this, a formal request was drawn up by the Antiwar-Campaign and the latter is now able to pass on the information to the Peace Brigades for further processing by the Balkan Peace Team. At the next meeting in co-ordinating the Balkan Peace Team on 19th July in Verona, this request becomes in effect a ticket to Zagreb.

The idea of getting a foot in the door for work in Croatia takes on form at this meeting. Three experienced volunteers in Croatia are to be sent as quickly as possible on an orientation phase. Afterwards, the final decision about staying will be made, and the possible areas of intensive work for a further four months clarified. The first announcements are made in the relevant magazines belonging to the movement: *"The Balkan Peace Team seeks volunteers with experience in non-violent activity to work for at least half a year in either Croatia or Serbia."* However, in September of the same year things come to an abrupt halt because there are not enough qualified personnel to set up a team. January comes into consideration as a possible alternative timeline. Things don't look too rosy for the next meeting of the Balkan Peace Team meeting in September! On the other hand, there is no sense in making premature decisions merely to fulfil expectations.

On 15th September, twenty-one people from fourteen different organisations from France, Germany and Switzerland meet in Paris together with the international offices of the large network of the Fellowship of Reconciliation and WRI as well as other organisations such as the Peace Brigades. A volunteer organisation called the 'Brethren Peace Service', a US-American is also represented whose members also work in crisis areas in Europe. However, there is no hope yet of an entry into Kosovo or a quick access to Croatia, and this could rapidly dampen developing interest in the project. Notwithstanding, the meeting ended with what the coordinator summed up as *"a whole lot of important decisions".* They are what give the Balkan Peace Team its substantial structure. These are: the description of concrete task plans, what the function of individual bodies is to be, making decisions about what direction to take as far as the main tasks of the teams are concerned, which are supporting local activists in their work for peace and the establishment of human rights. It also decides not to develop its own independent activities. Financial contributions of future member organisations should lay down a firm basis. Now it is time for those who have shown interest so far to decide whether and in what form they wish to accept responsibility.

Between Principles and Pragmatism: The Internal Dynamics of the Balkan Peace Team

The Peace Brigades International finds itself faced with several dilemmas. As far as its commitment in Yugoslavia is concerned, it is in two minds. Jacques B., its representative, would like to make use of the experiences of the Peace Brigades International in the Balkan Peace Team. And not only this; there is much debate about a Peace Brigades' coalition. Finally, the office of an international co-ordinator is thoroughly examined. John M, who from this position co-operates in looking after the interests of the Balkan Peace Team, finds himself more and more under pressure from all sides within the organisation during the autumn of 1993.

For the International Council of the Peace Brigades, the steering committee, it is important that the Balkan Peace Team's project development closely follow its own principles. This claim leads to numerous demands and improvements from the Peace Brigades to the Balkan Peace Team, so that a proper handbook has came into being which is referred to as 'the yellow bible' because the suggestions in it were printed on yellow paper. This 'bible' then formed the basic principles of the project. To it also belonged a questionnaire for volunteers as well as most of the criteria of selection relevant to volunteers, the concept of training and the process of selection. Later, the principle of impartiality for teamwork in Croatia is precisely defined, the Croatian project overhauled, rules introduced for the alarm network and a duty agreement worked out. The planned exploration in Kosovo is postponed until some time in the future. The other organisations also have their standards. However, the role of critical observer of principles is something adopted by the peace brigades. Basically speaking, this role is a task which is freely accorded them, but not one which could act as brake on affairs.

The internal background and disputes within the peace brigades is a matter which remains pretty obscure for outsiders. Delays which make it possible to consider experiences are interpreted as taking a superior attitude, while the Federation for Social Defence urges more speed. As the organisation, which has contributed most money, it suffers under the pressure of getting things put into practice and the fear of losing funds. These combine to produce a most uncomfortable pace. Internal pressure from the organisation is also felt as a burden for the Balkan Peace Team co-ordinators and consequently makes the work of co-operation all the more difficult. The tension between the main participants increases and finally comes to a head in the autumn of 1993.

The determination not to allow the project to collapse, to continue the general desire to put matters to the test and also the recognition that the project cannot belong simply to one organisation alone welds the organisations together in a common obligation. More than this, the Balkan Peace Team is open to criticism. Up to the general assembly in Paris planned for the beginning of 1994, it strengthens its structure as much as it can.

Financial bottlenecks and those pertaining to personnel typify the scene as a whole and cannot be overcome individually, but, despite this, all the partners finally come together just before the final assembly.

Lining up the Balkan Peace Team for the Start

All the effort was worthwhile. One of the participants still warmly recalls the meeting in Paris, on 2nd February 1994 as *"a great introduction"*. The hard work had provided a solid foundation for further tasks in the future. Of the eighteen participants at this meeting who represent thirteen organisations, five register directly as members. In so doing, they commit themselves to various operations which will further the project. This involves publicity work, the finding of volunteers, work on committees, financial support and providing personnel or material assistance. Shortly afterwards, six other organisations clarify their status, above all the seven different French groups which will now have to co-ordinate things among themselves.

The General Assembly of member organisations is one which has ultimate power to decide, but which, unfortunately, only seldom convenes. Current business is dealt with by the Co-ordinating Committee into which some of the member organisations can send one representative. Later, the co-ordinator of the International Office and a member of the Team also become members. The job of the Co-ordinating Committee is to check on and evaluate the progress and administration of the project. The planning and supervision of financial resources, providing support during crises as well a generally promoting the project within the organisation is also a part of its responsibility. It is clear from this that the project is properly managed. The chosen structure is now something, which has come into being; it has not been strategically planned. It has its drawbacks inasmuch as it creates different classes of members, those, for example, who have a place on the Co-ordinating Committee and those that do not. Whether one would choose do this a second time, Eugene D. leaves as an open issue. Nevertheless, he suggests leaving things as they are, since this is what the Assembly has put forward. Subsequent to this self-critical introduction, it has decided to follow his recommendation.

The critical enquiry as to whether the project organisation is strong enough is a justified one. The members of the Co-ordination Committee put a tremendous amount of work into the preparatory phase alone. A number of organisations limit the amount of dedication of 'their' people. To find members willing to put in the hours required is a difficult job. In the publicity sector, behind the scenes and within the participating associations, organisations and networks the wires buzz to harness various resources for the Balkan Peace Team. Within the International Fellowship of Reconciliation there is a lot going on to mobilize money, volunteers and facilitate possible access to Kosovo, and within the Peace Brigades organisation, people are being sought for their own committee. Jacques will advise these and other interested persons to work for national country groups who are at hand for every project and who form an important part of the support structure.

Furnishing funds is the second, self-critical weak point brought forward. It is important at this stage to receive the go-ahead from a German peace group which will invest in the project regardless of the state of uncertainty. On 11th August, the Münchner Friedensrunde had this to say, *"Since we know in the meantime that the work in Kosovo is extremely difficult, and its commencement not yet certain, but possibly dependent on the activities of the Balkan Peace Team in other regions of former Yugoslavia, our decision is valid here, too."* The 'decision' happens to be DM 21,000.-! For donors this reveals an unusual degree of far-sightedness and flexibility, and for the project it constitutes an important factor in stabilization. At the end of November, the organizers learn of a positive decision taken by the Heinrich-Boell Foundation, which will save them financially. *"We can now work on in the knowledge that we're not going to fail for lack of money!"* says the co-ordinator jubilantly. In Paris, the member organisations are obliged to pay their contributions, but the real basic principle goes: *"No one may be excluded because he can't pay his contributions!"* As a consequence, this means that permanent fund-raising will be the material basis of the project, and that this will always mean a situation of short-term security.

With 'open eyes'(Otvorene Oci) into Croatia: The First Team

The final timetable has now been drawn up since mid-November and the choice personnel has in the main been made. Those selected for the job are to be instructed in preparatory training in mid-February and immediately after this will drive to Zagreb where the Antiwar Campaign will cater for their language course. On 11th February, 1994, the first 10-day Balkan Peace Team training course will take place in a village not far from Minden in Germany. *"Training together for Peace: Nine activists in Päpinghausen prepare themselves for duty in former Yugoslavia"*, the local press reports.

Above all, there are four things for the team members to do in the first few weeks: they will have to learn the language, discover the possibilities of a health insurance and the registration of the project in Croatia, and, in addition, make contact with likeminded peace or human rights groups. As soon as the team has gained an impression of the lie of the land, it can then take up contact with other groups and organisations; members can introduce themselves to the embassy personnel of sender countries, human rights representatives in the Croatian government as well as representatives of the United Nations and other international committees. After that, they are then able to undertake actual operations.

Eventually, the moment has come where there is nothing more to prepare. One of the participants recalls the final departure of the teams from trainers and representatives: *"...then we all went off and had a meal in the town, and then we put all of these - crazy people in a car, into this beat-up, old car and said, 'Bye, go on down there now and start doing it'."*

On 28th February, four days after the volunteers had experienced an adventurous journey, they nevertheless arrive safely in Zagreb. The co-ordinator writes the first 'Balkan Peace Team Newsletter' and reminds the members' organiser that, *"It is now very urgent to begin with the fundraising!"*

The Balkan Peace Team, which is now an 'international project' with the following members: Brethren Service, Bund für Soziale Verteidigung, (Federation for Social Defence), 'Collectiv du jumelage des sociétés civiles de Genève et Pristhine', 'Helsinki Citizens' Assembly Geneva', International Fellowship of Reconciliation, Mouvement pour une alternative nonviolente, Peace Brigades International, War Resisters' International and the 'World Peace and Relief Team'. Later members are the 'Working Group Former Yugoslavia of the Dutch Mennonites', 'Eirene International', the 'Österreichischen Friedensdienste' (Austrian Peace Services) and shortly before the end, the 'Quakers Peace and Service'.

Organisation, fund-raising and the finding and training of volunteers remain one of the central tasks of the Balkan Peace Team together with the further development of the Kosovo project sector. However, with the arrival of the 'Otvorene Oci' (Open Eyes) in Zagreb, another era begins. From now on, the pulse of the project beats here in Croatia, and this is where experience in the practice of non-violent intervention comes in.

Sources

Antiwar Campaign Zagreb 18.7.93; BPT 13. 5. 93; 30.5.-2.6. 93; 7.6. 93; 15.6.93; 6.7.93, 1f.; 19.7.93;14.9.93; 1.11.93 non-partisanship; 1.11.93 Defense; 23.11.93; 22.9.93; 24.8.93; 7.-9.11.93; 14.11.93 letter; 14.11.93, fax; 14.11.93 cirular; 23.11.93 Agreement; telephone conference; 27.11.93; 30.11.93; 22.12.93; 2.1.94; 7.11.93; 24.2.94; 28.2.94; BPT CC minutes, 1.2.94; BPT GA minutes, 2.2.94; BSV Nov. 1993; BSV cirular 3.1993, 3; Calic 1996, 179, 106-109, 178f., 183. 199-201; IFOR 7.8.93; 9.8. 93; 12. 7. 93; IFOR SC Minutes, September 1993; January 1994, 5f.; Interviews Anna D. 1998; Daniel M. 1998; Eugene D. 1998; Jacques B. 1998; John M. 1998; Sabine M. 1997; Meder/ Reimann 1996, 12; Müller/Büttner 1996, 40; Münchner Friedensrunde 11.8.93, letter; Neue Westfälische (newspaper) 19.2.94; PBI 17.11.93; 20.8.93; 5.8.93; 19.11.93; 4.-10.1.94; PBI 1.9.93, 4; Pyronnet 1993, 38f.; Schweitzer 1993, 3.; Schweitzer 1996, 47; WRI Execmins, 17.-19.12.93.

Chapter 2 The 'Otvorene Oci' Teams: With "eyes open" in Croatia

(1) Team Start and the First Year

At the end of February 1994, the team arrives separately in Zagreb, and for this stay everything has already been arranged. One of the activists of the Antiwar Campaign has found accommodation for its members in an old house on the outskirts of the city. The four of the them settle in and learn to live with the regular electricity cuts and nevertheless somehow manage to use their computer, fax and e-mail apparatus according the whims of the power supply. In August, the team moves to a larger, more pleasant apartment, while a washing machine, refrigerator, TV-set and another car is organized for them by another volunteer from Germany.

The team is obliged to live with the minimum of equipment. Volunteers provide the computer and one of the 'tired' cars already alluded to. The computer, the modems belonging to it, and the old cars provide the team with constant problems. The cars either won't move or simply fall apart. The computers are either 'sick' or not compatible with other apparatus, and the modem chooses to enter the network only according to its own internal laws. Living close together, managing with the minimum, and getting on as best you can on your own – this seems to be the philosophy of the volunteer project, Balkan Peace Team. It was different from other international projects. One volunteer expressed the situation in a report about a conference held by the aid organisation, Oxfam, located in a luxury hotel, *"It was tough going after staying two nights in a luxury hotel with three-course meals three times a day, but we suffered through it."*

The first team consists of three men and one woman ranging in age from 24 to 32. They come from USA, Norway and Great Britain. Three of them have already had experience in Croatia working for peace or aid organisations or have already studied the language. At home, they have belonged to human rights and peace organisations and are active in the networks there or their families live in a tradition of volunteer work. They feel their moral duty is to do more than it is possible to do while at home and find the Balkan Peace Team attractive, since it is concerned here about working with conflict. Because of this, their expectations are vague and in some cases unrealistic. *"The reason I joined Balkan Peace Team and from my previous interest, was that I wanted us to be doing mediation and conflict resolution workshops or getting into the field with - the religious leaders perhaps. I was so naive about the situation, I didn't know where we would fit. What, you know could we even be doing between the two sides, trying to do something."* Personal previous experience is varied. In June, the first changes in personnel take place, and up to the end of the year, three other men join the team, a German, a Dutchman and an American.

The Balkan Peace Team has many ideas about what a team could do. It is meant to prevent threats and other acts of violence against other activists by its very presence. Members' public appearance at peace demonstrations is to help prevent intimidation. If required to do so, they are to accompany activists on tricky missions. Where evictions are undertaken and during legal proceedings at court; their presence is to signalise international interest. As foreigners, they can try to set up contacts and communication between the different ethnic groups in various parts of the country. From this standpoint they can use their outsider position to create opportunity to conduct dialogues and act as mediators. They can offer training themselves or relay the need for trainers as well as provide the means of relaying other support issues which do not fit into their own mandate. That's probably more than *"they will ever be in a position to realize"*, a coordinator writes in her circular. Having said this, the volunteers are to orientate themselves to the needs of their local groups.

For Ruth S. from the Antiwar-Campaign in Zagreb, it was a surprise to find that the team did not arrive with a complete plan of action, but used the first weeks to set up an analysis of its needs. *"And I found it really an extremely good way of functioning."* She was quite astonished to recognize people among the members of the peace team whom she knew well and not 'experts' whom she had expected. *"So now when they started this Balkan Peace Team, I knew there would be a group of people from the Balkan Peace Team who would come with some extremely experienced people that I had never heard of, people who are really experts in their field... and then I discovered that there is no such expertise to be found in the world."*

Ruth finds the first team well mixed. In it there are people with plenty of experience in the region and others who are familiar with human rights. *"And they did a lot; they did a good job,"* The first thing to do here was to get an idea of the kind of work the Co-ordinating Committee had in mind, and so bring it into line with what are the requirements of the local situation.

Anna D. from the Antiwar-Campaign in Zagreb had her own plans for the team. She supplies recommendations, addresses and telephone numbers and also makes it clear that making such connections possible will also have its consequences. Not all institutions and organisations in Croatia are well inclined to the Antiwar-Campaign. A certain distance is therefore necessary, and also important for the team to be effective. Anna's conceptions extend further. She would like to see the team working in Split. The activists there entertain considerable reservations about foreigners. The fear that well-meaning hippies could impair their cause by irresponsible behaviour is something to be reckoned with so for this reason a carefully planned strategy of introduction is necessary. A few weeks later, this comes into being.

It is not yet clear, however, whether the tourist visa issued to volunteers will allow them to work. It doesn't seem an important requirement to register the organisation; a report to the local police of one's presence seems to be enough. However, it was clear on arrival at the border that volunteers were dependent on the good grace of officials there obliged to stamp their passports. 'What do you want in Croatia? How long do you intend to stay?' What can the volunteers say in answer? They decide to tell the truth and the first team was shortly to discover that reactions were very different. They enter the country separately and some were not even asked what their business was, while others were simply refused entry or they were sent away and had to re-enter the country later. Other volunteers who arrive afterwards experience a similar state of affairs.

An official status for the Balkan Peace Team would put an end to all that. Added to this is the fact that during the next few months the activities of 'Open Eyes' expand with the result that their existence is noticeable to both the police and the authorities. In September, a lawyer who is also a friend, warmly advises registration. *"We also don't have much of a leg to stand on if we have to deal with government officials who distrust us, even when we are trying to make positive contact with them. ...Such officials, if we make them nervous, have only to look into the legal status of Otoc [Otvorene Oci, Open Eyes], and we could be on the next train out."* Thus, the fears of one of the team members. The private side of their presence begins to bear upon their freedom to act as a peace team. *"I think that they'll be a lot more strict on this if things heat up here."*

Not all volunteers see things so dramatically, and certainly not the participants of the Balkan Peace Team. In the months of September and October, the Co-ordinating Committee and the General Assembly alternately consider the problem at their meetings. At these, there is some reservation about the need to register. To try to endow a strong institutional status upon what is a loose coalition would be to destroy the Balkan Peace Team. Suddenly, there are a lot of things to consider which, on the spot in Croatia, are of no importance. The business of institutionalising their efforts is kept at a low profile, and in the course of the year, a non-profit making association comes into being in Germany. The team in Croatia remains a private undertaking.

Although the first four weeks are taken up with the language course, the impatience of volunteers is such that after the third week they begin to make contact with various initiatives and organisations in Zagreb, Istria, Ossijek, Karlovac and Split. Proceeding from their own personal contacts, which are easy to activate, the team expands its circle of contacts more and more until they are in a position to engage with so-called 'cold contacts', whereby unknown organisations are called and a request made for a meeting. Over forty such meetings come about as a result. The first official meetings are not sufficient to establish good contacts; it is necessary to build up from these initial connections. One volunteer describes this in his own words: *"We would go for coffees with various different people and come to the offices and come along to their meetings and then we would start to discuss the contents of their work and their projects while they were working on them, and not just as an outsider coming in from a third party to look, but really to be engaged with the organisations and what they were doing. Not necessarily engaged in their work but engaged in the process of their work".*

The range of things to talk about is enormous and encompasses such themes as conscientious objectors, refugees, human rights work, research, organisation consultation and translation work. 'How big is the threat here?' they want to know – after all that's why we've come. Apropos of this, one volunteer recalls:

"Yeah, some were directly attacked. There was one of the presidents of one of the organisations who had a bomb thrown into his office. A lawyer had a bomb thrown into his office. Another activist was beaten up by the Military Police when he was trying to intervene in a case. Another one had his car vandalized, and another was told by somebody in the police that she was on the list of people to be liquidated, which I do not think was actually true, but it certainly scared her."

The visits provide the volunteers with their own impressions for possible starting points. After all, they will have to find out what their role and their place is to be. The range is great and the material contradictory. Some recommend them to individual cases, whereas others dismiss this idea. *"They want us to work for them and gave us an probably mutable all or nothing alternative".* This was the guideline of another organisation. *"We don't need you here"* is the message in Ossijek. *"We need you here",* is that from Karlovac. A trip to Istria reveals that there are *"possibilities everywhere".* Then, again, things are different in Split. Looking back to that time, one volunteer notes:

> *"I was in Split, and in Split there were really only 3 or 4 groups that we really thought were a priority. So we devoted our time to those groups. And we would go and meet other organisations, especially with regard to the need to be impartial and non-partisan, it is important to be seen as open to engagement with other groups. But there were certain groups that were having real problems, and those were the groups that were an obvious priority, and so we devoted lots more time to them. Within a month we had good working relationships with most of them because they were eager for us to come as well. They did not know what it was that we were going to do, and they were eager for us to come for reasons that were outside of our mandate in the sense of what we were supposed to be doing. One activist really wanted us to translate for example".*

How and by what standards should future activities be chosen? In the seventh week, shortly before the decisive meeting with members of the Balkan Peace Team Co-ordinating Committee, there is deliberation about the evaluation of all this differing information. The talents of the volunteers play an important role here in tailoring programmes. The project is now in its decisive phase. From rough-hewn orientation material and some general principles, steps to practical implementation and work programmes for everyday now have to be forged.

At the beginning of May, the Co-ordinating Committee arrives in Zagreb. By this time, the human rights situation, despite the threatening circumstances mentioned above, has considerably relaxed, the team reports. Three or four members of the co-ordinating group question the necessity of a team in Croatia. The Team, however, has some ideas. It presents 10 programme points, which can be realized by dividing up resources into two teams working in Zagreb and Split. Among other things, the team members want to be present at court proceedings, be able to advise activists and, as a kind of 'fire brigade', act in the case where there is the danger of an infringement of human rights and so give support to a local organisation.

The subjects of conscientious objection, demobilization and the refugee problem can serve as essential points on the agenda to be discussed. They would like to support an international NGO project in Pakrac. A data bank on and for NGO's is to be established, and research undertaken on various points such as privatisation, and repatriation as well as the setting up of free media. Finally, its members want to find out how the Balkan Peace Team can extend its activities to Bosnia where, at that moment, war is raging. This plan is one which the Team has put together itself. Another volunteer recalls the complications of the process:

> *"We did not get much guidance from the CC in doing that. They were very much in the spirit, you know, this has to be led from the activists on the ground and the advice that they gave, but we were getting conflicting advice from people on the ground, everybody wanted us to do something else. So we really needed an independent measure to be able to evaluate if we should do this or that, and so we drew up, it was an extremely laborious procedure where we drew up plans of all the different things we could do, and the CC finally decided we could do any of them, and it wasn't very helpful, but eventually, I don't remember exactly how we came to the decision, but we came to the decision to have two offices, one in Split and one in Zagreb. We had the sort of mission statement of what we would be doing, but it did not actually mean anything."*

The recollections of one of the members of the Co-ordinating Committee are somewhat different in character: *"It was this inevitable thing that will happen between the sort of fathers and mothers of such an operation. And the people who actually put it into practice say, yeah, but we're the ones on the ground here. And we know better than you."*

Where should the main focus of attention lie? A difficult decision indeed. The members of the Co-ordinating Committee would want to distribute the emphasis in a different way. Again, within the team itself, not everything has been thoroughly discussed; and the result, therefore, is a compromise. The investigation for a further extension of the Team's activities into Bosnia turns out to be the only point that is struck out of the programme. The other points, with a few qualifications, are accepted. Another worthwhile objective is to find local groups or local people to whom, where possible, they can allocate tasks contained in the programme points.

With these guidelines in mind, the first team divide up the work into two offices, one in Zagreb and one in Split. Very soon, the team in Split shows itself active during the observation of court proceedings in the city. Members of a regional party, which had been observed by the central government in Zagreb with certain misgivings, were said to have blown up their own office. In Istria, the Zagreb Team commits itself to helping the inhabitants of a refugee camp whose enforced evacuation it cannot prevent.

In December, the 'Open Eyes' go out into the streets in Split on the day celebrating human rights with its own pamphlet and inform the public about human rights organisations in Croatia. Within forty minutes, their information material has been already distributed to an interested public. *"Local activists are reluctant or afraid of public actions, and so we wanted to start this to prove that, Yes, it can be done!"*, say those participating in this voluntary action.

In many respects this first team is a group of pioneers, not only because they have got to know each other during training, but because of the close association imposed upon them in cramped circumstances which had brought about a certain closeness and familiarity among them, one which did not deteriorate even when two of them went to live several hundred kilometres away to Split on the Adriatic coast. They develop their rituals and procedures and are the prototypes of the Team. How much pocket money is necessary? How much money does the Team need to get by? How can the work in the Team be efficiently organised? Office work and family life – everything developed with this Team.

In the summer, there was the first 'team summit', a private meeting at which both groups meet each other, exchange their experiences, spend time with each other, hatch new strategies, relax and spend their free time with one another. This will become a regular part of team life They consider the idea of integrating new volunteers into their esprit de corps, but it is difficult to initiate others into this close-knit community. Integration is a business which succeeds only more or less well, now for the better, now for the worse.

Any enlargement of the team is not possible in the first year. Since there is little money at hand, vacancies that become free cannot be immediately occupied, and in the summer for a period of several weeks there is only one person in each office respectively to manage its business. This is not good experience. Accordingly, it is decided that there be one month's overlapping period. The Co-ordinating Committee feels responsible for the emotional accompaniment of the volunteers and reacts appropriately with offers. However, it turns out that problems arising between volunteers within the Team either remain or later come too late to the surface and, as a consequence, cannot be satisfactorily resolved. This, too, is something that accompanies the first teams' activities and which continues.

In the summer, the Team draws up a 'handbook' in which the everyday life and work of the Team is described. Tolerance and the ability to be emotionally detached are two central abilities prescribed to keep a team functioning together. This implies tolerating differences until it hurts! The Team develops a daily routine of work. Mornings are devoted to going through e-mail lists and then arranging meetings. In the afternoon, the meetings are then realized in clothes appropriate to the occasion and clear objectives discussed. Important on these occasions is the sharing of information and ideas. Individuals may seize the initiative for the Team, but they must justify their decisions in front of the others. For this, a clear discriminative faculty is necessary. What are my objectives and wishes – and what are the Team's?

The discriminative faculty must also be active when it comes to writing reports. Is it, for example, internal information for the Co-ordinating Committee? Are there parts of it which may not be relayed to the public? The balancing act between being, on the one hand, an independent channel for information and, on the other, in fact giving vent one's views, leads to such distinctions. Similarly, making fine or delicate distinctions between much that is confidential information and that which may be disseminated is another consideration.

Nine months later, at the beginning of 1995, a revision of the Team's daily routine is due. *"Work seemed to be a continuous 'fire brigade' programme."* The day was filled with the 'good deeds' such as translation for example. *"In other words, December meant that OtOc Split was not sleeping enough, eating on the go, and personal time was an imaginary luxury. Not a good plan,"* volunteers said in summing up. And so at the end of the year 94 and in early 95, the Team devises a new order. This included regulated 'consultation times', regular meetings with activists, regular explorations of the vicinity, and regular workshops.

Before that, in October 1994, an important date marks the General Assembly of the Balkan Peace Team which included the first revision of teamwork and mandate. The principal tasks of the daily work of both offices have developed during the summer. Zagreb has kept up its contact with local NGO's. Split has worked with many human rights organisations as well as keeping an eye on the human rights situation. Out of the blue as it were, the General Assembly was suddenly at the door in October, and volunteers were obliged to evaluate their programme points for the month of May. One volunteer notes at this point:

> "...then, all of a sudden, came time for a GA, the General Assembly, and we suddenly had to look like we knew what we were doing. So, it was literally on the phone - because at that time we had very few people as well - sub-divided, you know. We thought about what we were doing, and decided that we were doing civil society development, support for non violent conflict resolution and human rights. I don't remember the phrasing exactly. We had to go to the GA and look like we had a plan and so on. I just think that is the way every organisation in the world works. It is common sense. The plan comes out of what makes sense. Xaver was not very happy with it. He thought we should sit down, make a plan and we should carry out the plan. But life is not that easy."

A certain distance has developed between the Team and the 'rest' of the Balkan Peace Team, here described in the following words by a volunteer:

> "It was a completely different world. They were on a completely different planet than the teams. It was an extremely educational experience, because very often we thought we were entirely alone in the field. We were a war project sponsored by a coalition of organisations that were absolutely invisible, that were just names on a paper, that come together once a year, that send us money. But we felt very alone in the field and going to the CC meetings we saw exactly how alone we were because they were like 'Yes, great we have this wonderful conflict resolution', and 'we have this blah-blah project in Croatia', and you actually have no idea what it was like, what we were actually doing on a day-today basis. After going to a CC meeting, I think everybody had the experience that we came back and said 'OK, we give up, we are on our own, we can do whatever we want to; they are happy, and they are going to describe it in whatever terms they want to.'"

There might have been another reason playing a part here. During the implementation of the initial idea which was the prevention of war in Kosovo or, say, the presence of the team in war areas, something rather new had developed. The teams experience 'presence' as something quite different from that envisaged by the others. Which new vision, then, characterizes the experiences of the reality actually lived through, and how does one distinguish between the latter and the original idea? No conceptual discussion takes place on this point within the Balkan Peace Team.

But then there is a brief moment when the possibility is there, and this occurs at the meetings in May in Zagreb. While the Balkan Peace Team is trying to realize its original dream in Kosovo, the team in Croatia is just in the process of developing that vision. The 'Meta-Plan' is a high-flying plan that seeks to mobilise the 'maximum potential' of the peace movement in the Balkans war. At the meeting of the Co-ordinating Committee in Zagreb at the beginning of 1994, this plan is not discussed. *"It lies too much outside any kind of achievable range",* one of the participants at the meeting notes. The opportunity to integrate new experiences into the old vision dissolves during attention given wholly to practical matters concerned with the next few months which, strategically speaking, included access to Kosovo as the next big obstacle to overcome.

In the following autumn, too, the adjustments to the mandate necessary at that time are principally concerned with its adjustment to lived, practical experience. The objectives on the horizon are concrete. The teams concentrate on the work of local activists in order to make this more efficient. That is their yardstick. In carrying out their activities, they follow what has been described by their partners as 'useful', and to this end regularly follow their suggestions. They can only indirectly speak of their own contributions to dealing with conflict in Croatia. If human rights were more consistently acknowledged in Croatia, then the Serbs in Krajina could relinquish their claim to an independent state, and the re-integration of Krajina could take place in a peaceful way...

Most regrettably, material limitation puts the brake on the work. In May, emergency plans are put forward, since money is restricted. Future activities – and the enlargement of the Team – stands or falls by the sole fact of whether fund-raising will have been successful by the summer! Too little mobility and too few personal resources limit the activities of the Team to act as a 'fire brigade at hot spots'. In the matter of acquiring money, there is no lack of applications or activity in the member organisations; it is a fact that not all are successful, however. When, finally, 100,000 crowns are paid in by the Swedish Branch of the Fellowship of Reconciliation, no further emergency plans for the reduction of costs and programmes need to be developed.

There is no lack of creativity either. Since there is no payable insurance for volunteers, the Balkan Peace Team initiates its own insurance fund until the Social Service Agency of the Evangelical Church in Germany takes over insurance matters at the end of 1995.

Lack of money dogs us. In November, the teams complain, *"Due to either miscalculation or unexpected expenditures, both the Split office and the Zagreb office are in a difficult financial situation. To be more precise: the Split office has no money. Except for personal money which will have to be used until maybe the end of the month."*

The Balkan Peace Team and 'The War'

In 1994, war rages in Bosnia. The war there has hung like a sword of Damocles over the whole region. Can the war finally be stopped? Is it going to spread? What can the international community do to increase its efficiency? Bosnian Croatians and Muslims form an alliance and agree to a model as to how a state could look which is their common heritage. Pressure on Bosnian Serbs increases, first in the political field and later, towards the spring, in that of the military. NATO proceeds from threat to deed when, at the end of March, Serbian planes that ignore the flight zones, are shot down. NATO bombards the protected zone around the town of Goradze in order to secure it.

In Mostar, steps are even taken to establish an order which is to come into being after the war. Hans Koschnik, from the European Union is employed there as administrator. Under pressure from the United Nations, Bosnia agrees to a cease-fire which indeed is actually kept to by the warring parties. The questions as to who is to blame and what is just or unjust are considered in November of this year at the newly inaugurated tribunal of Yugoslavia in Den Haag.

The Balkan Peace Team is not engaged in Bosnia. The building up of teams in Croatia and Kosovo occupies its current attention. In the articles of the circular on the BPT in the summer of 1994, the post, 'pre-war' situation in Croatia and the prevention of war in Kosovo have occupied primary attention. These are not particularly spectacular histories of actions taken there.

Volunteer peace initiatives have come into being in the former Yugoslavian republics which demand a more lasting commitment from those who work for peace. Much has taken place since things began in 1991. A provocative open letter is addressed to the 'Peace Movements', which states that

"To appeal for peace is not the same...as to make peace. Mass actions such as the Peace Caravan in 1991 and 'Mir Sada' – Peace Now in 1993 [are] ineffective and a waste of energy...Those who either come as individuals or in small groups and who co-operate with us on concrete projects help us much more. Hard, long-term work is something which is understood in this. Illusions which suggest quick and easy solutions must be rejected."

This is in line with the initial ideas of the Balkan Peace Team which recognises long-term commitment, painstaking work and stalwart perseverance. Work on problems, which are the expression of conflict, is tedious and undramatic. A volunteer describes the atmosphere of that time:

"I know it was always an issue of exactly why is it necessary for us to be in Croatia because Croatia wasn't making headlines, it wasn't in the news, it was not even the subject of human rights reports and alternative-type things. Most things seemed to show that the situation was stable. The situation was OK. Things happened more on a day to day basis. We spent a lot of time sitting in cafes with people talking conspiracy theories and we did not feel like this was a situation of urgency. The BPT was spending a lot of money so that we could sit in cafes and talk conspiracy theories with people. But looking at things from outside, there was a lot happening, and it was important, and I think our presence was needed, and was useful. It is still useful, certainly now. [1997. BM] I find it extremely valuable. There is nobody else doing that sort of thing at all. Somebody needs to be doing it."

In 1994, one of the most important themes in Croatia is the eviction of tenants from their apartments. With respect to all the differing views and assessments, the parties discussing these issues are united in one thing as a volunteer in Croatia recalls that: *"we've had enough specifics, and that we knew we would be doing some accompanying in the field. And this was, you know, suggested by everyone and that was a good thing. Especially at evictions. A lot of people were talking about evictions."* The need for 'Open Eyes' first proved itself with regard to this subject in Croatia.

Sources

BPT, 18.1.94; BPT CC minutes, 2.- 4.5.94; 5.-7.9.94; 14./17.10.94; BPT GA minutes 15.-16.10.94, 6,11, 18; BPT Newsletter, 1.3.94, 1f.; 1.5.94, 2; Friedenszeitung (Peace News) November 1994, 10f.; Interviews Albert P. 1/1997; Anselm F. 1997; Daniel M. 1997; Eugene D. 1998; Rosa T.

1997; Ruth S. 1997; Xaver A. 1997; Information Sabine M. April 2003; Oskar K. 8.5.2003, Personal liability insurance and accident insurance from 1.12. 95; health insurance from 1.1.97. Association and Liability Ins. for the car; OtOc 29.3.94; 31.3.94; 5.1994; 13.-14.8.94, 3; no date, summer 94; 10.1994,1-3; no date, ca 10.94, Complicated, 3; 12.94, 2,5; OtOc Sp 25.9.94; OtOc Sp Biweekly, 15.-30.8.94, 1; 1.-15.9. 94, 1; 1.-15.11.94, 1-3; 1.-15.12.94, 2.; 15.12.94-15.1.95, 1f.; OtOc Weekly Report, 1.-7.3.94,1; 8.-12.3.94, 1-3; 13.-20.3.94; 21.-27.3.94; 28.3.-3.4.94; 4.-10.4.94; 11.-18.4.94; 17.-24.4.94, 1; OtOc Zg 28.11.94; OtOc Zg Bi-weekly, 2/8.94, 1; 1/9.94, 1; 2/10.94, 1, 2, 3; Peace News, September 1994, 6. German quotation after: WRI Das Zerbrochene Gewehr (The Broken Rifle) 9.1994, 4f.; Schweitzer 1996, 47f.; WRI, Execmins, 1.-2.10.94, 2.

(2) Presence at Violent Evictions in Croatia, 1994/5

Ethnic Expulsion from House to House

On the morning of 14th September 1994, there was a knock on the door at Mrs Bronkovic' house in Zagreb. The police are there and want to drive this woman, who is nine months pregnant, out of her home. Apparently, she is living there illegally. Mrs Bronkovic is prepared for the visit. Friends and relatives, journalists and representatives of human rights groups are already ensconced in her apartment. Altogether there are thirty-four persons present according to a count taken by one Otvorene Oci volunteer. They wish to hinder the expulsion. Four policemen, two state attorneys, five armed soldiers and two civilians whom one cannot quite place stand at the door and demand that those present leave. These latter refuse. An hour later, the police have all the personal details of those present, and again demand that they all leave. The police then call for re-enforcements. When, later, these men appear, the foreign observer from Otvorene Oci does in fact leave the apartment in order not to come into conflict with the host country. He then watches what goes on from the street. The scene is not a particularly friendly one. One of the policemen almost manages to push an elderly woman down the steps. Others are either carried or pushed to a waiting police vehicle; some of them are in handcuffs. One can hear loud remonstrations from the house. Within ten minutes of the commencement of the eviction, eight men and women have been arrested and taken away.

The volunteer takes photographs and remains at the scene despite being told to leave the street. An ambulance arrives. After a short visit to the apartment, the doctor goes away again. The police, too, move away. Eight activists decide to go to the parliament and protest against this eviction. However, all is not lost. Mrs Bronkovic is still in her apartment. On their arrival at the parliament building, activists and volunteers from Otvorene Oci manage to speak to the vice president. One of the activists begins a hunger strike. Later, it is learned that this particular eviction has been temporarily broken off because of Mrs Bronkovic' condition. This happens to be a fortunate coincidence, a temporary respite, but no solution to a situation of conflict which, between 1992 and 1997, takes place thousands of times in Croatia and which is brought to the attention of human rights organisations and Amnesty International. For the volunteers of Otvorene Oci, this is first big testing ground.

'Ethnic Cleansing' with the Assistance of Law, Brute Force and Violence

Who are the victims and who the villains of the piece in this conflict? Mrs Bronkovic changed her apartment in December 1991. This was quite common in former Yugoslavia. Above all, those apartments belonging to the state often changed hands. However, during the course of the deterioration within the Yugoslavian state, habits also changed. What up to quite recently was acceptable, has now become the expression of a condition from which one disassociates oneself. In December 1991, Croatia complains about the ownership and rights of distribution of apartments that was once part of the Tito regime and also refuses to continue to acknowledge the transitional ruling valid at one time. People lose their right to residence simply because they behave in a way to which they have accustomed themselves for decades.

Since 1992, the state of Croatia has begun to claim what, in their eyes, are 'illegally' occupied residences in order to allocate them to war veterans. It has not been a matter of co-incidence that ethnic minorities have been called upon to vacate their abodes and then, under the influence of threat and violence, put out onto the street. These evictions are authorized by courts and known about by those affected. It can, however, happen that soldiers stand at the door and say, 'This apartment now belongs to me!' and, so saying, simply take the people out and put them into the street. Once the folks have been forced from their homes, resort to legal assistance won't help them anymore.

Although many of the courts recognise after many years of legal procedure that the laws pertaining to tenancy are in order. However, the apartment is not rendered as so much free accommodation by this fact. Rather, it is the present occupant of the house, who is frequently the same person who has evicted a family who should himself be evicted, but this is virtually impossible. Those affected by this situation turn to groups responsible for human rights for help.

For the human rights organisations, this state procedure means a flagrant infringement of elementary human rights as well as scandalously undemocratic practice. They therefore demand justice through the introduction of laws which are non-discriminative, an end to violence, intimidation and threat.

The Croatian state need not trouble itself too much about this however. Public opinion is lined up on the side of the heroes of independence. Anyone who exerts himself for the rights of the hated Serbs is in any case regarded as a traitor. And so it is that *"this battle for houses over the years has become a symbol for human rights infringement along ethnic lines"* according to a report by the Otvorene Oci in May, 1996: *"Despite constant government assurances that all Croatian citizens are treated equally and justly, human rights violations along ethnic lines continue. One of the most pressing human rights issues in Croatia continues to be the illegal eviction of Croatian citizens from their houses or apartments."*

Croatian Civil Society organizes Resistance

After a particularly violent eviction in Ossijek, which is later imitated in Zagreb and then in the whole of the country, the Antiwar Campaign has been faced since 1993 with the fact that its protests and attempts at resistance have failed to effect any change. When, in February 1994, the first Balkan Peace Team arrives on the scene in Zagreb, the problem of eviction is in fact, and one which concerns everyone. It becomes a theme to tackle for the Team both in the capital, Zagreb, as well as in the Dalmatian coastal town of Split. Split is the centre of the former armed forces, and that means that here a particularly large number of residences have fallen into state ownership and also that, in particular, many soldiers of the new Croatian army who have received accommodation there as a form of reward. It is in Split that the most violent evictions have taken place. At least two people have died during these operations. Amnesty International documents three of these having taken place in Split in the summer of 1996 and complains that, *"military personnel have shown a serious lack of restraint and have used force to intimidate those resisting eviction from their apartments. When violence has occurred, military or civilian police have failed to provide appropriate protection, and little or no effort has been made to discipline the perpetrators."*

Escalation in 1994: Zagreb

During the course of the autumn months of 1994 in Zagreb, the wave of authorized evictions escalates, so that each week three to four evictions are ordered. However, many of those intended are not carried out after all, and so the insecurity among the occupants remains. A group of armed personnel can appear at the door at any time and literally kick the inhabitants out into the street. On one of these occasions taking place in October 1994, a human rights activist was maltreated; the attack is documented and made public abroad. At the end of October, the 'Croatian Helsinki Committee' organizes a round table conference. Members of parliament, ministers, civil service officials of the Residence Commission and the courts, representatives of the army, but also non-governmental organisations confer in public about these evictions, and at the end of the month there is a talk-show on TV dealing with the subject in which, however, the majority of participants represent those active in expelling residents. Notwithstanding, the subject has at last attracted public attention in Croatia.

The constitutional court instructs the government to revise its conduct in the matter of evictions, and until new operational procedures are established, a moratorium is constituted to provide a short pause in these activities. The expectations from this are nevertheless pessimistic. In a report on the background to these events, Otvorene Oci proceeds from the assumption that the government will merely wait until international indignation on the issue has ebbed in order then to continue in the old way without hindrance.

Eviction and the Role of Military Personnel: Split 1994

Just how military personnel has behaved at this time is given in the case of family Sepic. In the summer of 1994, a war invalid forcibly quartered himself with the family and since the family would not submit itself to his violence and so be driven out, the man settled to the uneasy compromise of living with the family in the same apartment. In August, he left the apartment and went 'on holiday'. At the end of October, he then moved back into the same apartment. As a result, the Otovorene Oci spent several days ringing up several people, among them the administrative headquarters of the military police in Zagreb. The day after, in the evening, the military police arrived at the apartment in order to take the soldier with them, ostensibly on instructions from Zagreb, but it so happened that just at that moment the man in question had left the apartment. When, after his return the next morning, the family, as requested alarmed the police again, but no one turned up. The soldier, however, now cleared and arranged the apartment in such a way that the family could be turned out according to the legal terms of an eviction. The family then received notice to get out by the middle of the next month. As the day of their official eviction drew nearer, news of this judicial misdemeanour had got around, and caused uproar in many places.

Family Sepic for their part could now see a chance to keep their apartment and so its members decided to resist the officially authorized expulsion. This is the first such case in Split and for the activists of human rights organisations here the first opportunity to show themselves in strong support of the family. In fact Family Sepic did receive hoped-for confirmation from the constitutional court to the effect that it would not have to vacate the apartment. On the day of the planned eviction, human rights activists and other volunteers had already firmly placed themselves in the apartment just in case something unexpected took place, but in fact on this particular day everything remained quiet. However, on the day following, the war invalid appeared with a number of his former colleagues-in-arms carrying three hand grenades and threatened to blow up the apartment if he were not allowed into the apartment. Mrs Sepic then had to leave and settles in with neighbours. Otvorene Oci volunteers, together with a journalist friend of theirs hurry to the scene, but are intercepted by the 'invalid's' comrades and threatened. They are obliged to leave having achieved nothing. The civilian police do nothing to rectify matters either. The only thing that is finally accomplished is the writing of an official protest, which is later distributed by human rights groups all over the country in various newspapers and magazines. Nothing seems to help, and frustration is the order of the day.

In a new attempt to get things straight, another volunteer, accompanied by a journalist, together visit this invalid soldier in order to hear the other side of the story. The latter tells of his suffering in the last few years, and that he is obliged to do something against what he recognizes as his ruined life. Whether this is due to the pressure he has been subjected to by those responsible or, in spite of it, is uncertain, but the news gets round that the upshot is that this war veteran had been accorded another apartment and that Mrs Sepic could return to her own dwelling. Finally, in November, the old soldier moves out. However, in doing so, he gives the apartment key to a comrade who had lost both legs in the war, and this man now uses this dwelling on the fifth floor in a building without a lift! No one feels responsible for this new situation either, and everything starts all over again.

Family Sepic continues to live for a further year with her neighbours. But she does not give up the struggle for her rights and again goes to court. At court, the war invalid gives evidence of the fact that he had occupied the apartment with the permission of the accommodation authorities. Mrs Sepic nevertheless stubbornly insists on something being done in her case by those responsible in military circles, and the accommodation authority. In this, she is supported by the 'Dalmatian Committee for Solidarity', by the 'Dalmatian Committee for Human Rights' and by the 'Croatian-

Helsinki Committee' as well as Otvorene Oci .The activists in Split organize a national campaign by fax which is put together by the 'Croatian Co-ordination for Human Rights'. Finally, Mrs Sepic wins the day, but not before the war invalid can be provided with another apartment. By this time it is already May 1995. Despite this setback, return to her apartment is duly celebrated in an atmosphere where *"wine flowed in abundance and everybody was in a good mood."* Family Sepic is an exception. According to estimates submitted by activists, 280 violent evictions occurred in Split between 1992 and the early summer of 1994, and only five families were been able to return to their former dwellings.

"Enemy Activity" – The New Weapon Against Refractory Tenants

The struggles in court are not primarily concerned with who is in the right about a controversial apartment. A new element is to be seen at work in the affairs of tenants who kick up a fuss about their residences. These are now accused by the public prosecutor's office as indulging in what it refers to as culpable, 'hostile activity' towards the state of Croatia. This article of law is worded as follows: *"Apartment rights are not valid for anyone who has participated or is participating in enemy activity against the Republic of Croatia".* The consequence of this is that the tenant loses his legal right to occupy property (apartment). Since 1994, more and more people have been obliged to see themselves as persons involved in 'enemy activity'. Up to the middle of 1995, there have been 6000 recorded cases throughout the country, 600 of these alone in Split. Human rights groups and Otvorene Oci accompany the lawyers of those affected into the courtrooms.

One of these cases is that of family Petrov. It is a case concerning a law which has been in operation since 1992, but which is nevertheless only occasionally put into effect, and one which often has unsuspected consequences. If family Petrov is pronounced guilty of enemy activity, then this will be seen as a precedent in Croatia. What, in fact, are the Petrovs guilty of? They themselves are actually guilty of nothing directly, but Mrs Petrov's parents are persons under suspicion. These, namely, were the original tenants who left Croatia in 1992 and passed on the apartment to her daughter.

However, when the parents attempt to return to Croatia later, they are accused by the Split court of being guilty of 'enemy activity'. But what have they done? The fact alone that the Petrovs did not return to Croatia immediately is seen as sufficient proof for the court that *"the defendants do not accept this state or its politics."* (This is taken from the official verdict). In this way, the daughter and her family lose the right to live in the apartment. The family's lawyer contests this verdict at the final court of appeal. In the summer of 1995, the administration undertakes the eviction even before the constitutional court has come to a decision. The eviction can then in this way be postponed, but the next date for official eviction is fixed, and in the meantime the Petrov family is put under pressure. Soldiers arrive and threaten Mr Petrov. The police fetch the family for interrogation, for the reason that the judge feels herself threatened by Mr Petrov. A few days later, the police question Mr Petrov's mother, while he, Petrov, calls for a revision of the whole issue. The family gives up. Its members ask the activists not to demonstrate anymore or to take part in other activities on their behalf. They make further enquires as to what possibilities there are to emigrate to another country. Finally, Mr Petrov leaves his homeland, having been supplied with a number of contacts by volunteers of the Otvorene Oci.

The Military no Longer under Restraint: The Wave of Evictions in 1995

In August 1995, there is the hint of a new kind of eviction in Split. The role of military personnel which, after the violent takeovers in Western Slavonia and Krajina, now enjoys overwhelming approval for their actions among the people, begins to play an important role in carrying out evictions. Soldiers knock on doors and introduce themselves as the representatives of a so-called 'Military Accommodation Commission.' When the inhabitants then open the door, soldiers forcibly occupy the apartment and drive out the tenants. Anyone resisting entry is faced with a summons from the so-called 'Sub-commission of the Military Housing Commission'. This is a 'committee' that simply doesn't exist, but how is the tenant to know that? The court summons is to see to it that the tenant leaves his apartment for a time. In the intervening time, the soldiers then forcibly enter the apartment. In principle, the inhabitants have both the civilian police and the military police on their side, but in practical terms, the local police force declares itself incapable of intervening in military affairs, and the military police for its part remains as a rule passive in such situations.

Members of human rights organisations and international observers as well as Otvorene Oci members also enter the apartment and these, too, are placed more frequently under increasing pressure. Activists, who are known all too well by the authorities in question, and who are responsible for these intrusions are frequently the victims of murder threats. Family members are threatened with violence or rape. In those disputes arising in the apartments themselves, activists and family members are forcibly prevented from using the telephone to ask for assistance. These acts of violence are exclusively directed at women.

In December 1995, such evictions grow to take on the proportions of a campaign. In this month alone, nine such attempts at eviction are registered on a Saturday by Otvorene Oci and Split human rights groups. In each case, the families are either allowed to return to their homes or the operation remains a future threat. Such a large number of attempts has not yet occurred and so it seems that a certain means of carrying out these operations has been previously agreed to. It is appalling to realise that the military police do not attempt to prevent them or to intervene. However, this state of affairs comes to an end in the early part of the following week when an inspector of the Criminal Department of the Military Police puts an end to this arbitrary activity on the part of soldiers by both preventing a forthcoming eviction and by threatening perpetrators with legal action.

Privatisation or the Solving of Conflicts?

Since the summer of 1994, the Dalmatian Committee for Solidarity (DOS) has been making a plea for tenants living in controversial accommodation to buy their apartments. Since this requires a corresponding amendment to the existing law, the DOS has been busy lobbying in this direction. Fax messages are sent and international organisations, co-ordinated by Otvorene Oci , have also been requested to write to appropriate governmental departments to bring about their wishes. And in November 1994, the law is indeed amended in this direction. However, it does not conform with the wishes of human rights organisations in many important points. From a practical point of view, it tends rather to hinder those tenants who have been illegally removed from their homes from buying them and so from being in a position to return to their former accommodation.

The passing of this law brings about a new element within the eviction scene. Anyone who wishes to buy his apartment now has 60 days time to get all the documents together so as to make an application. From this it is clear that there will be a final decision on the question of ownership in the near future. If, then, this is the case, the forcible occupation of apartments will no longer be a rewarding activity, which, in turn, raises pressure until such time as facts are presented. The evictions now escalate to unsuspected proportions, reaching dimensions whereby evictions are not even announced beforehand, so that no one can prepare for the eventuality of being on the spot to deal with the situation or put up resistance. *"It doesn't look too good"*, the Otvorene Oci says, summing up the situation, hoping at the same time that the tension will die down as soon as the time limit has run out. However, the next few weeks give no indication of calming down.

A similar wave of evictions engulfs Zagreb. Here, too, there is no opportunity for activists to cope anymore with the situation. One reason for this powerlessness is the incalculability of an eviction strike, and another is the claims being made on them as a result of the new situation by Krajina and Western Slavonia. Almost all of them are concerned with projects in these areas. The only hope at the moment is that the courts will, after all, finally regulate matters fairly.

The Never-ending Theme of Eviction

The subject of eviction is something which occupies the concern of Otvorene Oci and will do time and again in the years which follow. Some of these go on for years, during which those affected are accompanied into the courts by teams. They either defend themselves against the accusations about being 'hostile to the state', or oppose eviction and strive to claim legal title against the occupiers of their houses. In the years which follow, Otvorene Oci tries – often unsuccessfully - to accompany attempts to oust unlawful tenants from their houses or apartments. Lawyers and activists are not satisfied with the situation either. Again and again, their attention is diverted from what is actually going on. One of them recalls the situation as follows:

> *"After that come other problems, and everybody has forgotten over the years, and we have forgotten what happened to people who cannot return to their flats, and they can't receive even their furniture back, their things, and so on. The soldiers generally stole everything, and also they looted everything from flats, including even pictures, even photos of children, everything. And for me this is terrible, even to talk about it, and even the victims finally understood that they could not get back into their apartments by simply waiting for the court to come to them."*

Lawyers and activists wish to keep the people affected by eviction as well as international authorities in touch and active on their behalf by setting up intensive documentation and information about these wrangles and disputes regarding eviction. In this regard, Otvorene Oci is of help by drawing up project applications which publicise these cases both in book form and in other publications.

"They have contributed a lot to getting things done": Otvorene Oci in Action

At the end of 1997 as the interviews for this book were being prepared, many former volunteers and their colleagues look back on their time in Split and the critical time of battling for houses. Respect and admiration accompany their assessments of team members active there at the time.

> *"They were very courageous. I remember Rosa and Xaver, they were the first activists here in 1994, and when they came, this kind of eviction stopped. But we have had other problems with apartments, and with people who weren't able to get back to their apartments and so on, and they were incredibly courageous. They had more courage than activists here. They were able even to enter a flat and to talk with a soldier, and as they were from abroad, it was less of a problem for them than, for example, to a journalist from the media at Split because you must know this element of character in people in the east; they appreciate people from abroad too much and it's good to take advantage of, and it's necessary to remember it when we think about BPT."*

Activists recall other volunteers from Otvorene Oci: *"I was fascinated by their courage, these foreigners who showed so much courage and had a great wish to really get at the basic truth. I mean, it isn't important what side you're on, but that you're on the side of truth and justice. That's how we became good friends. We've fought together all the time."* Judges, too, are impressed by the presence of foreign observers, and one lawyer recalls that, *"but if they're alone, the judge is able to say, 'Okay, I will call you when I have collected all the documents', but doesn't mention a date, and this could mean one, two or three years, but when observers - especially from abroad - are in the courtroom, the judge doesn't have the courage to say something like that, and they generally mention date, and so we observe it."* Here, Otvorene Oci takes up its place with other international observers.

A journalist from an independent newspaper in Split emphasizes what is special about the Balkan Peace Team: *"They were the only organisation at that time interested in evictions."* He goes on: *"And also not only interested, they'd also been the most effective, more effective than any local organisation".* Why was this? *"They helped local organisations, which were not sure what to do precisely. They got hold of information from the families, sought to obtain information from soldiers, put pressure on local authorities as well as international organisations to get them interested in the evictions..."* Another important factor was that the foreigners stood by local activists during threatening situations when, for example, they both entered apartments together.

> *"There was then no difference between them and us. Further, it was very important for those doing the evicting to realize that there were foreign observers on the spot to note what was happening. That put them off a bit at least and they were therefore less inclined to be more aggressive, although on the other hand there were situations where there was no consideration for their presence and attacks on 'Open Eyes' people took place, all the way from rough treatment, threats and actual bodily harm, matters which were later reported in the local press."*

Even when the two groups have been shipwrecked once together, the experience has nevertheless welded them together. One activists has this to say on the subject: *"But the eviction was continued and we would sit on the floor and try to stop them. But it wasn't a success and we had to go out of the flat and it was the same stress for us as for Otoc [Otvorene Oci]. It was a big experience for them and for us, too. And in that moment we were totally united, and it was so nice for us."*

The volunteers of Otvorene Oci, too, in retrospect had the impression that a solid contribution had been made, of *"having really done something worthwhile".* This hangs together with the fact that the volunteers, too, felt that the presence of foreigners had an influence on the police, even if this was only small. Seen as a 'grass roots' organisation, the Balkan Peace Team exerted no direct influence on the Croatian government. In this sense, however, it cannot be looked upon in the same way or compete with other organisations like the OSCE of the EU, and, in addition, has no political weight to exert. On the other hand, it cannot quite be assessed. and this fact urges the police and authorities to be more careful than they might otherwise be. In the course of time, the volunteers do not feel treated in any way differently than 'the rest' of the activists whose cause they support. In contrast to their Croatian colleagues, the volunteers do not regard themselves as being in such an active role. They see themselves rather as supporters of local activists: if these are active, then so are they, if not, they are not either. In no circumstances should Otvorene Oci 'go it alone', and take local organisations by surprise or try even to take over leadership. This would go against the declared policies of the Balkan Peace Team.

Having said this much, the matter remains a tricky tightrope crossing. Practice requires constant decision-making. Local partners expect an active role without telling them what to do. The volunteers see so many possibilities. Nevertheless, there are chances for them only to build bridges, as it were, to help local activists to expand their scope of action. After all, it is they who have to carry on the work when the Balkan Peace Team is no longer on the scene. In this way, Rosa is quite aware of her task when to the head of the military police wants to speak to her. She takes a local activist with her to the meeting and does not herself take part in the proceedings, a conversation which then begins to develop of itself. The police officer and the local colleague then get down to talking about everything which is necessary to talk about with each other directly, there and then.

The Otvorene Oci teams also lay down bridges between themselves and other national organisations and international organisations such as the European Community Monitoring Mission or with members within the offices of the OSCE which have established themselves in Croatia. Again and again, meetings are arranged to talk about strategy and in order to reach an agreed objective. In the critical period of October, 1994, things are ripe: activists of various organisations in Zagreb are to be put together with observers from the EU Mission. Otvorene Oci organizes everything, sends out invitations – and precisely on this day, many activists are arrested at a particularly dramatic eviction. *"Of course, the meeting was cancelled,"* the office in Zagreb reports in its transcript of proceedings. *"The only good thing was that a rather influential member of the Swedish delegation to ECMM (in fact the head of the delegation) attended the – cancelled - meeting and the fact that all the invited participants were in jail made quite and impression on him. We believe he'll use his influence to help seek a legislative solution for the problem."*

Sources

Amnesty International, April 1996; Interviews: Albert P. 1/1997; Andrea Z. 1997; Anselm F. 1997; Horst T. 1997; Ivan J. 1997; Rosa T. 1997; Raj S. 1997; Xaver A. 1997; OtOc 24.8.94, no date, ca 10.94, Evictions; 25.5.1995; 26.7.95; OtOc Sp 8.12.95; 17.12.95; 19.12.95; 26.2.97; OtOc Sp Bi-weekly, 15.-30.8.94; 16.-31.10.94; 1.-15.11.94;16.-30.11.94; 16.-31.5.95; 15.-31.7.95; 1.-15.8.95; 15.-31.8.95; 1.-15.9.95; 1.-15.11.95; OtOc Zg.16.5.96; OtOc Zg Bi-weekly 1/9.94; 2/10.94; 2/11.94; 2/9.95.

(3) Human Rights Monitoring after Military Attacks, Western Slavonia and Krajina, 1995

The 30th April, 1995 is a Sunday. Anselm and Xaver, volunteers from the Otvorene Oci Team in Zagreb are spending their weekend with other volunteers attached to an international aid project in Pakrac. Pakrac is the town in Western Slavonia through which the Croatian inner front line runs and which is largely (two thirds) uninhabitable. Croatian state territory and that controlled by Serbian forces collide with one another here. The border is supervised by UN troops and has been since 1992. The Social Reconstruction Programme, brought into being by the United Nations in 1993 is at work in this town. A part of this programme is the 'Volunteer Project Pakrac', which is run by CARE (Austria) and a Croatian peace organisation, initiated by the Anti-War-Campaign. Their volunteers work in both sections of the divided town and try to bring humanitarian help, re-establish material resources and generally help in the matter of bringing the alienated population together, in this way sustaining the hope that a common future which could re-unite Serbs and Croatians is possible.

Sunday is picnic day. But the situation is tense. Shots are to be heard in the night along the border between Croatia and the so-called 'liberated zone' taken over by the Serbs. Shell attacks can be heard in the distance. On their way from Zagreb to Pakrac, Anselm and Xaver come across a train carrying tanks. The Croatian government has announced 'limited exercises' along the front line. The actual movement of 7000 men and preparations for a military counter-attack remain a secret – not only for the civilian volunteers working on their projects, but also the United Nations and their troops.

What, then, happens in Western Slavonia is the beginning of a military day of reckoning in Croatia. Since the blue-helmeted UN troops have moved in, it has been temporarily quiet in the Krajina area, West and East Slavonia. Prior to this and above all in Western Slavonia, but also in Eastern Slavonia with the town, Vukovar, and in areas to the south, Krajina, with its capital, Knin, the Croatian National Guard, Serbian paramilitary men and the Yugoslavian federal Army have exchanged heavy fire in the period between 1991 and 1992. In Western Slavonia, with a diameter from east to west of about 23 kilometres (ca. 14 miles) and 30 kilometres (ca. 19 miles) from north to south, these bitter struggles have accounted for thousands of lives, especially among civilians. These people not only die in the hail of rifle and shellfire, but are also brutally murdered. Thousands of others flee simply to save their skins. Whole villages and towns are razed to the ground.

In the Krajina area, the symbols of the 'infidel', such as Catholic churches or cemeteries are desecrated and partly or wholly destroyed. The upshot of this brief struggle is that many matters are left unsettled. After the war, Croatia becomes a reception area for refugees from Bosnia. In the spring of 1992 alone, more than 400,000 flee to Croatia.

This respite is a chance to come to a decision about the future by negotiation and peaceful means. However, the desire to come to an understanding among those representing the opinions of the conflicting parties is not very marked. They are much more inclined towards roping in the 'international community' in this case, the UN and its soldiers to fight for their specific interests. In the Krajina region, for example, the Serbs have declared the area as 'autonomous' and called for an independent 'Serbian Republic of Krajina'. In this way, UN troops secure their liberated areas. On the other hand, for the Croatians, UN troops are primarily there to ensure the quickest possible negotiations towards integration, so bringing these so-called 'liberated' areas back into the fold. The United Nations for their part exert themselves to knit the severed parties together again by carrying out a programme of disarmament and by re-establishing the infrastructure of the country. However, a dialogue between Serbs and Croatians on the subject of peacefully forging a common future fails to get off the ground. At the beginning of 1995, the Croatian government openly threatens not to extend the UN mandate and so bring the territory under its control by force of arms.

Securing peaceful integration of Serb dominated areas constitutes an important motivation factor among the peace and human rights groups in Croatia, but also among other international organisations. To this end, therefore, Otvorene Oci undertakes an exploration trip into the Krajina region in spring 1995 in order to seek out persons and groups who would be willing to work towards bringing hostile parties together or towards a change of attitude. Perhaps it is possible for the Balkan Peace Team to help build a bridge between the two inarticulate parties and for this purpose to set up an office in Knin. The prospect of playing a meaningful role in this context of conflict provides strong motivation for the volunteers. In addition, the work of human rights in Croatia itself would be given more credibility if one could supply viable proof of the fact that one is active where Croatia's rights have been curtailed. Military or civil integration of the controversial territories? That is the question. In the spring of 1995, a decision is made and the volunteers of Otvorene Oci are in the middle of it all.

Prelude in Western Slavonia

As evening closed in on the day of the spring picnic there are people in uniform to be seen. Rumours about shell attacks continue to circulate. A call to the UN troops' headquarters in the city is assuring: 'Alert stage I, green, everything OK.' Around midnight, however, the local director of CARE insists on the evacuation of international volunteers. Despite the curfew, a convoy of vehicles draws up heading in the direction of Zagreb. At an intermediate stop, a camp for UN troops, the volunteers learn that war has returned to Western Slavonia.

At ten to six in the morning, a major Croatian offensive begins along the whole course of the front. Only at one point, namely in the suburb, Okucani, can one speak of anything resembling military resistance. Like the UN troops, the Serbian units are apparently entirely oblivious of what is going on. The Croatian government proclaims the action as an 'anti-terrorist measure' and speaks of an attack on a motorway where two people in a car were shot at. The approximately 2750 UN troops remain in their barracks.

Back in Zagreb, the volunteers there ask themselves what they can do in such a situation. Their concern for the civilian population in the war area gives them much to think about. The Croatian government for its part has given an assurance that the rights of minorities will be respected. The volunteers, however, recall the assault of Croatian units in Serb controlled regions during 1993. At that time, soldiers had left an appalling picture of cruelty behind them in terms of brutally murdered civilians. Now volunteers want to do everything in their power to guarantee the well being of everybody in the area to make sure that what has been said is not mere propaganda. They want to witness what is actually happening with their own eyes and subsequently inform the public. That indeed is the one thing they can do: be eyewitness and supply tangible evidence of what they have observed.

In the first place they write letters to members of the parliament and offer their services as accompanying personnel and observers. They also encourage members of parliament to accompany them to Western Slavonia. In the meantime, the war takes on new proportions. The once 'limited action' an 'operation of limited scope and local character' threatens to get out of hand. On Tuesday, 2nd May, a shell hits the market place in Zagreb, killing several people and injuring many more. It is the first of its kind that falls on Zagreb in this war. In the days following and in other Croatian cities, shells rain on other cities which have been fired from Serbian areas. The United

Nations negotiate between 'Krajina Serbs' and the government in Zagreb. On Friday, 5th May, the defenders of Western Slavonia capitulate. Everywhere there are white flags. The Croatian army proceeds then to arrest all men fit for military service and take them to camps for interrogation. Houses are searched for weapons.

This weekend, Otvorene Oci personnel are on the spot with the first politicians. They find cowed inhabitants who want to flee the war area like those 7000 who fled in the first few days of hostilities. There will be several thousand others in the weeks and months following the visit. Most of them will be accompanied by UN troops to the border. They refuse to believe the promises of the Croatian government that they will treated as citizens with equal rights. They fear revenge and assault and suspect that the villains of the piece will get off scot-free. They fear that they will be treated as second-class individuals who will be denied jobs and training opportunities. Many of their fears will be substantiated.

After this first visit, the volunteers belonging to Otvorene Oci decide that, together with volunteers of other international projects, they want to establish a continuous presence of observers in Western Slavonia. Added to this, there is a new task ahead of them in talking to the deputy mayor of Gavrinica, a Serb who had already experienced interrogation by Croatian authorities and was allowed to return home. He belongs to a small circle of well-known, moderate Serbian leaders who now, under Croatian domination, would have to fear for his life.

Because they are known, they would probably be the targets of Croatian extremists. While it is true that he would have personal protection from United Nations soldiers, these soldiers go off duty at 7 pm and so leave the people in their charge exposed to possible attack. While, on the other hand it is true that the Croatian police are there to protect the house, they nevertheless assure us that they cannot effectively hinder anyone who really wants to gain entry. So it was, then, that a member of the Otvorene Oci spent the night and the following night in the politician's house so that he would be present to witness what went on, should anything happen. Only after the American ambassador and other politicians from Zagreb had visited the local politician could the latter muster enough confidence in the promise that the UN surveillance was enough to ensure his safety.

Unarmed protection of persons is also requested elsewhere. In a house next to which soldiers have found temporary accommodation, nineteen women with their children have gathered together to wait for their husbands who have been arrested. They fear that their uniformed neighbours might well try to pay them an unsolicited and unpleasant 'visit'. International volunteers who, as possible witnesses to assault, are also there to hinder molestation. The volunteers of various organisations spend four nights near the women's quarters. The women are tense and distraught. They don't say anything about what they have experienced. Every time there is an explosion in the neighbourhood, they cower together in fright. Could it be that a drunken soldier has shot into the air or has someone just been executed? After four days, the soldiers leave their quarters and the volunteers, too, can end their task of playing watchdogs.

To track down human rights infringement and later document them is Andrea's job, an activist belonging to the Croatian human rights organisation 'Group for Direct Protection of Human Rights' in Zagreb. Driving down to Western Slavonia on the 10th May, she is accompanied by volunteer from Otvorene Oci. They stop where there are freshly dug graves and at places where larger excavations have been recently undertaken. No grass is to grow over mass graves. They take note of assaults on neighbours by neighbours, of plundering, and they register threats and demands on remaining Serbs to leave.

On the whole, they are able to register correct behaviour on the part of the Croatian army. Assaults by army personnel have occurred, but these are not the rule, and do not appear to be part of a premeditated strategy. The police, too, who take over when the army departs, also carry out their duties with a certain degree of respect. Sensibly enough, the units have been recruited from other regions, so that the danger of someone wishing to settle old bills is considerably reduced. All this is scrupulously written down in reports every evening by local organisations, but also by the Team, since the gathering of information for later dissemination is the be and end-all of their presence on the spot.

In all this they are able to ascertain that people of Serbian nationality have difficulty in adapting themselves to the new situation. These do not know what rights they have now when their men are released from the interrogation centre and how one can get hold of the necessary papers in order to leave the country. Added to this, there is fear of having to do with the new people in power and one automatically avoids visiting local authorities.

Rumours circulate about what horrors Croatians are capable of perpetrating when abroad and are only too readily believed. Volunteers establish communication channels. They collect, filter and collate information from Croatian government locations,

UN organisations, international aid organisations and others and in this way are able to differentiate between rumour, half-truths, false information and propaganda. What they are able to filter out in this way they pass on to the population on their journeys from place to place. At the same time, they are able to give 'individual help' and accompany people to local authorities so that they can make the appropriate applications for papers and so on.

The journeys undertaken by the Team together with their colleagues in the country are confined to the region around the centre of Pakrac. Many of the remote villages spread around the countryside are not visited at all. It "seemed to become a veritable free supermarket for anyone with a vehicle or cart", one member of the Team writes in a report for the month of November. Abandoned houses are cleared out. Nothing of any value is left behind. What is left is destroyed, dirtied and scattered. Cattle, which cannot be taken along, are 'looked after' by Croatian helpers against what is referred to as a 'small sum', that is, between 5 and 10 deutschmarks per animal. Small wonder that at these horrendous prices for 'care' soon no one can pay anymore. Only little by little do these deplorable circumstance come to light, and it takes even longer of course for them to be halted.

In May the soldiers gradually pull out. More and more men return from the interrogation camps, and tension becomes noticeably less. The Croatian government issues its balance of Serbian casualties during the blitz attack which it alludes to as 'Operation Flash': There are some 188 persons involved, among these a possible 54 civilians. Otvorene Oci is able to collect information from various sources and later produces a higher number of casualties.

In the following months, the Team documents everyday discrimination with meticulous accuracy and exposes governmental propaganda as lies. However, it also registers the fact that steps were in fact taken towards normalization, and that efforts to realize equal rights for everyone were indeed undertaken.

Despite their many efforts, the members of the Team are deeply frustrated and disappointed. Instead of contributing to the development of peace, they feel that their presence, and their researches, their dissemination of information has only been helpful insofar as it has prevented the region from falling under the total shadow of war. *"Many people say that this conflict would have been much worse were it not for the presence of internationals after the fighting. People are beginning to worry about the future when, they fear, the press and international volunteers will leave the area."* - So one report. At least the attention of the Balkan Peace Team has remained focused on them, even if the war in Western Slavonia is only the beginning.

Decision in Krajina

At the end of July 1995, press reports are full of rumours, which suggest that the next offensive is about to begin. And so it is. Croatian troops break through the Serbian front on 29th July from the Serbian side and within a few days manage to conquer the 'Serbian Republic of Krajina'. The attack, which involves the deployment of 100,000 men, results in an enormous wave of fleeing refugees, so that on 8th August, 200,000 of these are expected in Banja Luka. Then stillness settles on the region. International observers are not admitted, regardless of whether they belong to the EU or whether they call themselves Otvorene Oci or local human rights helpers. On TV, the Croatian government calls on the people in the newly occupied regions to stay where they are and vouches for their safety. It is mostly older people who stay. Without their families they are dependent on help from the outside.

At the end of August, the UN accuses the Croatian army of human rights infringements during the offensive. These include arson, plunder and torture. At this point in time, the army had loosened its grip on the occupied territories, and, bit-by-bit, the truth begins to emerge. On 13th August, the Zagreb Team drives into the northern part of Krajina. Access from the south is still not possible. The Split Team manages on the 17th August merely to reach the first village behind the border before being sent back by military police at the next sentry post. The objective, Drnis, is not accessible. The situation is 'too dangerous', say the policeman on duty, and in any case their papers are not such which will allow them to go on into the country. On the 19th August, two days later, the second attempt is successful. Together with the Dalmatian Solidarity Committee, they get as far as Knin and so gain their first impressions.

The extent of the destruction can only be recorded in mere figures, but not in words. Eighty per cent of the houses have been damaged. Some villages, Kistanje, for example, having about 2000 inhabitants, has been utterly destroyed. One volunteer recalls the scene:

> *"We got in and it was just devastation, absolute; we were walking into people's houses, you know, people that had obviously ten minutes to pack, and, you know, they left everything.*

That was the first, and I remember coming back in the car that day and pulling over and just breaking down and crying and crying. And then, for the next two weeks after that I was really emotional, found it really hard to deal with. But, we started going in, quite a lot, just going up into more villages, and seeing who was left, seeing if anyone was taking care of them, if they were getting visits. Because none of the big organisations, like UNHCR and OXFAM [were there] - because it was so removed in the countryside, it was villages everywhere - and we weren't really geared up yet. ... "

Otvorene Oci and activists from Split and Zagreb belong to those who concern themselves with the collection and providing of evidence. They drive to the villages in Krajina, speak to those few who have remained and listen to the reports of murders of villagers who did not want to leave. The military re-conquest of Krajina is long over. The Croatian authorities need no longer to fear armed resistance.

However, the situation in Western Slavonia is quite different than that in Krajina where an end to violence is not yet in sight. A witness reports later from Knin that the troops invading the city had at first behaved correctly in the first few days of occupation. These, however, were then followed by other units and it was these latter which began to plunder and lay fires. The murder of older Serbs who had believed the promises of the government, now even increase and reach the figure of nine dead in one single village, Varivode, a tragic high point.

An Otvorene Oci report called 'The Krajina Murders' sums up its interim balance, a balance of murdered civilians, mostly old people. These old people had their homes in remote villages that had been plundered and deserted, now desolate and surrounded by ruins and dead farm animals. One volunteer speaks of his findings in a strictly confidential report:

"A very old woman lives alone in a very remote village. She says: 'I was four years old when the First World War came through here. Then I saw the Second World War. We had to hide in the woods. Now this war- I don't really know why I'm still alive.' Every day the soldiers come to take something away from her. Yesterday it was the generator, so that she has no electricity. The day before, it was one of her few remaining cows. With

each thing stolen, they take a bit of her life. They are killing her slowly, and the police do nothing to stop them.

She shows them her old, gnarled hands and says to them, 'Look, how can you steal from me.'

They laugh and reply, 'We've got to feed the soldiers, old woman!'

One of them points a gun at her head. 'I should just shoot you now. '

She's tough. 'Well, why don't you then? '

'You're not worth the bullet.'

Nine old people are shot dead in the village of Vrhovina. Someone dragged them out of her house, and shot her on the front porch of her house. You can see the hole in the wall where the bullet exited the back of her head. It's surrounded by blood, bits of bone and hair. Nine old people, no threat to anybody, died like this, and somebody pulled the trigger. Some humanitarian groups estimate that up to six elderly people are murdered every day in their homes in the former Krajina. The authorities release no information.

We drive through kilometres of burnt-out villages. Each house has been plundered, and then burnt. The large rib cage of a cow sticks out of the ashes of one barn. The bones of other cows litter the road. In one village, dead cows and horses lie all along the road and in the front yards of burnt-out houses. They rot in the sun, and the stench is unbelievable. Millions of maggots squirm in the rotting holes in the bodies. One horse rots next to the body of its small offspring. Another, further down the road, lies in two halves, hit by an anti-tank rocket. Someone has come through this village in an orgy of violence, massacring every living thing, burning all the buildings.

My friend's mom grew up in this village. She walks through the ashes of her house, and has no words. Her husband pokes around in an unburned part of the attic. He finds a woven rope of garlic, something to save, and holds it aloft in triumph. He starts to call out to his wife, then looks at the garlic string and realizes what a pathetic thing it is amidst all this destruction. He lets it fall."

As under the focus of a magnifying glass, things begin to increase in intensity as Otvorene Oci volunteers describe the impressions gained in stories like this since the summer.

Since the middle of August, the volunteers from Otvorene Oci drive together with human rights activists from the neighbouring region into Krajina. The Zagreb office is responsible for the north, while the Split office looks after its business in the south. What these young people are faced with is difficult to process. In the reports which they prepare and send to the co-ordination committee, the reader easily overlooks the anguish they experience. Despite this, these volunteers themselves become private detectives making their own investigations.

Together with a representative from the Croatian Helsinki Committee, an Otvorene Oci volunteer follows up the rumour that in Orton Brdo another corpse might be lying there whose owner was supposed to have been killed on 21st August. A witness takes the two observers into the house of a Mrs Vujnovic, 85, and there after a while they do in fact find her corpse. The report on the Krajina murders is a sober one: *"The initial search was without result, but a closer look revealed the decomposed body hidden under a sleeping bag on the floor beside a bed. The UN HRAT [UN Human Rights Action Team] has been informed."*

The United Nations established Action Teams to enquire into the human rights issue. Four such teams are underway in Krajina, only with full freedom to move around since 8th and 11th August respectively. It is important to local human rights activists and the Otvorene Oci to employ such teams. The local police force is not 100% reliable, and again and again, the suspected murder is presented as suicide. For those representing the interests of human rights groups it is especially important for them to establish with absolute certainty how the individuals they find as corpses actually came to die. Only in this way can they contest the reduced figures issued by the government which are supposed to fully account for the deaths of older Serbs.

But why take the trouble at all? The dead are dead and the perpetrators of these crimes will probably never be caught.

However, at the beginning of July, 1996, the first court proceedings take place concerned with murders committed in Krajina, where eight men were accused of committing murder involving the deaths of eighteen civilians. After three months of legal investigation, two of these men were sentenced and the others acquitted, since it wasn't possible to establish their guilt beyond all doubt. During proceedings it was discovered that the experts could only poorly re-construct the course of events leading up to the crime. Too much time was lost before the investigation, the investigation itself was carelessly carried out, the ballistics expert, for example, cannot precisely establish which weapon was actually used to kill the victim. Another irregularity also comes to light: all those accused insist that they were members of the armed forces at the time. On the other hand, they all possess papers, which testify to the fact that at the time of the murders they had already been demobilized. They indignantly deny this prior dating. They speak, too, of the administration of torture during interrogations.

In the summer of 1996, one year after 'Operation Storm', the Croatian government adjusts the figure of those dead in Krajina to 1000. Human rights workers contest this. The justification for their doubts is to be seen from the graves at the cemeteries. There are eight hundred identified graves alone in the Krajina area, half of them without names. In their eyes, the declaration is only an attempt to pacify the international community which is much concerned about the human rights issue in Croatia. The upshot of operations such as this one quite clearly demonstrates how important the painstaking work of collecting evidence is, but, at the same time, how difficult it is to arrive at justice. Notwithstanding, legal appraisal of this nature is at least one way of reaching this goal and Otvorene Oci are contributing to it.

Making sure that those among the civilian population who have survived murder still manage to carry on with their lives is a matter for the humanitarian organisations. The United Nations' High Commissioner for Refugees' Office has set up a service for refugees in Knin. The head of this organisation, UNHCR, together with a volunteer visits an old woman in order to bring her ready-made food. She lives alone in a village and is 94 years old. Like all the houses in the place, her house was also burned to the ground. Now she lives outside with nothing more than a blanket to keep her warm, together with three chairs on which she sleeps. Despite all attempt to persuade her to leave, she is too frightened to go. She therefore remains dependent on the life-saving rations delivered to her, although she doesn't quite know how to open the packages. Apart from what the helpers bring, she has nothing – not even water. Just how many people are in the same or a similar situation has not yet been officially stated by September. Nor is there any sort of overall assessment, since the villages lie so remotely situated from one another for the UNHCR to be able to investigate every single one.

It is not only transport which presents a problem. Without special identification papers allowing them freedom of movement, people in distress cannot get as far as the UNHCR office. They have first to acquire documents. This is a time consuming business which requires them, too, to put in a personal appearance at police headquarters in Knin.

Information Junction

In the course of time, the Otvorene Oci team members in Zagreb gradually become experts on information about Krajina. They supply groups with information, which includes details on Croatian groups, journalists from abroad, but also on international human rights organisations such as Human Rights Watch.
Together with two journalists from Holland, they go out to find partners to interview in the remote villages of Krajina, and to gather information about life there after the 'Storm'. On their way they pass a burning house – in the meantime it is November 1995! They film the house and suddenly men appear and start calling them names: *"'What do you want here? Haven't you ever seen a fire before?' While the journalists hastily pack up, our interpreter replies, 'Well, no, we haven't seen a fire like this before. Would you like to tell us something about it?'"* Then they drive off. The drunken men they had encountered follow them for a while in a car. The team reports the experience to a United Nations police unit at to the police headquarters in Vojnic. They describe the men. This time all went well, but whether the police will go after the men to establish their identity is highly unlikely.
On reflection, the volunteers have shown astonishingly little fear during their tours. Not enough, one of them notes, looking back, and draws attention to the many mines which are a constant danger. Once or twice he had driven through a minefield without knowing it. Making investigations in houses is also not without its risks. They aren't too worried about their security. Their local colleagues are there, they say, at first rather anxious about the presence of foreigners, but then in the first few weeks when familiarity has been established, the are glad that volunteers from abroad are with them. Later, when they become known to soldiers and police in the Krajina region it is above all the car which is much sought after as an attractive means of transport.
On the other hand, it is important to be able to make contact between the local activists and international organisations, especially with the UN civilian police and their Office for Civilian Matters. This, for both sides, is new ground, since both are not

used to co-operation and have first to discover what kind of people they are dealing with. Nevertheless, only when these organisations follow up cases which local human rights workers have unearthed will there be a chance of the authorities tracking down crime. The more publicity there is about murder and plunder, the more likely it is that protection of civilians becomes an actuality. This is why the researches and subsequent reports set up by Otvorene Oci from Krajina and local human rights activists are so important.

At the same time, there is frustration that one is not able to do more. One volunteer recalls:

> *"In those three months we probably went ten times, we just go and come back the same day. And when we were there, we would try to go many different places and see if we could find people. And if we found them we would try to talk to them; What do you need, what is going on here, what are the problems? But after two or three visits it's very obvious what the problems are. And then you feel in a situation that you need to help people. And there really wasn't much you could do – except to feel bad."*

The team in Split is also concerned with cases of murder. For the Zagreb team, on the other hand, the main focus of attention is the refugee camp in Kupljensko not far from Vojnic. There are up 25,000 people in this place literally living on the street. The confusion of this mad war is symbolized in a special way here in the fate of these people. Properly speaking, the people here stem from Bosnia and are followers of the Bosnian Muslim leader, Abdic. In the winter of 1994, they were driven for the first time into what was then Serbian Krajina. In the spring of 1995, they try to re-conquer lost ground in the neighbourhood of Bihac. At first they are successful and a return to their homeland seems within reach. Then the Krajina area falls into Croatian hands, and in Bosnia, Croatian and Bosnian, government troops once more gain the upper hand in and around Bihac.

The military balance of power drives refugees into a veritable dilemma. They are too fearful to return to the area around Bihac and find themselves settled in a narrow valley between Velika Kladusa and Vojnic. The provisional village stretches along some seven kilometres of road. The High Commission for Refugees and the UN Human Rights Action Team try to relieve the desperate supply situation, but the convoy of six trucks carrying provisions, water and including an ambulance is stopped by Croatian soldiers. The refugees become the plaything of regional interests. From the governmental point of view, there is an understanding between Croatian and Bosnia-Herzegovina that the refugees should be transported back to Bosnia. However, that is not what refugees want. In order to prevent the refugees from settling in for good, the Croatian army places obstacles in the way of the humanitarian organisations' supply when and wherever they can. Despite every obstacle, these organisations do in fact manage finally to establish an ordered plan of aid. The sad thing is that even the need to make the camp habitable for the winter is vehemently resisted, so that when the autumn returns to the mountains, the place is transformed into a muddy swamp in which the sanitary situation is truly catastrophic.

The Otvorene Oci is primarily concerned with whether the UN High Commission for Refugees can perhaps agree after all to a forced return of these people. Together with Médecins Sans Frontières (Doctors Without Borders) who are also active in this camp, team members get into touch with the camp inhabitants by asking them certain questions in order to introduce a dialogue the opinions and also get to know the opinions of sufferers. The team is criticized for this action in which it is revealed that many of those talked to expressed the wish to be taken in by a third country, *"but people told us we shouldn't have done that. We were keeping their hopes up,"* one volunteer remarks, looking back.

A second focus of attention is directed to the role of the Croatian military personnel and to the police in the camp. Whether these, too, we want to know, only do what is required of them in the course of their duties, and nothing more. There are regular visits up to the camp and regular reports follow. The camp is not accessible to local activists; only foreign personnel are allowed in.

Promises and Reality

In December 1995, Croatia guarantees the return of the refugees on signing the Dayton Accord. However, the Otvorene Oci report that the 'anniversary' of the 'Storm' in August 1996 reveals quite another side to the story. A year after this event, life in the Krajina region has still not properly returned to normal. There is no mentionable rebuilding of the villages in Serbia. Those formerly inhabited by 2000 people now only have two to three old inhabitants. The primary school in Knin is still not functioning. School textbooks in Cyrillic script lay scattered all over the hallway. The majority of churches have either been plundered or are still mined. *"Despite pressure from the organisations working in the area and the international community, the area remains without the basis of a working legal structure. Looting continues on a scale worse than before, and incidents of harassment and intimidation, although reported, continue to be ignored."*

Apparently, the return of refugees is not desired. In the course of 1996, about forty Serbs return per month. They have to prove that their house is still standing; otherwise they do not receive their papers. Many of them leave the area again after having been threatened and intimidated. About as many people leave to join their families in Serbia each month. In the Serbian village of Krcke, a group of Serbian inhabitants get together to rebuild their houses. Each week, they come up from the coast and set about their renovation work. One day they arrive in the usual way to find their houses in ruins again. 'Professionals' were at work, the police tell them. The police report is not available in this instance nor is the case to be brought to court. So much for the protection of the law!

Sometimes indeed human rights organisations ask themselves why do they trouble themselves to try and help. The Helsinki Committee helps a certain man from Serbia who would like to drive out to his house in the Krajina region. When he arrives and opens the door of his house he treads on an explosive charge, which explodes immediately and kills him on the spot. Repeatedly mined houses become a serious threat, because houses are being constantly mined again. There is no certainty that the house has not been tampered with, even if the owner is away even for an hour or two. So much, then, on the subject of survival of those returning home in the Krajina region a year after the 'Storm'.

Otvorene Oci continues to observe the situation in the years which follow. The team regularly drives into the region and documents graves and the condition of monasteries and also takes opportunity to visits the inhabitants of villages. The documentation of 'non-return' and of 'non-normality' is a salient consideration in their work.

Sources

Böhm 2001, 180-207; Calic 1996; Interview Anselm F. 1997; Chris N.1997; 17; Diana M. 1998; Rosa T. 1997; Xaver A. 1997; Meder / Reimann 1996, 24; OtOc 2.5.95; 7.5.95; 8.5.95; 9.5.95; 13.5.95; 27.5.95; 6.6.95; 1.11.95; 15.6.95; 18.7.96; 8.1996, 2-7 Assessment UNHCR; OtOc Sp 16.8.95; 17.8.95; 19.8.95; 26.8.95;14.10.95; 19.7.96; OtOc Sp Biweekly, 1.-15.8.95; 1.-15.11.95; OtOc Zg 9.95; 7.9.95; 22.9.95; OtOc Zg Biweekly 2/8.95; 1/11.95, Hearts and Minds, Definitely not for publication in any way, shape, or form! 2/11.95; Reuters 1.5.95.

(4) Encouraging and Networking with Local Activists Following Military Attack: Croatia, 1995

The brutal conquest of rebellious parts of Western Slavonia and the Krajina region dashed the hopes of many activists in Croatia. The integration of Western Slavonia and Eastern Slavonia and the Krajina region was to be facilitated by peaceful means employing political negotiation. Such symbols as the Pakrac-Volunteers-Project of the Croatian Antiwar Campaign stand for this intention. International volunteers who are working to reconstruct the area and who are helping on both sides of the demarcation line of a divided city are tangible proof that separation can be overcome. Since its beginnings in 1993, this project has developed very well. In retrospect, Anna D. recalls,

> *"The work was going very nicely until 1995 and we all got the idea that this is the place where peaceful integration will occur. And then there was a military police action in May 95. So out of that came that very clear picture that - you know, volunteers worked and worked and worked and worked for two years and it was all gone in five days, because the Serbian people - many were killed - and those who stayed were actually trapped, so that there's no choice to stay. And a very painful process started."*

The Shock

Many activists working with Otvorene Oci now ask themselves the basic question: *"What can we strive for now politically? ...Now that there is nothing left to fight for."* Military incursions cause such huge movements of refugees that these lose their minority status in Croatia. They are now no longer considered 'worthy of protection' and furnished with special rights according to the constitution – at least on paper. There is no minority question anymore and so no starting point for political activity. And more than this: many activists feel personally affected. Many have relatives in the Krajina region who have lost their parents' house.

One can deduce from experience with the authorities in Croatia what will happen to the remaining Serbs in the occupied areas. First, human rights infringements and assault on the part of the military, then discrimination via bureaucracy and the new elite. How can the few human rights and peace organisations stand by those seeking their rights and requiring advice? What can these few pit against the overwhelming wave of violence and the glorification of victory? While the conquest of West Slavonia in May surprises everybody and inspires intensive work in the region, the 'Krajina Storm' in the summer meets with an opposition fighting to its utmost capacity. By the time July comes round, it becomes clearer and clearer that a political opposition to match the military offensive in the Krajina region is quite out of the question. At the end of the month, Anna D. in conversation with a volunteer from the Otvorene Oci team asks sarcastically: *"Is there anyone here who would put non-violent intervention into practice? Lie down in the path of a tank, for example? Now's your chance!"* During this month, too, the Balkan Peace Team's Co-ordinating Committee takes its turn to meet in Germany. Here, too, there is only cursory talk about what can be done when hostilities begin. *"Perhaps, after all, one had hoped that nothing would happen,"* one of those present conjectures. In Croatia as well as in the west European peace movements there is the dominant feeling that there is nothing one can do against military might once the machinery grinds into action. And afterwards? Cynicism is the order of the day among the local activists in Split: *"If we go to Knin now, all we can do is ask the cows if they are Orthodox or Catholic."* The winner is the army which, during ostensible 'heavy fighting', has managed to free the fatherland from its bondage. It becomes what Anna describes as a 'holy, untouchable institution.'

Mindless Hate and Violence are Rife Everywhere

The Otvorene Oci in Zagreb, too, experience a storm running through their ranks, and towards the end of July the Team manages feverishly to set up a negotiative action at the last minute when the possibility to drive to Knin offers itself. But the plan evaporates during the offensive. At the beginning of August, the volunteers write an appeal to the Croatian president and request the member organisations of the Balkan Peace Team to write protests. When Croatian TV shows hundreds of letters from inland and from abroad in which the offensive is supported, then this should not go uncontested. In their appeal, the volunteers insist on access to the war areas for humanitarian and human rights organisations.

The office of the Ovorene Oci in Split is in any case closed and has been since the beginning of the offensive. One volunteer is on holiday while the other is at present busy at a workshop. The majority of the activists there are also busy elsewhere – on lecture tours, on holiday, at conferences or away on business. It takes a week before they are all at headquarters again. Deliberations begin as to what is the best and quickest way once we can get into the Krajina area.

Until then one has to put up with the intoxication of victory, nationalistic exuberance and the excessive euphoria of a trigger-happy people, which takes some beating to describe. In Zagreb, the day on which Knin – the fortress of the 'enemy' – capitulates, a procession streams through the centre of the city in jubilant demonstration, and the same scene is to be encountered in many other towns. For a considerable number of the 100,000 people who, in 1991/2, had been obliged to flee their homes in the Krajina region, the way home opens up again to them at last.

Others look upon this spectacle with mixed feelings. They have relatives and friends in the war zones or as soldiers with the troops. They are concerned about the whole affair and hope that it will soon come to an end. Those who are annoyed about the offensive itself are most certainly in the minority. The activists who work with Otvorene Oci are among these. But some of these, a few perhaps, who are pleased to see Krajina back in the hands of the Croatians. For the Croatians – about a thousand in all – who have remained in the 'Serbian Republic of Krajina', there is a volte face: from being a minority suffering under social discrimination, they are now rising to the rank of being a privileged majority.

However, for the volunteers it is something else which makes the situation insufferable. It is the fact that again they are obliged to be witnesses to outrage. The vicious circle of violence and revenge seems to have acquired its own inner dynamics that apparently has no end. Added to this, is the brazenfaced denial of responsibility and the refusal to recognize guilt. Two hundred thousand Serbs in flight from their homes? So what? The 400,000 refugees three years previously are twice as many! Six Serbian villages in flames? That was no doubt the work of Bosnians.

Or a little later, on one of their trips into Krajina territory in the village of Petrinja, where Croatians return to their houses which Serbian nationalists have destroyed. Now they move into their neighbours' houses which are empty and from which their Serbian inhabitants have fled. Otvorene Oci accompany an acquaintance of theirs who wishes to visit the house of an aunt. The aunt's former neighbours have moved into the house and refuses let her in. *"Your family did nothing to stop them from blowing up our house. There's nothing left here for you. If you try to get in, I'll kill you,"* were some of the things the husband said. *"We're going to live here until we re-*

build our house, and then I'm going to blow this one up. I have nothing to say to Chetniks, and all Serbs are Chetniks." His wife added, *"Why didn't they warn us what was going to happen? They didn't save our photos, so why should I let you save theirs?"* High feeling and bitterness are rife. On the same excursion and only a few kilometres away from the blazing villages, they come across an area which has quite a different atmosphere. Here, there are no burning villages, astonishingly few signs of plunder, and many people who have returned to their homes. So this is also possible apparently. Here, there is respect and neighbourliness which will not allow itself to be undermined.

The Otvorene Oci now ask themselves what they have to do anymore in Croatia. The essential question as to a 'solution' of this major conflict inside the country has been answered. Bringing 'peace to the country' is just in progress – with violence. What peace are we talking about here? Isn't the question of the purpose of existence now cleared up for the Balkan Peace Team? Democracy? That can be insisted upon in many societies. One doesn't need to be in Croatia for that. On the other hand, it is ridiculous to withdraw just at this time, at a time, that is, when the country is entering a decisive phase when it comes to human rights and the development of a civil society. There's a lot of consternation about the fact that things should turn out this way and that the last curtain should fall on the scene in such a way. A volunteer puts it like this: *"Yes I'm depressed. It's not a nice feeling being here at the moment, hopelessness and helplessness abound; the thought however that this is it, the final curtain, which makes me really angry."*

Staying On

During these conversations within the Team, there is a significant remark. *"We have been meeting with many local activists to discuss the situation and to try to give them more moral support than we can offer ourselves."* Moral support. This is to be able to share hopelessness at times when events have taken the upper hand and seem unending, and together put up with situations and phases where the presence and experience of power is almost insupportable.

Despite the gnawing conviction of having suffered a decisive defeat, Otvorene Oci of the Balkan Peace Team remain in Croatia. They do in fact offer moral support on this more passive level, but also a great deal of practical help. Volunteers, for example, can fall back on those resources available to them, which can be supportive. Some of the activities, such as observation and the making of reports on human rights infringement have already been alluded to in a previous chapter. Here, we are concerned with the establishment of inter-connections with other organisations and groups. The majority of volunteers have been on location for long enough in order to know their way round. As 'internationals' themselves, they can make contacts with other large international organisations with relative ease. For this reason, they can move around in the areas that have been conquered more easily by and large than local activists.

Creating Networks

The volunteers are full of energy in helping to set up centres in the integrated areas where humanitarian assistance is to hand, where human rights activities are in progress and where information can be organised and collated.
"Otoc volunteers did a really extremely important job in West Slavonia," says Ruth S., looking back to the activities of the teams in West Slavonia. She was working at this time with the volunteer project of the Antiwar Campaign in Pakrac. Their work has to be more closely orientated to human rights issues. Here, Otvorene Oci volunteers help in the matter of advising people. They are also busy setting up an 'Info-Centre' in order to co-ordinate the many human rights and peace groups which have come into the region with varying objectives. Energy is to be harnessed so that double work can be avoided. Everybody must be informed of who does what and where.
"So then they, Anselm and Xaver, took a really important role in that, like weekly meetings with UN agencies, helping them set up this Info Center, which we were doing. Even being on a kind of weekly meeting - Anselm, then was half a week in Pakrac taking care of the office there and helping setting it up."
It is in this way that the Gavrinica Human Rights and Information Centre came into being. The special thing about this particular centre is the fact that NGO's can make use of the infrastructure such as telephone and computer connections when they are in the area and can so come together for talks and other purposes. A room has been rented to this end. The costs of this are carried by the office responsible for civil affairs of the United Nations, and these are glad of the presence of the centre. Otvorene Oci volunteers are instrumental in bringing these very different partners together. They know what the local groups need and how one has to express oneself in order for something to be done in dealing with such a bureaucratic organisation as the UN.

More than that, they have also been able to convince the new manager of the UN office, who is very open on questions of human rights, that co-operation with knowledgeable and committed local groups is also an advantage to him. This ability to tactically negotiate pays off. As early as May 1995, they receive the 'green light' for the setting up of an Info Centre, which is to be opened directly above the newly opened Gavrinica Centre for Human Rights. This centre is already an important place to go to for volunteers, but also for activists working in the region. Many operations such as visits to villages, informing people of their rights with information material and so on begin here. In the meantime there are many organisations working here in connection with human rights. Almost all the groups have attached themselves to a human rights Co-ordinating Committee.

Initial Assistance

In July, all the preparatory work for the Info Centre seems to be ready. Together with Ruth S. from the Pakrac project and Paul Stubbs from the University of Zagreb, the Otvorene Oci are to permanently manage the build-up phase and the subsequent activities of the Info-Centre. This is an attractive offer and falls in line with the wish of the volunteers to be able to play a more active, personal role and to carry out tasks, which are more substantially helpful. The main tasks fall in any case to those working in Western Slavonia and it is here that the volunteers would like to open their own Balkan Peace Team office.

In Germany during July the role of the Team in developing the Info Centre is something that appears on the agenda for consideration. However, to undertake the co-ordination of the Info Centre is a matter, which goes against an important basic tenet of the BPT. This prescribes that members do not take over tasks accorded to local workers when they are capable of undertaking their own activities. It is also not quite clear how much say in the design of the Centre the Balkan Peace Team still has or whether it will be a body receiving orders from the UN which will place the means to hand for the material basis of the centre. The meeting then decides that the best thing to do is to only approach the matter when the time comes to determine the rules for itself. Otvorene Oci will have to make a start and then find a suitable person from Croatia who will take over the job. A negotiating committee is agreed upon which also includes the co-ordinator at the BPT International Office, since here we have to do with financial responsibility and commitment. Money at this point is just something the Balkan Peace Team doesn't have. The volunteers now have to keep their eyes and ears open in order to find someone, and then, at the end of July, a suitable candidate is in fact found, a former activist from the volunteer project in Pakrac. Until he is actually available, the Otvorene Oci does the work of building up the Info Centre, later hands it over and subsequently plays a supporting role. *"That it is perhaps a bit disappointing for you personally to have to hand over responsibility, I can understand. But really it is what international projects are there for - not to replace local initiatives, but to support them."* Sabine M. says by way of consolation. She is one of those who determines how things later take their course within the Co-ordinating Committee.

Military escalation, however, follows another timetable than that of civil organisations. Hardly have the human rights and peace organisations in Western Slavonia had more or less got to grips with its organisational problems, when a military operation in the Krajina area breaks in upon them. However, the experience of co-operation in Western Slavonia is transferable, and as a result the human rights office in Gavrinica becomes an exemplary one. In the Dalmatian Solidarity Committee in Split, there is now the idea of setting up a human rights office in Knin similar to that in Gavrinica.

As soon as Krajina is accessible once more, the idea is pursued and talks with the mayor of Knin, representatives of the police and the army, together with civil servants working for the UN High Commission for Refugees and Human Rights Action Teams are subsequently undertaken. Here, too, representatives of the United Nations encourage participants to pursue the plan further. The Dalmatian Solidarity Committee then works on plans for its realization, and fight through applications and paperwork requesting help from the Otvorene Oci when necessary, and in all this, are steadfastly supported by them. As to the point whether international volunteers can permanently work in the office is something they ask the Otvorene Oci about. Financial bottlenecks, however, will not allow the placement of another, additional volunteer. It is also a questionable matter whether the teams would, in addition to their own work, have the capacity to introduce, instruct and accompany another person.

Our Very Own Project?

Centres become fashionable and the Otvorene Oci as an international organisation with the best contacts locally is an attractive partner for large donors. OXFAM, an English humanitarian NGO with large funds at its back, arrives in September and suggests co-operation towards opening an office in Vojnic for the Otvorene Oci. This is near the large refugee camp at a place which Otvorene Oci workers have already had an eye on. The office, which is to be called the 'Community Advice Centre Vojnic', is above all to serve refugees in the Kupljensko Camp. To the tune of 100,000 British pounds it is to furnish refugees with humanitarian assistance and give them advice as to their rights. In conjunction with local groups like the Antiwar Campaign in Karlovac, Otvorene Oci is to co-ordinate the activities of the centre. OXFAM requires an answer within a week. The question now is whether "slow bureaucracy", an ironical, self-critical term used by the International Office' co-ordinator in the Balkan Peace Team, will be equal to the time pressure imposed upon it to come to a decision. In the meantime - it is now September - the Info Centre at Gavrinica has undergone its first test. *"OtOc gave the first interview in the centre, answering the questions of journalists from Japan and Norway."*

After a time, requests for help from Pakrac and Gavrinica become less and less frequent, and even the human rights and information centre finally manages to stand on its own feet. Now the challenge from OXFAM project in Vojnic and that of the office in Knin remain. The 'slow bureaucracy' of the Balkan Peace Team is indeed capable of quick decision for once. Negotiations with this partner become more concrete and the demands on behalf of the Balkan Peace Team clearer. At the end of September, when the BPT sits down to another regular meeting, this time in France, there is a fully negotiated contract on the table – but it comes to nothing. As in the case of Gavrinica, the decision turns upon the same considerations, viz. an independent, self-guided project run by local co-workers. Acting as external consultants, volunteers from Otvorene Oci can be hired for special work when, for example, the in-built, conflict arbitration mechanism becomes effective.

In a letter to volunteers, Daniel M. from the Co-ordinating Committee gives reasons for his reserve. Neither from the point of view of his preparation, he says, nor from the point of view of a concept does it make any sense, to bind his volunteers to long-term projects. 'Flexibility and nearness to those affected' - these are the decisive criteria for the employment of his volunteers. Participation in the distribution of humanitarian help and also to co-operate with others in this is a means to an end for the Balkan Peace Team, above all in those cases where it helps to create access. The management of distribution programme for humanitarian assistance in a region is quite another matter. Contact with local inhabitants is not necessarily part of the picture. Volunteers from Otvorene Oci for their part are not trained either for setting up, supervising or carrying out volunteer programmes. If, on the other hand, individual volunteers obviously bring these talents and experience with them, then, of course, this is an extra advantage. However, the Balkan Peace Team as an organisation is not obliged to appropriately support volunteers with such potential. To bind one volunteer firmly into a project contradicts the central concept of the Balkan Peace Team, which desires to deploy flexible teams who are capable of reacting to a situation quickly and adequately.

The Humanitarian and Security Situation

In compliance, then, with this concept, the volunteers help the Vojnic project through its teething stage in that they maintain meetings between the local groups and the large international humanitarian organisations, and also assist in the search for candidates. They find accommodation, find the materials for the setting up of an office and co-operate in electing co-ordinating personnel. They also continue to accompany the project and are only active in such cases as when conflict arises. At the end of October, everything is ready for the word, 'Go!'; positions are filled exclusively with local inhabitants, and the necessary vehicles provided. The project is co-ordinated from Karlovac, since office accommodation is in short supply in Vojnic some 30 kilometres away where property of this nature cannot be purchased for a reasonable price.

Winter is approaching and this means that humanitarian need will increase. Paradoxically at this point the helper infrastructure deteriorates. The International Red Cross has a mandate to assist in this region only up to the New Year, and is already not in a position to supply remote villages with aid. The UN Commission for Refugees has food supplies, it is true, but not enough people to distribute them. Consequently, it is dependent on military observers and UN police! UN military observers, however, have had orders to reduce their presence in the area and to use less petrol. In this way, they are less able to move and therefore less effective - even when they remain in the area!

In view of this situation in the case of the 'big fellows', the responsibility among the smaller, local organisations with projects like that in Vojnic increases. These unequal partners now begin to forge their future which entails concrete co-operation projects during the course of tedious negotiation. During these transactions, Otvorene Oci play a central part and help the parties to come together. At a later date, too, they stand by as the new, full-time co-ordinators, working in a technically well-furnished office having a computer and co-operating with paid employees, cannot at first come to terms with the need for a monthly report and the demands of accountancy. The contrast between this scene and the work of that of a small group with only two or three part-time volunteers could not be more glaring. Until the new project leaders come to terms with their new functions, these Ovorene Oci workers, employed here in an honorary capacity, provide what could be called 'coaching' to those who need it.

Enlarging the Networks

Building out networking doesn't just happen on the spot. It belongs to the essential 'business' of the volunteers to make use of every opportunity to make contact. Large-scale conferences like that of the Helsinki Citizens' Assembly taking place in Tuzla in October, 1995, offers just such an occasion.

At a meeting of this kind, activists are to be found who are working in conflict areas and who are from other - for the most part - European countries. Who's doing what? How are things going with this or that project? What new contacts are at hand? What kind of initiative can eventually be taken? All over Eastern Slavonia, the last region which has not yet been 'integrated' and which is still under Serbian domination, new networks are being established. The future is uncertain, but the possibilities of peaceful integration have not been completely lost, and so the interested parties talk about how they can co-ordinate their human rights activity. They draw up a paper outlining their concepts on how a peaceful repatriation in this region can be facilitated so as to bring the process once more into the Croatian state. Here, too, the Otvorene Oci are active when the groups meet in Hungary. Afterwards, it is they who publicize and promote the ideas that were developed by civil societies' organisations at that time, since, they argue, *"The important task for the OtOc was to show the international community that citizens' initiatives for peace and human rights do already exist in the area, and should be nurtured and supported."*

And the human rights centre in Knin is making progress, albeit not so rapidly as hoped. The lack of activists is noticeable. Even within Croatia itself it is difficult to assemble enough people to be present in Knin. A team member of Otvorene Oci confers with representatives of the DOS, the Dalmatian Solidarity Committee as to whether an application to the European Union could not help to place paid personnel in the office there. Other applications to OXFAM and to the American Development Programme still hang in the air and assistance is promised for the middle of November, but as yet nothing has happened. Then, at the end of that month, things start to move and the office finds itself with two, and later with three, full-time employees. The Otvorene Oci can well use this as a starting point for activities in the area. At the same time, they use the variety of member organisations within the BPT in order to find international volunteers for co-operative work in the Knin human rights office.

Breakthroughs and Breaks

At the turn of the year between 1995 and 1996, the Balkan Peace Team itself experiences a phase of change. Many long-serving volunteers will leave the organisation in the spring of 1996. This alone will change relationships for those in our care. New volunteers will bring new competencies with them and will focus on new areas, and the two teams in Split and Zagreb now develop new strategies. At the 'summit' in December 1995 in Ciovo, both teams prepare for their departure and their eventual break with the support of the offices in the Krajina region. Zagreb had always felt responsible for Karlovac, Split for Knin.

In Karlovac there seem to be problems on the horizon between the employees there for whom a local mediator should be found. These problems then develop into an out-and-out clash of opinion in the following weeks, and since mediation cannot be effected in time, some of the full-time employees leave. In order for work to go smoothly in future, Otvorene Oci volunteers organize workshops in making decisions and in dealing with conflict, later extending these to the subjects of co-operation and the clarification of roles. From these workshops concrete plans develop for immediate activities.

However, not only the activists in Karlovac are having problems getting along with one another. Co-operation in Split, too, suffers from division and controversy. The volunteers from Otvorene Oci ask themselves what they could have done wrong, since, after all, they have come with the objective of helping and strengthening local groups.

In Gavrinica, too, there are tensions, this time between the donors and those managing the human rights centre. *"Mediation and a lot of meetings will be needed."* Thus, the assessment of the situation by volunteers after a visit in March 1996. And, for good measure, there is contention and dissent in the Knin office where there is wrangling about a changeover in management personnel. Otvorene Oci is asked to rig up workshops for communication and work planning.

Competition and Dependence

Information and human rights centres present a very effective way of observing the human rights situation. They are favoured by international donors as concrete projects and consequently well promoted. Competition is therefore inevitable. From time to time, there is competition from the human rights organisation HOMO, from Pula, which has plans for an office in Vrhovnica and which it wants run by activists from northern Croatia. Finally, OXFAM finances all three.

Once financing has been finally secured, this does necessarily mean that the basis is laid for permanent working conditions. In the autumn of the following year, OXFAM has to deliberate on the possibility of further support for the office in Knin. It seems pretty certain that the donor organisation will drop out by the end of the year. In this situation, no long-term plan of work can be made, rather, projects, which in general last about a year, now begin to move into the foreground. Again and again, new projects must be found, or, to put it another way, one's own activities have to be expressed in a project and application, a process which, for activists, is something quite alien.

Financial problems belong to everyday experience of NGO's in addition to everything else that makes life difficult. Make-do-and-mend becomes a technique for survival. In conversation with British civil service personnel from the embassy, Otvorene Oci workers discover these people's interest in exact information from the Krajina area. For the journey back to Zagreb together with the ambassador, they arrange a drop- in visit to Knin with the human rights office as a starting point. Short and to the point, the Dalmatian Solidarity Commission is able to give its account of the situation with the result that, with a few, not very subtle hints as to the financial state of affairs, the embassy tentatively opens possibilities for support.

A go-between such as the Otvorene Oci which brings foreign donors and local project organisers together without seeking an advantage for itself is worth its weight in gold in this business.

Powerlessness and Possibilities

Everyday successes cannot make up for the sense of failure. The experience of personal impotence is too deep-seated. This is made clear at the assembly in November 1995 of all the member organisations together with Balkan Peace Team in the Netherlands for the first time since the military coup. Volunteers from Croatia report that the local activists have gradually overcome their shock and have re-organized themselves. For Xaver, one of the longest serving volunteers, and one who has been with the group from the first, disappointment just will not dissolve. There is a feeling that the project has failed, as if 18 months of work had been just wiped out. *"Why are we doing this?" "Is our work that so unimportant?"* Other team members don't see the situation as so extreme. The Balkan Peace Team as a small organisation cannot be expected to tip the scales between war and peace. This is something, which has to be painfully digested.

The role that can be played by the Balkan Peace Team is one of a faithful partner accompanying activists who, at the end of 1995, find themselves increasingly under pressure. During a speech, the President of Croatia referred to Croatia's 'enemies' as the country's opposition parties, its independent media, human rights organisations and foreign embassies. Once again, the General Secretary of the United Nations had pilloried Croatia for its infringements of human rights, and this was the return shot. International interest in the Krajina area has diminished since January 1996. All the sub-organisations of the United Nations, such as the police, the Department for Civil Affairs and human rights teams have moved out of the southern part of the country. Only the UNHCR is still in situ.

What, however, is new in Knin is the establishment of an 'Organisation for Security and Co-operation in Europe' branch in the town. Its employees call upon the Otvorene Oci workers to arrange a meeting of lawyers and solicitors in order to inform them about their work and their function. At this meeting the OSCE members are first obliged to learn of the intense frustration of local activists. There is still not room enough to build up a common strategy. This, too, belongs to the business of bridge building – and constitutes a high degree of resistance to frustration!

In spring, 1996, the European Council refuses again to accept Croatia into its ranks. As a result, the row about internal 'enemies' increases in vehemence. In the shadow of a grand public appearance, the Croatian president refers to the chairman of the Croatian Helsinki Committee as a 'shame to Croatia'. A well-known, right-wing extremist organisation produces a pamphlet headed: 'The 50 Most Prominent Interior Enemies' and proceeds then to slander them individually by name. Among the persons listed are some who work in co-operation with Otvorene Oci. In July, a bomb attack is made on the house of the chairman of the Croatian Helsinki Committee.

The human rights office in Vrhovnica is the most remote. In September, this, too, becomes a target, this time of an arson attack. While on a visit volunteers of Otvorene Oci can still see the marks on the wall. Without either fax or a telephone, the workers there are pretty lonely and would like an international volunteer to work with them. At the next opportunity, the Otvorene Oci volunteers draw the attention of the UN High Commission for Refugees to the plight of this small office, which up to now had overlooked its work. Shortly afterwards, direct contact is set up between the two, and, impressed by the work achieved by the human rights office, closer co-operation for the future is talked about. However, the pleasure at learning this doesn't last long. In the same night after the UNHCR visit took place, two of the women activists were attacked and injured. The attacker is known to them and threatens to kill them. The police briefly interrogate the man and then release him. Otvorene Oci find themselves in trouble. They now no longer have the capacity to maintain permanent residence. They can only visit the office from time to time. Nevertheless, they take time off during the re-opening of the office to stay for several days.

Nevertheless, this is not much more than moral support, but then not less either. In this way, the circle closes on what the Otvorene Oci can do in working alongside its partners.

Sources

BPT CC minutes, 16.- 18.7.95; 30.9.-1.10.95; 14.-15.9.96; BPT CC Daniel M., 2.10.95; Sabine M., 1.8.95, Slavonia;1.8.95, War; 26.8.95; BPT GA minutes, 4.-5.11.95; BPT IO 8.9.95; Bozicevic 1995; Interview Anna D. 1997; Anselm F. 1997; Ruth S. 1997; Xaver A. 1997; Kat, 1995; OtOc 28.7.95; 4.8.95; 11.8.95; 27.8.95; 14.9.95; 25.9.95; 11.10.95; 20.10.95; 29.12.95; OtOc Sp 16.8.95; 1.96, Hearts and Minds; OtOc Sp Biweekly, 16. -30.6.95; 1.-15.8.95; 15.-31.8.95; 16.-31.10.95; 1.-15.11.95, Confidential; 15.-30.11.95, Confidential; 15.-30.11.95; 1.-15.12.95; 2/12.95, Internal; 2.-22.1.96, Confidential; 23.4.- 6.6.96; 19.8.-7.9.96; 8.-22.10.96; 23.10.-7.11.96, Confidential; 23.10.-7.11.96; 8.-22.12.96; OtOc Zg 3.8.95; 18.8.95; OtOc Zg, Biweekly 2/5.95; 1/6.95; 1/7.95; 2/7.95; 1/8.95; 2/8.95; 1/9.95; 1/10.95; 2/10.95; 1/11.95; 2/11.95; 1/1.96; 2.96; 1/3.96; 2/3.96; 2/5.96; 2/7.96; 2/9.96; The Centre is variously described as: NGO Information Coordination Center, Human Rights Information Center.

(5) International Alert: Conscientious Objector is Assaulted: Croatia, 1996

Niksa Violic is alone when, on the 14th May 1996, he receives his call-up papers for duty in the Croatian army. He goes along to the barracks and explains that he is a convinced Jehovah's Witness and as such cannot be placed under arms. Two days later he is arrested and taken to the military prison in Split. Here, he is so badly treated by the military police there that he is later taken unconscious to the military hospital where he is constantly under the observation of a military policeman. Efforts are being made to bring the man to trial before a military court in Split.

In the meantime, however, Niksa Violic is not alone anymore. On the 23rd May, Elisabeth, a volunteer from the Ovorene Oci in Split informs the WRI, the Antiwar Campaign in Zagreb, which is active on behalf of conscientious objectors in Croatia and also Amnesty International. The alarm network set up in these organisations is activated. People in dozens of countries are informed by e-mail of the incident and at the same time asked to write letters of protest to those responsible. Names, addresses, telephone and fax numbers are added. In the days following, faxes and letters land on the desks of the ministers of defence and of justice, in the offices of the judges in the case, and at the address of the state attorney at the military court as well as the prison in Split. The Croatian embassies in the respective countries belonging to the writers of the letters are also the target of the letters of protest. Elisabeth, too, writes to the most varied addresses in Croatia who are responsible for military matters. The Antiwar Campaign and its network is busy doing the same thing.

Then, on the 24th May 1996, Niksa Violic is to appear before court. He is threatened with the possibility of landing in jail for ten years if the judge sees fit to giving him the severest sentence. Hans S., a human rights activist from Split, together with Elisabeth, is on the way to the hospital to accompany Violic to the place of his trial. On the way there, Violic is beaten again. Hans who later publishes his photo in a critical paper in Split photographs this incident. In court, Violic' lawyer pleads strongly for Violic and contests the legal competence in this case of the military court. Proceedings are postponed. A medical expert's report on Violic' physical condition is carried out at the hospital. Only after this has been done is the court to proceed with the case. A few days later, Violic is allowed to go home. Hans assesses this as an encouraging sign, despite the fact that the military state attorney after the hearing still insists that Violic must be arraigned. However, in the months that follow, Violic remains unmolested.

In preparing an article appearing in the summer of 1996 in the magazine 'Peace News' in London dealing with this case, volunteers evaluate the effect of this protest campaign. According to Hans, Violic' release from prison is the direct result of campaign pressure.

In spring, 1997, the human rights organisation, Amnesty International, opens its campaign for the rights of conscientious objectors in Europe. For this purpose, it places a dossier at its disposal in which many European countries are criticized for their treatment of conscientious objectors. Croatia is among them:

"Those imprisoned for avoiding military service, including conscientious objectors, have frequently avoided publicity, and it is difficult to document the number of cases. Among the most recent known cases was Niksa Violic from the Split area ... although the current status of the case against him is unclear as he has reportedly been exempted from military service temporarily on medical grounds. Amnesty International urges the Croatian Authorities not to pursue criminal charges against Niksa Violic. Should Niksa Violic be imprisoned at a future date for refusing to perform military service because of his religious convictions, Amnesty International would adopt him as a prisoner of conscience."

Amnesty International has Niksa Violic in mind. The story behind the man begins with an alarm sounded by Elisabeth and the Otvorene Oci volunteers. Most human rights organisations, acting much like a fire brigade, have installed a sophisticated warning system that functions around the world. The conditions for this are that an individual case becomes known at all. In the case of Niksa Violic it is not only the moral power behind the Balkan Peace Team and its member organisations which becomes apparent; the network of human rights organisations range far beyond the group consisting of the Balkan Peace Team and its organisation. This network brought its potential into play in a highly concentrated way for someone under threat.

A Glimpse behind the Scenes

In the struggle for human rights in Croatia, local activists and organisations work in co-operation with international organisations. The case of Niksa Violic makes this co-operative activity clear. Local personnel deal with research and documentation, while the foreign organisations exert pressure on the Croatian state. The local organisations for human rights in Croatia have come into existence as a response to the challenges brought about through war and human rights infringements of appalling dimensions. In 1997, there are four such organisations: the Croatian branch of Amnesty International, the 'Croatian Helsinki Committee for Human Rights', the 'Centre for the Promotion of Human Rights', and the 'Group for the Direct Protection of Human Rights'. Although it is difficult to find mention of the fact in the media, it is nevertheless true that the Croatian Helsinki Committee is continuously present in the country's media. The price for this is high. The media and those supporting it make sure of securing enemies as is shown by the attack of the chairman of the organisation in 1996. However, its effectiveness is limited. The state authorities can, if they want to, simply throw its demands overboard and generally ignore its activities. Until news occurs in international newspapers or is noted by international organisations, nothing happens. Seen from this point of view, local organisations are dependent on international partners such as Amnesty International or Human Rights Watch. The social scientist, HANS-PETER SCHMITZ, has noted that organisations such as these, which today are in operation worldwide, nevertheless discover their limits when it comes to the introduction and maintenance of human rights in an individual country.

Happily, the network of human rights observers is widening. In Croatia, for example, the United States of America plays a central role when it comes to the protection of human rights. They and the United Nations publicize regular critical articles and reports on Croatia. The United Nations has named its own special rapporteur for the region who, among other things collects facts during visits to the country, for example, or uses information from local human rights organisations. Considered over the years, these reports indicate certain improvements in individual areas and then continue to offer a long list of new recommendations.

Even when not very much changes for those affected, human rights activists nevertheless recognize an important tool in naming of cases. Stubborn persistence, a certain degree of stolid obstinacy, and a high amount of plucky risk are necessary characteristics in this political work. Activists receive hardly any recognition in their own country, and are generally dubbed as 'enemies of the state'. They carry the main burden of research and are the people who have been most industrious in continuously uncovering cases of the infringement of human rights in the re-conquered areas since 1996 after the departure of the UN Commission for Refugees. They are still documenting these transgressions and making demands for change. This sometimes makes them the targets of attack.

The acknowledgement of their work set down in these reports is considerable in international circles, making up to a degree for what is denied them at home. This confirms them at least a little in their commitment. They are expressly mentioned in a United Nations report. *"Local, non-governmental organisations that have been especially helpful include the Croatian Helsinki Committee for Human Rights, the Anti-War Campaign, the Serb Democratic Forum, the Dalmatian Committee for Solidarity, HOMO, the Committee for Human Rights in Zagreb, Pakrac and Karlovac, Otvorene Oi (Open Eyes), Papa Giovanni XXIII and the Civic Committee for Human Rights."*

The individual cases are taken up, but also incidents of personal assault such as that reported here by a volunteer of the Balkan Peace Team at the end of 1996: *"Another attack against a human rights NGO active in the former Sectors occurred on 9th December 1996 in Split, when a foreign national working with Otvorene Oci (Open Eyes) was severely beaten and injured by a neighbour who accused her of 'spying against Croatia'. Despite a police investigation, the assailant has so far not been arrested."*

International press and electronic media coverage does not stop at moral support. It also offers a basis from which to organize political pressure, and this needs a factual starting point. If the Croatian government is not of its own accord particularly eager to support the maintenance of human rights, then the latter can be brought into connection with matters which are important to Croatian politics, and one of these political levers is the maintenance of signed, contractual obligations. Up to 1997, Croatia had signed agreements, which make it partner to thirty-six human rights issues. Moreover, since 1992, an Ombudsman has been embodied in its constitution. Since the line-up of 1996, this post has increasingly concerned itself with human rights issues. In 1997, a critical report on the question of safety and of property ownership in the Krajina region was publicised from this quarter. The latter was particularly directed at sanctioning the appropriation of deserted Serbian property.

Another effective lever is that of not allowing Croatia to become a member of the European Council. Only in November 1996 can the country become the 40th member, and its application for membership has been turned down several times. In this, its poor performance in the human rights area has played a significant role. Indeed, the acceptance of Croatia as a member at all turns upon issues such as respect for minorities, encouraging these to return unmolested to their homes as also endeavours towards reconciliation. So much for the theory. In the light of everyday practice, things look quite different. Even in December of the same year, the Croatian Journalists' Association declared that pressure had increased on them since acceptance.

The American government exerts its pressure on Croatia via economic means, and its manipulatory lever is the maintenance of the terms of agreement of the Dayton Treaty in 1995. There, too, Croatia had recognized minorities. As a consequence of its not keeping to the terms of this agreement, the US blocked the planned loan of millions to that country from the World Bank, at the same time threatening to oust it from the European Council.

Another encouragement to toe the line is that of the close connections both countries have in the matter of American military aid for Croatia and the explorations as to how far Croatia has developed in order to become a potential candidate within the framework of NATO partnership for peace. Both these issues are coupled in the view of the American administration with the question of human rights, with concrete measures taken to repatriate refugees, for example, and with the practical application of the Dayton Agreement and, finally, with general democratisation of the country.

Acceptance into the European Union is a further inducement. Croatia is not an option here either at the end of the century, precisely because of its attitude towards human rights. However, its economic links with the European Union are of such importance that, at least from a pro forma point of view, it allows itself to be coerced into the maintenance of human rights norms. A case in point is that which occurred in 1998 where, under the threat of trade sanctions, the Croatian state was moved to act or – at least to pass a law – that would, in theory, allow refugees to return to Eastern Slavonia. This was sufficient to avert imminent sanctions, but the actual implementation of the law was subsequently made more difficult by bureaucratic interference.

Again, the difficult task falling to the Otvorene Oci and local partners is to discover during tedious, painstaking investigation, whether in fact 1998 is to be a 'Year of Return' as United Nations High Commissioner for Refugees, Mrs Ogata, called it or whether the whole affair remains a propagandistic lie. This persistent need to enquire and research, check, collate, explore, prove and demand is hard work, and a challenge for those taking part in it. However, as long as the Croatian government continues for its part to be obstinate and to regularly to employ rigid bureaucracy to hinder the implementation of human rights, so its opponents will be similarly stubborn in their demands. In other words, the Croatian workers towards these goals must not allow themselves to be browbeaten in their researches, nor the international groups who work together in their forums be thwarted in setting up reports and hatching political campaigns against injustice. These, and the representatives of the international community have to continue to work together consistently for the recognition of human rights by associating them with political and economic advantages.

Sources

Amnesty International 4.97, 25. 4.98; Antiwar Campaign Zagreb, 28.5.96; Fitz-Report 1997, 1; HRW 1998; OtOc, 5.96; OtOc Sp, 14.6.96; 14.6.96, Atmosphere; OtOc Sp Bi-weekly, 23.5.-7.6.96; 8. - 22.10.96; OtOc Zg Bi-weekly, 2/5.96; Peace News 7.96; Schmitz 1997, 27,65, 60; UN 4.11.94; 14.3.96; 17.10.97, No. 80, 82; 29.1.97; U.S. 31.1.95; 2.95; 3.96; 30.1.97; 0.1.98; WRI, 23.5.96.

(6) Reporting Uncomfortable Truths about Refugees' Return: Krajina, 1997/8

What, then, is peace? Is peace discovered when the shooting stops? When there are fewer than a thousand dead during hostilities? Or when a signature has been placed under a peace agreement? Or is peace a situation when all one's enemies have been annihilated or driven away?

In principle, everything is quite simple. Croatia was under obligation at the Dayton Agreement to facilitate the return of all those expelled from their homeland and to guarantee the same rights for everyone. Why? The Croatian nationalists are very satisfied with the current situation where the predominantly Serbian population has been driven out of conquered territories. That's their peace.

The Croatians who had to flee from Bosnia even fear those returning. They have been offered a new home in the Krajina region. They have taken over old property and possessions. And what happens to them when the former owners return? The way home is not a one-way route; the problem equally affects Serbia, Croatia and Bosnia-Herzegovina. It is the international community, which demands their return, because it doesn't want the persecutors to be successful. Its members do not want feelings of national hate to persist interminably, hate which is expressed in the perverse expression, 'ethnic cleansing', one of the most repulsive phrases that has come into the language this year. And, further, even countries of the international community where the refugees have found shelter, want to get rid of them again.

The international community leans heavily on Croatia to exercise concessions in the matter of the return of refugees. In this, Croatia does not voluntarily put its signature to the Dayton Peace Agreement. Finally, however, Croatia has the final say in the matter of implementation of the agreement, and here there are a number of possibilities to hand. Certain laws, the administration itself and a number of 'uncontrollable individual culprits' contribute in various ways to making the return to Krajina dangerous and so keep it the way it is. Croatia counters pressure from the international community during peace negotiations by resorting to both passive and active resistance.

The reports put out by Otvorene Oci on the possibilities and limits open to people returning to their homes is a mirror of power relationships between Croatia and the international community as, also, the earnestness of that community to put through its demands 'on the ground', i.e. to see them fulfilled as practical reality. Time is on

Croatia's side. The attention of the international community wanders from one crisis area to another in the natural course of events. Permanent, serious commitment requires constant stimulation. The question is: can the reports and the activities of the Balkan Peace Team do anything to help?

Reports with Added Value

The writing of reports is an activity with a tradition in the Balkan Peace Team. *"The Balkan Peace Team is that project where people have to write the most reports"*, says Monique Z. in an interview which distinguishes the Otvorene Oci from other volunteer projects in the Balkan states to which her organisation, the 'Brethren Volunteer Service', regularly sends volunteers every two years. It's a lot of reports. In the first place, it is the writing of a report every 14 days which every office writes to the Co-ordinating Committee.

Every six months a summary or 'Field Report' has to be written. At the beginning it was intended in this way to keep the Co-ordinating Committee informed of what the volunteers were doing and how the situation could be assessed, and whether what they were doing was in fact *"a contribution to the implementation of human rights, and whether it was a furtherance of methods to resolve conflicts and such matters"*. It is an instrument of control for the project in the same way as regular feedback which the Balkan Peace Team receive directly from organisations and persons in Croatia and Serbia who co-operate with the Team. Anna D. from the Antiwar Campaign in Zagreb is such a person in a position of trust. The quality of the reports, which have been set up in the course of the years, is for her a pleasant surprise. *"The additional benefit which was not expected at the beginning, but which sort of became clear maybe after a year or something like that – were the reports - and this was something we hat not envisioned at all when we negotiated about Open Eyes. But it turned out that the reports were very useful."*

One use of the reports is that they provide a source of information for people committed to the cause of human rights in the country and in other countries which formerly made up the state of Yugoslavia and which is now breaking apart. They offer an alternative source of information which, apart for the new electronic media, provides another possibility for the people of Serbia to remain in contact with what is going on around them. These reports inform activists about developments in their country in those regions where they are not actively engaged. One knows, for example, what has happened or is happening in the Krajina region despite the fact that one is not working there oneself. Independent newspapers, moreover, use these reports as sources of reference and background.

Local activists value the reports put out by Otvorene Oci, since these are frequently not in a position to write up reports owing to their own hectic activities during the day. Not all reports, however, are of the same good quality. Those coming from Western Slavonia and the Krajina region are much valued, as also those dealing with the topic of evictions which then find their way abroad and which exonerate the local groups. *"These people know the local language, so they can really speak to the people"*, Anna D. says of them from the Antiwar Campaign centre in Zagreb... *"and then the other thing is that they're not forced to use special official language."*

Along with the facts which the Helsinki Committee also includes in its human rights reports, the reports written by the Otvorene Oci speak, too, of the atmosphere and in this way they acquire an 'additional use'. At the beginning, the reports serve as a collection of facts flowing directly into one's own resources and also to those of colleagues in Zagreb and elsewhere for the further processing of cases. The principle is always appreciated: Otvorne Oci always reveals its knowledge and places it at the disposal of local activists. This helps them to make relevant information available which is the basis for use as international pressure in the matter of human rights. *"I keep all of their reports,"* Raj S. concludes and sends them on to colleagues at home and abroad. However, he doesn't believe that the Otvorene Oci reports have a direct influence on the issue. The organisation has not yet built up a reputation in this matter that could inspire the interest of the Croatian media.

Certain issues require volunteers to write reports on special topics such as those from Western Slavonia, the Krajina region, on evictions and other subjects. From time to time these develop into a comprehensive document such as that which reports the development in the Krajina region a year after the 'Storm' ('Operation Storm. One year after') or another report on Western - Slavonia looking back on six months of work in which evaluations are made.

Explorations undertaken by the Balkan Peace Team is also something which has been set down in reports. Among these is that reported on the situation in the Krajina region when it was still administered by the Serbs in the spring of 1995 as well as about Eastern Slavonia documented in the 'Vukovar Report' at the beginning of 1996. Both offices concern themselves with the question of the return of refugees. In the first six months of 1997, reports appear almost at the rate of one a month dealing with various facets and developments of this issue.

Part of a Country 'returns': Eastern Slavonia, 1998

At the turn of the 1997-98, a great change takes place. Eastern Slavonia is once more placed under Croatian rule in the middle of January. Contrary to Western Slavonia and the Krajina region, Eastern Slavonia remains unscathed from the ravages of reconquest. Although in the autumn of 1995, it was anticipated that Croatian forces would march into the area, the international community was successful in establishing a transitional government. In an agreement that took place in Erdut at the end of 1995, it is laid down that the Croatian government may only take over after two years have passed. Now we are at that point.

Eastern Slavonia has suffered heavy losses during the hostilities over the last few years. In 1991, 70,000 people left the area as refugees. Since that time it has become a place of refuge for Serbs from other parts of Croatia. At the beginning of 1998 this figure is already 60,000 people. In contradistinction to the Krajina region and Western Slavonia, the ranks of the police include both ethnic groups, Croatians and Serbs. In the case of judges, it is 60% Serbs. The international community now leaves it up to them how things shall be managed. Only 180 UN policemen remain for a further nine months in order to keep an eye on the situation. In the spring of 1998 Otvorene Oci publishes a report after the departure of the UNTAES (United Nations Transitional Administration in Eastern Slavonia).

The 'Return' Plan of 1998

Since 1998, the Split office of the OSCE (Organisation for Security and Co-operation in Europe) has been trying to better co-ordinate the work of many NGO'S. From these exertions, well-organised work groups develop which concern themselves with the spontaneous return of refugees, with the health situation and with the re-establishment of the infrastructure. The work of these groups becomes the basis of a larger report set up by the Otvorene Oci in the summer. In this report the organisation draws a balance as to whether for 1998, the promised 'Year of Return' can really amount to something. The commitment and the success of exertions on the part of the international community is also assessed in this balance. There is no doubt about their committed engagement, but what have they in fact achieved?

Flashback and change of scene on the political stage. In April, we witness the tug-of-war on the practical implementation of refugees entering its critical stage. Above all, the UN High Commissioner for Refugees, but also the OSCE and the transitional government of the UN in Eastern Slavonia work together with the Croatian government towards laying down concrete operational procedures. During these tough negotiations, the representatives of the Zagreb administration come up with more and more objections and reservations. Finally, in April, the issue comes to a culminating point. The commission, consisting of twenty-one ambassadors responsible for the maintenance of the Dayton Peace Treaties and the Erdut Agreement, threaten to boycott the donor conference for the reconstruction of Croatia, which is just about to begin. This conference, however, is a central factor for financing this reconstruction from international resources. Suddenly, the Zagreb administration withdraws its suggestions for modification!

By the summer there is to be a plan that will allow the ousted Serbs to return within thirty days. In June, Croatia has worked out a plan which, before it is passed, must be scrutinized by the watchful eyes of an international community still ready to administer economic sanctions. At the end of July, the ministers of the EU states meet one another in order to consider whether the plan is a balanced one. If this is not the case, then there is the danger of Croatia losing the 'most favoured nation treatment' in negotiation with the EU and the final cancellation of the already postponed donor conference. However, the 'Plan' goes through, and when, in July, it finally becomes law, the Croatian translation is discovered as a radical departure in meaning from the original document in English. Now we will have to see what substance there is behind such an ambitious title, 'Return and Welfare Plan for Displaced Persons, Refugees and Migrants', say observers at the scene.

Return to the Rogues - Amnesty-Report, 1998

In August, Amnesty International publishes an explosive report on the new situation in the Krajina region three years after the 'Storm' and draws its own dark conclusions. After this time, it say, criminals still go unpunished and asserts that immunity for these people still obtains. For years, the authorities remain idle even in cases, which have been known since 1995. In the AI report, the figures proclaimed by the government in Zagreb about ostensible punishment of wrongdoers is simply dismissed as so much eyewash. The consequences of such exemption from punishment they say is, a massive and permanent intimidation of the Croatian Serbs left behind in the conquered areas. The international community does nothing to counteract this state of affairs, while at the same time it has actively committed itself to securing the return of refugees. One new element has occurred, the report says, and that is that, since the middle of 1997, and for the most varied reasons, more and more offenders and witnesses have begun to talk about their involvement in crime either as actual perpetrators or onlookers. Now, these are regarded as traitors in some quarters and in a number of cases have been physically attacked.

It is possible, the Amnesty report goes on to say, that the passive attitude of the Croatian state authorities towards registered criminal activity will be successful in the long run. There is the great risk that the Croatian authorities will wait for international interest to wane and hope for it to pass on to the next point on the agenda by just sitting out the scandal and criticism of world opinion.

There are other noticeable tendencies, the report continues, ones where the flow of information to NGO's from authorities concerned with tracking down criminals is to be halted. There is also the further tendency to channel the information flow from these sources in order to make observation of individual incidents more difficult. The minister of the interior in Zagreb has reacted to the report by saying that he has emphasized the number of cases which have already been solved and that he attributes the responsibility for the murders to 'uncontrollable individuals'. *"This type of response had already been strongly criticised in the AI report as a means of avoiding the issue of continuing impunity"*, comments Otoc.

In this way, Croatia has become an example for a phenomenon which, for SCHMITZ as a scientist, is something of a headache. *"To an increasing degree, governments which are attacked improve their means of defence or, after every wave of accusation, modify their tactics with new instruments of oppression. At the same time, the world's attention undergoes another process of getting used to the situation so that, finally, even the most brutal human rights infringements hardly gain any more attention or need justification."*

Return of refugees is more than local authorities can deal with

The return of refugees only takes place on paper. Apparently, in Serbia, after completing and receiving all the necessary documents, 1300 people are still waiting for transport. International organisations envisage the repatriation of several thousand people from Serbia once local authorities have got over their problems in putting the 'Plan' into action. Now, in the summer, the human rights organisations are at their limits in helping people solve their problems. In Gracac, where the Otvorene Oci team visits the new office members in the Dalmatian Solidarity Committee, more than twenty people come each day seeking advice because they have returned to find their house occupied and don't know what to do about the situation. In addition to these, there are enquiries about humanitarian assistance in the human rights office, which are so many that personnel cannot cope with them, for the simple reason that this is not part of their job.

Together with 'Hocu Kuci', another organisation which is directly concerned with the return of refugees, Otvorene Oci volunteers drive to Plavno in order to inform thirty refugees waiting in Serbia or Eastern Slavonia who wish to return to their homes just what the situation is like. In what kind of condition are the houses, etc? Apart from researching for their report, these volunteers bring their local colleagues in contact with an Italian humanitarian organisation that happens to be working in this area at the moment. Here, one could speak of 'networking en route'.

1998: Not a Year of Return

The Otvorene Oci report comes out at the end of August. The conclusions it draws are sobering. The 'Year of Return' has come to nothing. *"The 'Year of Return' is moving into its closing months without large scale return having taken place. Only time will tell whether this return is realised in 1999 or not."* The report gives a survey on how the government in Zagreb, the international community, local organisations and the Bosnian-Croatian population on the spot regard the process of repatriation. It reviews the recent phases of return and concentrates on the most important points which, as before, persuade people still living in refugee camps not to return yet. These are the problems connected with acquiring papers, fear and, lastly, the gloomy prospects of perhaps not being able to earn enough to live. The lack of information or contradictory information about the actual situation is another reason for their hesitancy. For those who actually return, there is the lack of personal safety, the lack of infrastructure, houses occupied by strangers and the bureaucratic barricades which block the way to assistance which present the biggest obstacles. The second part of the report outlines what organisations in the region are active in supplying humanitarian assistance, in offering legal advice and the observation of human rights, in reconstructing the infrastructure and the economy of the country and in re-establishing psychological and social consultation and support, and just what these organisations do. It goes on to claim that, if the repatriation is to be a permanent operation, then, in particular, the needs for safety and reconciliation must be taken seriously into consideration together with that of offering people an economic perspective for recent expatriates. *"I want to stay, but if I can't find a job in 6 months or a year, I will have to leave"* is a phrase that the volunteers hear again and again.

Observations in the following months underline the concerns that are reported in the account.

"Large numbers of people queue outside the municipal offices, police station and offices of local NGO's. The queues are for applications for documents (birth, marriage, employment certificates etc.) which are essential for returnees to make applications for any sort of assistance and to begin the process of reoccupying their homes. Municipal authorities and the local ODPR office are reported to be understaffed and lacking sufficient resources; delays can be long." This describes the situation at the beginning of September. As for the 'Plan', exactly those vague instructions have arrived which do not bring us much further. *"Although having received their instructions almost two weeks ago, most Housing Commissions have yet to begin work. Many local and international organisations think that the two pages of instructions are quite vague and are afraid that when they do start, they will not be able to accomplish much due to these vague instructions."*

What Effect Do Reports Have? Looking for Evidence in Croatia

What does Otvorene Oci achieve with its regular reporting? In the situation report at the end of 1998, volunteers register their satisfaction with the response to the report on repatriation has had both in Croatia and abroad. The Austrian Embassy which, just at the moment occupies the presidency in the EU, has received permission to distribute the report to all the embassies of the EU members. In addition, an academic version of the statement is being prepared. One can content oneself with the fact that useful information is disseminated to important bodies responsible for decisions. Further, it is revealing to learn that OXOFAM has called upon the BPT to be one of its consultants in the future. In this connection, it will write a monthly report on the political and human rights situation in the country. So much, then, for this report.

Generally speaking, immediate reactions are a measure of whether a report has 'struck home' and where. It happens, for example, that a volunteer is on a lecture tour abroad and someone will come up to him or her and say: *"Oh yeah, I found your report while on a conference and I published it in this Italian peace magazine".* Publishing reports in developing electronic networks such as ZAMIR secures worldwide distribution – and frequently enough – vehement counter-reaction. Teams react in different ways to this. Anselm, for example, uses criticism to make contacts: *"Yeah, sometimes they would send us responses and sometimes we'd make contacts with other people who disagreed with a report, and so we'd meet with them for coffee and talk about it. It was a good way to meet people. They were probably the harshest critics."* Diane speaks of the many articles sent to her by people and from which volunteers can see that their information has been further processed. The many telephone calls requiring more details are another indication of the processing of information.

Otvorene Oci uses these reports to inform those who are already in the know. Of these is, for example, the UN High Commission for Refugees. One of the people working there at the end of 1997 while being asked about the Balkan Peace Team and its reports tells us that they regarded them as credible accounts and allowed them to flow into the information pool. They are part of the control which international organisations can use to check the doings of Croatian authorities and exert pressure if this is felt to be necessary. The reports are albeit 'critical', but not 'aggressive'.

Sybille M. from the OSCE office in Split sends her new employees to Otvorene Oci so that they can become acquainted and so gain some insight in their work. The volunteers, she says, *"...have a good idea of what's going on".* In their reports, they used to bring what might be called an 'additional viewpoint', namely, that of local human rights organisations. Added to this, they have investigated cases over a long period of time and tried to maintain an overall view of matters without, however, directly intervening in them. Contrary to the OSCE, which is always regarded and treated as an outsider, they were less formal in dealing with people and problems, and people consequently had more trust in them. In this way, they could delve more deeply into problem situations, which remained a closed book for the OSCE considered as an organisation.

The Consequences of Reporting: Tracking Down Evidence in Europe

Activists in Croatia feel that an influence originates from quite another place. The Balkan Peace Team is one the largest peace projects in Europe. Up to thirteen organisations combine together in order to send volunteers to Croatia and Serbia. *"The reports are probably influencing some things in WRI or IFOR,"* Ruth suspects. Anna D. feels the same, and it has come to her notice that

> *"one interesting thing is that the international peace community, peace activists or whatever you want to call these people who are committed to nonviolence, they very closely follow what Open Eyes are doing. You know, they wouldn't follow, what UN agencies are doing, or any kind of already established human rights networks are doing. It seems to be that somehow they feel that it is their province, and somehow, they feel connected. So it's essential information for them what Open Eyes are doing. What they do helps them to understand the situation."*

The Balkan Peace Team member organisations have to adapt the reports received from the team so that these can be further disseminated in their own publication channels. In this way, a 'snowball effect' comes into being which then comes to the attention of other organisations.

From time to time, in individual cases this can be proved as, for example, when, say, in Austria, where the Austrian Peace Service has its headquarters, Amnesty International avails itself of further information. Charles O., the representative of the Austrian Peace Service in the Co-ordinating Committee, and with a glance at the situation in Austria, says that the *"assessment of Croatian politics has already changed a little in the last few years."* He is of the opinion that, *"in the meantime there is much more attention directed to what happens in Croatia with regard to human rights, the freedom of the media and themes such as these, and I feel that a part of this is due to the work of the Balkan Peace Team."*

Information Policies and the Limits and Complications of Transference

The Balkan Peace Team is dependent for much of its publicity and information work on its member organisations. Its International Office in Minden, Germany, for example, collects team reports and sends them -also on enquiry - on or distributes them as information material. It cannot perform publicity or lobbying work. It cannot attend to the latter since this is the task of member organisations. Furthermore, it has not the working capacity to work in the former area, since it is completely overloaded with its own work. In addition to this, it has come to light that the reports are too specialised for a general public, which is not immediately concerned with the themes in question. As a general rule, they demand too much prior knowledge from their prospective readers, and neither the International Office nor those of the member organisations have the facility to process or simplify reports. If, in some cases, they manage to be instrumental in forming opinion within political parties, then so much the better, and one can speak then of success. More cannot be expected.

This is precisely where frustration enters the game since, in the case of many volunteers, it is a matter of seeing their researches, their energy and their heart's blood landing somewhere up on a dusty shelf. They speak of their disappointment to the coordinators in the International Office, and it is here where the Balkan Peace Team is confronted with a barrier, which can only be crossed now and again as in the case of Niksa Violic.

There is another phase whereby concrete enquiries coming from member organisations land on the Team's table. These can come from the War Resisters' International or Peace Services like Eirene International. For Frances, who experienced these times as a volunteer, the role which the team plays is changing: *"And that's a very different role than Otoc had been playing before, but it could work as long as we also had feedback from them."*

While the Balkan Peace Team is not busy establishing itself as an international lobbyist, the member organisations are for their part freer on this point. They *"again and again use material or things for their work which originate in the Balkan Peace*

Team." An example of this, according to Sabine M. from the Co-ordinating Committee, is that *"member organisations use it, for example, when they wish to hinder refugees being sent back to Kosovo or it could be something heard about the fate of those returning home which is useful for their national campaign in the country. That is not something the teams would do; it's not their job."*
The job of the teams is something different. *"The job of the teams is more to report what is happening in the country and so report on what different sides have to say. It is not made much use of or not used at all in larger political questions and issues."* It is understandable that team members entertain great expectations, but the philosophy of writing reports constantly changes with each team generation. One writer who well expresses the spirit of the reporting of this period is Frances. Here, she is adhering to the watchdog function:

"We also saw ourselves as watchdogs, watching internationals to see if they were fulfilling their mandates. And if the international community were to say that the return of Serbs must happen, in two months or so, then we could see that it was being implemented. And that was something very easy for us to do, and something that no one else was doing. And we tried to find our role then, because there are enough people quoting and reporting human rights. We wanted to be able to fill in the blanks."

Sources

Amnesty International 8.98; Interview Andrea Z. 1997; Anna D. 1998; Anselm F. 1997; Charles O. 1997; Diana M. 1998; Frances E. 1998; Friedhelm D. 1/1997; Helena P. 1998; Raj S. 1998; Ruth S. 1997; Sabine M.1997; Simone V. 1997; Monique Z.1998; Sebastian K. 1998; Stefan K. 1998; Sybille M. 1998; Umberto U.1997; OtOc 6.98. 8.98, 5; 11.12.98; OtOc Sp Biweekly, 23.12.97-22.1.98; 23.1.-7.2.98; 23.4.-7.5.98; 8.-22.5.98; 8.-22.6.98; 8.-22.7.98; 22.8.- 7.9.98.

(7) A "dignified departure": The Process of Leaving Croatia

The offices in Zagreb and Split were closed in October 1998 and November 1999 respectively. The Balkan Peace Team withdraws from Croatia. In one sense this is a simple matter. The mission has been completed, the objectives reached and now we can all go home. In reality, however, the whole thing is much more complex. The Balkan Peace team has long since developed to a project, which has its own interests in the region. Member organisations meet the needs for information via the Balkan Peace Team. These are the people who maintain and secure contact with local activists. Only a few other organisations such as the WRI have other structures in which Croatian groups and organisations are represented.

Added to this is the matter of objectives. In the declaration of its basic objectives, the Balkan Peace Team revealed these goals as being very vague and general. And even at later date it has not formulated its objectives in any more concrete way. It has described many of its activities in a way, which depicts how it can put its tasks into action. It has never, however, laid down what the conditions are for carrying out that task. In the first few years of its existence it was clear what these tasks were, above all, in the case of the violent conquest of the Krajina area. There, it was not a question of what to do, but where the main emphasis was to be laid. When, in the spring of 1997, local activists were asked when the Balkan Peace Team's time was up, no definite answer could be given. *"When things have normalised"*, was the answer. Even when several volunteers who, a year later, meet at the regular, rotating conferences of the Balkan Peace Team and consider the possibility of leaving, they find it difficult to hit upon definite criteria for doing so...and they, of all people, should certainly be able to do so from their own experience, and from the vantage point of years which have passed, and also from the fact that their knowledge of the region and the situation within it has increased in that time.

The routines of Otvorene Oci run on as usual in every generation of teams. One meets up with activists, does research on the spot, and turns up at the meetings of international organisations to exchange information. All this finds room for commentary in the six-monthly reports. In June 1998, the Balkan Peace Team met in Cologne, Germany for its general assembly. At that juncture, something became visible which, for some time had been unconsciously realized, namely, that the future of the Otvorene Oci offices in northern Croatia were out on a limb. In the next few months, options are discussed as to how one can carry on. Everything is at stake. Even closure is debated. What has happened?

In spring, 1997, that is to say, a year before, Albert P. had set up a rotating assessment of the Team's work for the perusal of the Co-ordinating Committee's activities, and for this purpose had conducted twelve interviews with activists in Croatia. For the first time, he touched directly upon this topic and put forward an 'exit strategy' with three worked-out options. These theoretical flourishes are not a revelation to everyone present, and some even consider them *"unrealistic"*. Nonetheless, their evaluation of teamwork has its aftermath. As a result, the WRI increasingly places the offices in Zagreb in question. In June of this year at a meeting in Camaux in France, the Balkan Peace Team is evaluated. Ruth, from the Antiwar Campaign Zagreb, knows from her own experience with project work how important it is to think of the end of a thing when one begins with it. She had experienced the long process of dying in the case of one project and had noticed during it that volunteers always found reasons enough to continue.

The volunteers of Otvorene Oci, however, have been thinking about giving up since 1997. A *"dignified departure"* is one of the four strategies, which they have wanted to pursue since the summer of 1997. Apart from that, there is nothing new about volunteers considering leaving. And, moreover, they are used to non-voluntary departure when there is no more money to hand. One volunteer sketches the relationship between money and the ability to work:*"We are all fully aware that, as an NGO, money will always be a problem. However, this does not mean that it is acceptable for the money worries to a) hamper our job in the field by not having enough petrol to drive to Knin, Glina, etc., and b) create the need for us to over justify our expenditures in the field with respect to normal food and team items; c) be told that the office only has enough money for xx more months and then, at the same time, be presented with unrealistic exit strategies."* The weak financial basis on which the Balkan Peace Team stands is a problem. The lack of a clear perspectives for the future another. This applies to the project as a whole.

In autumn, 1997, a 'strategy debate' is deliberated, the upshot of which is a 'Three-Year Plan.' The central issue of this plan is the self-imposed obligation to stay on for a further three years in the region and thereby strengthen the Team's structures.

When, in the autumn of the same year, another comprehensive change of team presents itself in Zagreb, this time an experienced former volunteer is found for several months as a support. Both Otvorene Oci teams make use of this reinforcement in order to develop their strategies with more considered reflection than is usually the case.

The Split team has somehow worked out the means of strengthening its presence in Knin at this time, and accordingly systematically sized up the NGO scene there. The other team, which by now has moved from Karlovac to Zagreb, is faced with profound changes in orientation. It has to re-establish lost contacts, create new working relations and find out what is needed. When in March 1998, the two teams meet for a 'summit' and swap experience, they decide to complete their plans by the next general assembly in May. *"Also by then a discussion is planned on how best to decide when OtOc should leave Croatia."* The general meeting is a good opportunity to moot their generally shared doubts on the further purpose of Otoc.

The General Assembly this time taking place in Cologne in 1998 is over shadowed by a further financial crisis and also by the intensification of strife in Kosovo. Back in Zagreb in mid-June, the team gets down to work. In this, it is supported by a former volunteer. In a veritable brainstorm of deliberations, they offer their ideas to each other: who needs them, what are the needs, whether the team is equal to these tasks when formulated, and how they can best put them into action? They finally come to the conclusion that they have three options to choose from: to carry on as before; to do what others do which has proved satisfactory; not to content themselves with that which proves satisfactory for others, but, instead, to carefully investigate what needs are there. The team decides to risk tackling the last exercise, takes stock of what it is actually doing, and interviews key people in Croatia.

During the conversations which follow, it comes to light that much of that which was considered as a strength is now outdated. Now, it is not so important, for example, that an international project is ready to offer support at the same shoulder level, so to speak. Other matters, such as monitoring, for instance, have in the meantime long been taken over by internal groups. The accompanying of activists, moreover, has also in the meantime proved itself to be counter-productive, since it is felt that these should develop a sense of self-confidence. And as far as international contacts are concerned, there are enough groups in Zagreb for that. In Split, it may well be that everything looks different, but as far as the scene in Zagreb goes, a team such as Otvorene Oci is no longer support, but simply a part of the infrastructure. These speak, too, to Anna D. from the Antiwar Campaign Zagreb. Yes, a team is needed in Croatia, but the question is only: Do we need one or two? The need for Otvorene Oci is more evident in the south.

By August, the team has worked out seven options and is pressing for a definitive decision from the Co-ordinating Committee, which is going to meet in September. Option 1 is closure; options 2 –4 describe the removal of the office into other areas of the country. Option 5 means further development, while option 6 means a change of mandate and option 7 is 'Other alternatives'. They vote for the first, because this shows that the Balkan Peace Team is in a position to adapt itself to changing conditions and knows when it's time to go. Their main concern is how to get the Co-ordinating Committee to agree to what they have decided.

However, it turns out that this worry is unfounded. Apparently impressed by the thoroughness of the analysis, which takes its own principles seriously, the Co-ordinating Committee decides in December 1998, to disband the office in Zagreb. As part of this process, there is to be a farewell visit of one of the members to the most important partners in Zagreb. In November, the General Assembly will finally have to confirm the decision, but these are merely formal steps in the process. Up to that time, the office had already been closed. The Balkan Peace Team justifies its withdrawal in a circular: *"There are of course still many roles for international peace groups and volunteers in this area, but the BPT is able to recognise that what we have to offer to North Croatia is no longer appropriate, and therefore we will withdraw."* The official farewell is celebrated on 31st October 1998, in Zagreb. Up to that time, the local activists suffering from a loss of attention and input are catered for in terms of moral and material support. It is emphasized that the office in Split continues to be important and that contact there will not be broken. Where there is a need, member organisations are to send volunteers directly into Croatian groups.

A year later at the end of November 1999, the General Assembly state that there is to be a complete withdrawal of the Balkan Peace Team from Croatia. Other than in Zagreb, it is not the volunteers who analyse their work and come to a conclusion not to be able to deliver what is needed. This time it is the organisation itself, which comes to the decision no longer to have the energy for a new beginning in Split. At the same time, the BPT feels that it no longer possesses the appropriate answers to solving problems and attending to needs in Croatia after dissolving the newly appointed team in June 1999.

Internal reasons have brought about the breakdown of the team. In the first place, the basis of confidence between the Team and the 'rest' of the organisation has been undermined. This implicit mutual confidence is something which holds the Balkan Peace Team together and which, up to now, has functioned well. The isolation in which the teams work, the limited means of making personal contact with members of the Co-ordinating Committee and the Sub-groups which, on the one hand, were set up to support the teams in Croatia and Serbia/ Kosovo, require a modicum of common trust for the whole tenuous affair to hold together. In the case of the last team in Split, there wasn't a workable bond between team and Sub-group, and, added to this, there was division, especially within the team itself. This was made clear at the first meetings with the Co-ordinating Committee at the end of May, 1999 when the Sub-group for Croatia met volunteers. A mutual attempt in June to focus the work anew and to integrate other volunteers into the work fails. Too late. Perhaps in spring, 1999, there might still have been an opportunity, but at this point all eyes were on the war in Kosovo, the evacuation of the team from there and the immediate future.

And so it was that in June 1999, the Balkan Peace Team found itself without a team in Split. A long-standing volunteer leaves before time, another breaks off his introductory phase, and a new arrival holds the fort for a period before she, too, leaves. She experiences too little support, she feels, in order to see herself as forming the core of a new team. During the summer, a former volunteer who happens to live in the area, sees to the post and e-mails.

In September on the occasion of the next meeting of the Co-ordinating Committee, the criteria for a new start are laid down: the strengthening of the respective Sub-group and that of the financial backbone belong as much to this new approach as the clearly declared needs on the part of local activists. But there are doubts. There is doubt whether energy and will are strong enough. Experience shows that a team with a clear task needs half a year from the word 'Go' to the point where it is really in a position to negotiate. And what is the task? The question of war or peace is no longer a relevant one as far as Croatia is concerned. And will the Balkan Peace Team be equal to the subtler problems connected with building up the country again? Has it a workable concept for this?

It also becomes clear how difficult it is to let go. There has long since been a change in generations in operation in the Balkan Peace Team. The 'new' folks demand precisely defined tasks and are ready to take radical steps to curtail and reduce, while the 'old' see their presence in Croatia in the context of the whole, see what, in the meantime, has become the old, reliable relationships with partners gradually disappearing and above all, they recognize loss. The maintenance of the Split office implies rest for the activists in Croatia after the closing of the Zagreb office. Perhaps it is also an unadmitted opportunity for activists in the Balkan Peace Team to take a rest.

The heavy weather of coming to a decision finally persuades the Balkan Peace Team to arrive at a compromise: no immediate new start, but, after having made investigations, a final decision in November is to be taken by the General Assembly. There, the Sub-group also recommends the closure of the office in Split. This difficult decision poised between the original intention of prevention and that of hanging on to stable associations which have taken time to mature is finally one in favour of the first. With painful reluctance, the General Assembly then puts what has been decided into action not, however, without thinking of new projects developing in other parts of the Balkans in order to readjust the balance. The office will be 'wound up' by February 2000, the apartment owners given notice and the flat cleared out, the computer overhauled and made fit for operation for the Kosovo team.

"That was not the way we wanted to go", one of the participants remarks, looking back. To hang on to the team and to experience the change of heart in Croatia in 2000 as the new elections introduce a change of power at the top and then to leave -that would have been a successful policy to pursue in leaving Croatia. But it was not to be.

Sources

BPT CC minutes, 13.-14.6.98; 4.-6.9.98; 10.-12.9.99; 11.-12.2.2000; BPT CC Edgar E., 15.11.99; BPT volunteer, Frances 30.5.97; BPT GA minutes 20.-21.11.98; 20.-21.11.99; Information, Charles O., 7.2003; OtOc 9.4.98; no date, ca 7.98; 11.98; OtOc Zg 16.6.98; 8.98, What; 8.98, Centre; 8.98, Anti-war; 8.98, Zagreb; 16.-30.9.98.

Chapter 3 "Balkan Peace Team FRY" in Serbia and in Kosovo

(1) A Start with Obstacles. The Long Process to Develop an Effective Team in Kosovo and Serbia (1994-1996)

In Kosovo, everything is different. In contrast to Croatia, there are partners here, but not the one partner organisation such as the Antiwar Campaign in Zagreb. Croatia, for example, is a country, which establishes itself as an independent state fighting out its struggles for power within its own territory. In Kosovo, on the other hand, one has here to do with a population majority, which at this very moment is still carrying on a non-violent struggle for freedom. Strict isolation within population groups belongs as much to the strategy of resistance as the policy of holding out and not hitting back against the police and military authority, despite rape, torture, arbitrary arrest or the random disappearance of people, all of which constitute a programme of suppression. Polarisation here is very strongly pronounced: there are either friends or enemies, and foreigners are immediately pigeon-holed into the one category or the other.

It will be three years, from 1994 until the end of 1996, before the Balkan Peace Team aspire to an independent, recognised position in Serbia or Kosovo. The threat of expulsion from the country constantly hangs like a sword of Damocles above the heads of those conducting exploration and team members alike. The Yugoslavian authorities carefully sift through the possibilities of issue, duration or refusal of a submitted visa or even decide upon banishment in some cases. In this way, they severely control the degree of freedom of activity among those entering the country. Here, too, the state grip on local activists is more direct and menacing. This also applies to those who have issued a personal invitation to foreigners in order to help them acquire a visa, and to those who accommodate them. Just what might trigger off an expulsion or encourage the state authorities to interfere cannot be prognosticated beforehand. *"They might tolerate you for a while"*, one of the representatives of the UN refugee organisations in Belgrade remarks on the occasion of an exploratory trip into the country. The chance of working without being intimidated is not something that can be predicted by anyone.

As far as the member organisations of the Balkan Peace team is concerned, loyalty to Albanians in resistance movements varies greatly in intensity. For the first time, considerable differences of opinion arise within the project itself or in the analysis of the conflict or the parties within it. This differs from the activities in Croatia where human rights observation was one of the most prominent features of volunteers' work while dialogue plays an essential role in the Federal Republic of Yugoslavia. In Kosovo, these two are apparently incompatible with one another. Anyone putting himself out in the interests of human rights is stigmatised as 'pro-Albanian', and anyone who strongly supports dialogue is 'pro-Serbian' and so undermines the resistance strategy of non-co-operation.

For anyone wishing to succeed on this tightrope without giving way to either prejudice, great tact and diplomatic delicacy is required. He or she must first have founded a sound basis of mutual trust within both camps, and also possess great strategic acumen with regard to the work of the team. How, for example, can volunteers who will be in the region for six months, say, be able to get to grips with the new situation? Many have had their typical preparatory training based on cases, which, as a general rule, took place in Croatia? Work in Croatia, for example, quickly gains contours and profile, whereas that in Kosovo long remains vague and uncertain. It is small wonder, then, that the charisma associated with work in Croatia – whether desired or not –has been assessed by some as a 'model', also fires the imaginations of volunteers presenting themselves for work in Kosovo. However, the lesson here that visible human rights work is not possible is one of the most bitter to be learned.

Contrary to the situation in Croatia, developments showed little or no continuity at first as far as teamwork was concerned. Several new starts become necessary before what was referred to as 'the stupid foreigner syndrome' is finally overcome. *"Wanting too much, too soon, too quickly, and all this without any clue of what is going on"* – this was the estimation levelled at the situation later by volunteers looking back. However, this judgement does not at all correspond with the careful, nay, almost timid attempts to get initial teamwork off to a good start in Kosovo in the early days. The very attempt, it seems, not to put a foot wrong can bring about just this result.

The Balkan Peace Team nevertheless pursues its mission with dogged determination, and precisely because it is not blind in its persistency, but thoughtful in encountering problems, these abortive 'new starts' in fact allow it certain insights into the risks with which projects of this kind are connected.

1994: Sounding out in Kosovo and the Pilot Phase, Part I

When, in 1994, the Balkan Peace Team was founded in Paris, and sent off its volunteers into Croatia for preparation, it found itself quite unarmed as far as Kosovo was concerned. Just how things should proceed in this direction was a matter of debate. The representatives for MAN (Mouvement pour une Alternative nonviolente) put forward their concepts. According to these, a continuous series of delegations should constitute a permanent presence, one which widens the circle of contacts and which has the function of de-escalation. Kosovo has been the main area of activity for MAN since 1992. There, both competence and ambition are to be found. Although the movement is a member of the Balkan Peace Team, it considers itself to be marginal and is seldom represented at meetings. The French are more interested in non-violent training in France itself than in volunteer work in Kosovo. In Kosovo itself, MAN clearly adopts a position in favour of the Kosovo Albanians. For this reason the current associations are mainly exploited in favour of lobbying for Kosovo Albanians and for the setting up of school partnerships. As the result of frequent, short-term visits to Kosovo, contacts are cultivated with resistance leaders. MAN goes after people in Kosovo who can really take action in the organisation of non-violence, and these do not necessarily have to be those setting up non-violent resistance in the interests of Ibrahim Rugova's Democratic League.

The German idea is to establish an independent team in Serbia directly and to use this as a basis and point of departure for Kosovo. Thereupon, it is decided in February 1994, to investigate the situation anew, after which direct application will be made to the Yugoslavian authorities for permission to work on a pilot project. In this it is also felt that consultation with partners in Kosovo is necessary in order to determine just how much of a support it will be for them when there can be hardly any visible human rights watch (or none at all) and when the central issue in the work of co-operation is dialogue.

The exploratory team, consisting of Daniel M. and Ellen B. from the War Resisters' International, Lars C. from MAN, set off for Belgrade on 4th April 1994 and spend the first week in that city. Daniel in particular has built up a largish network of contacts there as a result of his many visits to the country. Possibilities are then discussed with these contacts, and from these conversations new ideas and concepts are developed. One positive aspect, for example, is the fact that in the Soros Foundation office a Serbian works in co-operation with an Albanian. This is carefully registered and listed among other matters in the exploration team's report sent back home. Another point noted is that where, on occasion, a Serb takes action against the discrimination of Albanians. Along with these matters, reservations with regard to the use of dialogue are also noted. Among these reports on Kosovo, individuals from both communities who are ready to take part in dialogue and who have been isolated or disciplined for doing so within their society are looked into. These meetings and discussions bring forth concrete proposals from which later action can be taken. One of these, for example, is the suggestion that the team should enter into co-operation with the UNHCR. Another issue arising from these talks is that developed in conversation with the 'Centre of Anti-War Actions' in Belgrade. Since the Balkan Peace Team is concerned with dialogue on a daily basis and not with high-ranking politicians, the Centre in Belgrade, acting as Serbian partner, and the 'Council for the Defence of Human Rights and Freedoms' in Prishtina, as partner for the Albanians found that they could adopt the Balkan Peace Team's project. The condition here is whether the Albanian side is willing to give the 'green light' to a dialogue project.

Thus armed with these ideas, the members of the exploration team now leave Belgrade and set off for Kosovo. In Prishtina, conversations are taken up with their Albanian partners. In the Soros office, *"The Soros people are, of course, all dialogue-minded, but rather gloomy about its prospects - they know exactly how difficult it is."* They are unable to offer any concrete terms. The 'Council for the Defence of Human Rights and Freedoms', the organisation which originally invited the Balkan Peace Team, can well understand the situation and realizes fully that an eventual team must be independent. In addition, dialogue between Albanians and Serbs must, they feel, provide the basis for interaction between them. One or two suggestions are put forward as to how to go about the problem. Their conversations bring team members into contact with the editors of various Serbian newspapers, with the Dean of Prishtina University, with the Secretary for Information at the government offices in Kosovo, with radio and newspaper journalists and with Serbian and Albanian politicians.

They come away with the most varied and the most contradictory of opinions. The head of the UNHCR office in Prishtina, for example, sees the BPT as an organisation in complete accord with the contract concerning 'preventative protection' and reflects on the idea of how a label could be designed so that the project could fall in line with the work of the UNHCR, and how this could receive his patronage. Participation in the weekly press conference held by the Albanian resistance leader, Ibrahim Rugova, leads later to success in that a committee executive of the LDK officially invites the exploration team members to coffee and personally offers his assistance.

The many impressions received are then discussed with people in Prishtina, people who, as a consequence of their many journeys through the country, have become good acquaintances and who do not necessarily directly belong to activist organisations. For the exploration team, these people serve as important 'sounding board' with whom one can speak and so gain an impression of what is actually going on. From what is said, they begin to sift the grain from the chaff in order to arrive at a considered opinion. It is important that the members of the exploration team don't stew in their own juice, since eventually they have to return to Belgrade.

There, a report had come in from the Co-ordinating Committee of the Balkan Peace Team which says how the 'adoption' and the co-operation with the UNHCR has been evaluated. It is April 1994, and war rages in Bosnia. NATO has bombarded Serbian units in Gorazde; Serbian troops have taken UN soldiers as hostages. It is not known for certain how far the United Nations will be caught up in this war. It is not known either how long UN organisations will continue to work in Yugoslavia. With this hanging over their heads, and judging the issue from their western European point of view, the members of the Co-ordinating Committee fear that the Balkan Peace Team could be compromised if the United Nations Organisation runs into trouble. If this problem can be evaded, then co-operation with the UNHCR is something for which one should strive.

The idea of adoption, too, is found to be a good one, so long as there are no visa problems to be encountered or annoyance connected with local partners. On the basis of these recommendations, the exploration team is given the green light to negotiate with Serbian authorities. It is suggested that the pilot team be given three months in Kosovo to promote a scheme of contact and dialogue between Serbs and Albanians on a day-to-day basis, and so with this as their objective, the team sets off for Belgrade and the government's ministry of foreign affairs where it is to be received by the ambassador, Budimir Kosutic. He spends two-and-a-half hours with his foreign guests, time which is felt by the team as 'impressive', only then to be informed that the time is not yet ripe to implement what they have in mind. In three or four months, he says, things may well be different.

The Co-ordinating Committee, which sits in Zagreb at the beginning of May to evaluate this experience, decides to take the ambassador at his word. In three months one will be ready. There are many things to prepare by then. The members of the WRI in the exploration team are convinced that the first team must fulfil high demands. Experience and practice in strategy development belong as much to the tasks ahead of them as the ability to create a 'resonance' group from local people. There must be young people in the team, and especially women, since these are the most important target groups. More than this: it will be their job to find a work level lying between the everyday and the political.

Daniel M. introduces an idea on how 'the conflict' can be influenced by this kind of work. The original concept stems from the peace researcher, Johan Galtung, who once spoke of 'the chain of non-violence'. According to this, societies change when their opinion of the other side changes. These changes are brought about by marginal groups who take their opinions into the centre of their own society. They create a bridge between the once 'hostile' society and their own. For the immediate situation in which the team finds itself, it is therefore important to bear in mind that the oppositional activists in Belgrade increasingly concern themselves with the subject of Kosovo. It is now that the 'links of the chain' in the two differing societies be found and the two brought into contact with one another.

There seems to be common ground on the topics of interest to women, on the needs of young people, and the fashionable discussion about computers. Since the Serbian opposition groups with which the Balkan Peace Team works are not so tightly organised as Kosovo-Albanian groups organised in the resistance, Serbian grassroots groups need more support from time to time. Then one has to look around and see whether there is opportunity for contact or even co-operation with the Kosovo-Albanian society. A team must therefore know what initiatives are being worked on in Belgrade by local activists.

Above all, the Balkan Peace Team wishes at all times to avoid giving the impression that it is supporting Albanian resistance. Indeed, to underline the fact that it is willing to speak with all sides, it is concerned to gain an invitation from the Greek Orthodox Church. The latter's position in Kosovo is quite clear: Kosovo is Serbian and that's the end of the matter. This 'courtship', so to speak, is successful enough to result in an offer of a study trip through the monasteries of Kosovo, so that this will strengthen the open-mindedness of its viewpoint.

At the same time, however, it is to open up avenues, provide more open doors and supply more backing, offer the opportunity to find more priests who are willing to enter into dialogue, and to take advantage of those connections existing between peace groups and the church. In August, the Co-ordinating Committee requests the patriarch in Belgrade to invite the team to a study excursion. Preparations run at full steam ahead, but are menaced with the threat that plans will again be smashed.

In September, the next training programme takes place. Volunteers of the pilot team get to know each other and work together on the mandate for their mission. At the next Balkan Peace Team General Assembly in October of the same year everything is on tenterhooks. The programme is in danger of collapsing. There is still no invitation from the Orthodox Church, and the volunteers have only limited time at their disposal. To make full use of their potential, no more time is lost in waiting, and invitations are supplied privately. So it is that on 3rd and 4th November, 1994, the last arrangements are made in Zurich with the team. The task ahead once more run over, emergency measures and communication pathways discussed. The main task awaiting them is to work out a project suggestion as to how a permanent presence can be continued in Kosovo coupled with the concrete ideas resulting from reconnaissance activities conducted in April. It is agreed that an intensive, mutual communication be set up.

The team arrives in Belgrade on 5th November, immediately begins to meet people and prepare for the study trip through Kosovo's monasteries. From 14th to 24th November, the team is underway on this tour through Kosovo and Sandzak. Meanwhile, back in Belgrade, the trip to Prishtina is prepared on 3rd December where the team remains until shortly before Christmas. One of the volunteers, as announced, leaves the team. A substitute for the woman is delayed because a visa is not forthcoming. The team, however, knows nothing of all this. Communication is appalling and for the most part doesn't function at all. *"I just couldn't understand that an e-mail in Belgrade could just disappear. And it disappeared; they disappeared continuously. Metres and metres of e-mails"* This is the experience of the team at that time. Consequently, it remained ignorant of any answers to questions and reaction to its reports. Its interim report at Christmas is not particularly encouraging either and reads: *"Thus at this moment we are reluctant to predict that the presence of a BPT team in Kosovo can be meaningful."* On the other hand, the idea of strengthening drivers for peace indirectly by providing them with goods and communication possibilities is something, which begins to ripen during discussions. This is to come into being by making regular visits and by bringing goods into areas where they are needed, and by the setting up of communication channels.

This concept is passed on to the Co-ordinating Committee on 6th January 1995 and discussed just over a week later at a meeting in Lyon. Here, the matter comes to a head, causing considerable consternation, less because of its content and the suggestion it contains than from feelings of disappointment on behalf the team and Co-ordinating Committee. The team came across and questioned 139 people and yet, despite this, has hardly taken advantage of the information resulting from the encounters. Surely there must be something amiss here! The team now finds itself entirely dependent upon its own resources, discovers that it has been badly prepared to deal with the situation and cut off from all means of communication. The most important people to whom one can refer, namely, Daniel and Sabine, were seconded to the three-year conference of the WRI in December and therefore not at hand to consult. Important points for the team, such as the timing of the deployment of volunteers has just not been considered.

The team does not feel that it has been taken seriously by the way in which its suggestion was reduced to formal issues like visa problems. It feels that its concerns were reduced in importance, and their contents ignored. Emotions run high. Finally, there is general agreement that one needs more time with each other in order to consider these matters in peace. Another agreement to meet is made without minutes and this is subsequently arranged for Paris in February. There is more to talk about. The team reveals in its reports that it has distanced itself from Albanian resistance, and that it is shocked by the consequences this has brought about, a matter which is unacceptable for the member organisations, since this kind of thing undermines the credibility of local partners. All this foreshadows a 'crunch' and must be substantiated.

1995: Pilot phase in Kosovo, Part Two

During the meeting in Lyon in January 1995, a decision is made to keep the pilot phase going. The next team is to make use of the information gleaned from the previous April. The next volunteer, Volker from the Netherlands, then sets out for Belgrade at the end of January 1995, and is introduced to contacts there by a member of the pilot team. From there, he journeys on to Prishtina where the next transfer takes place very quickly. On 11th February, Frauke, a volunteer from the United States, finally arrives after having sought various ways of getting into the country since November of the previous year.

Like the first team, the second, too, is deeply shocked by the polarisation of society in the country and by the explosiveness of the situation in general. Here, apparently, no prior training can be of assistance. The pressure exerted by Serbian police and military is unbelievable. For example, a jeep drives into an open market place and its occupants, policemen, drunk or mad or both, simply fire on people. A woman is raped in her own house, and despite all this, no revolution is sparked off. *"It is a very curious thing how they've managed not to explode."*

Frauke just cannot understand why the whole thing is not blown sky high. From time to time, people move along the streets in groups, because they don't know what is going to happen next. Then, just as inexplicably, tension relaxes again and no one knows why or how. That's everyday experience in Kosovo. For Frauke, the most appalling thing is the realisation of just how well organised state violence is. *"It was quite amazing to see this and say, 'Well, someone actually sat down and thought this through',"* she concludes. She has experienced many a divided society, but nothing like this.

The appearance of the first team has left its mark. *"In certain circles in the Albanian movement, the BPT is perceived as being pro-Serb, or as coming from the Serbs, etc. because of the Church tour, and because the Church is at one with the Serbian nationalist front. We are working on changing this perception of BPT."* Frauke und Volker report. To this end, they are working on the BPT information pamphlet so that it now can appear not only in Serbian, but also in Albanian.

They sit down and talk with notable hardliners for the Serbian cause and try to find a balance in their contacts. Right up to the end of February, they still cannot find contacts with important Albanian partners. They fail to make appointments either with representatives of the LDK or with the 'Human Rights Council', despite the fact that foreigners are always taken there directly. The phrase, 'causing some concern', turns up in their reports to the Co-ordinating Committee. They turn with some trepidation to another delicate area that of human rights work. They ask at the 'Kosovo Helsinki Committee' whether they might accompany their personnel on their research trips into the villages. At the same time, they check with the Co-ordinating Committee whether this is really a good idea or whether it might appear to the Serbian authorities as something undesirable because it is too much orientated to human rights issues.

Frauke finds it easier personally to make contact. Many new contacts arise at meetings organised by women, but at which men are not explicitly excluded, although they rarely attend. Other contacts are to be found in pubs: *"...and as for me, when I am there I chain smoke and drink tons of coffee and do all these things that I wouldn't do at home. But when I am there, that's where I make my contacts."* This makes things easier, she says.

At the beginning of March, the team are at last able to meet an LDK representative, and during the first of half of the month, the fog of alienation begins gradually to clear. *"Very slowly the pieces of the puzzle start fitting together; we understand more about the history and dynamics of the conflict. We hear things because people know us a bit, and the monitoring part of our mission seems to start functioning. Who knows how it will pay off one day?"*

They soon discover the answer to this question, but it turns out to be a different one that that desired. During this month they learn that the police is placing the inhabitants of the village of Grejkoc under huge pressure. Team members don't dare to drive into the village itself, but Frauke manages to get into contact with a few people from the village when these turn up in the town.

This incident acquaints the two volunteers with what is about to happen. As soon as the team approaches the theme of human rights, they attract the attention of the authorities: *"...and then with all that we did, we'd just started to do human rights work, which is actually the problem which drew a lot of attention to us."*

The weeks pass without incident and things begin in a harmless way until Detlef, a third volunteer member from France, reports his presence at the local police station. The officer at the desk asks the landlord who is also present for further information. Later, Frauke reports: *"Immediately afterwards he asked if the black girl was still living with the landlord. It was lucky that the landlord came in for Detlef's registration, the officer warned, because he had planned to send the police for me on Friday and search the apartment and neighbourhood. He knew that I had been working, since I was seen with a blond boy wearing a jacket and backpack, visiting offices."*

On registering earlier, Frauke had said that although she is here on behalf of the Balkan Peace Team, she does not actually work for the organisation. She should register her organisation, she was told on this occasion, otherwise she would not be allowed to work in the country.

The young woman then goes to the police in order to get the matter cleared up. What then followed was what was referred to as an 'informative talk', but which was really an interrogation at which she was carefully questioned about all the persons she had met, their names and the abbreviations for their names contained in her notebook which the police had taken from her. She was then loudly accused of being a spy and an informer.

Her landlords were also questioned as well as the volunteer who had just arrived, and later, a team colleague who at that very moment happened to be abroad. These good folks were then released on the provision that in future they were to respect the law and that this time they had been lucky enough to encounter indulgent police officers ready to overlook their misdemeanours.

Despite this assurance, police pressure did not let up. Telephone conversations seemed to be bugged; police cars followed acquaintances. Frauke was asked again for interview, but later the summons was withdrawn. In short, the team was placed under pressure resulting from Frauke's earlier interrogation. Decision is taken for her to leave the country immediately. In the meantime it is Monday, the whole business having begun on the Friday before. Only now can she contact the International Office in Minden to explain the situation. She drives to Belgrade to inform people of the possible problems they can be faced with, and from there she goes on to Germany. From Germany, she travels down to Zurich in May to a meeting of the Co-ordinating Committee which is to come together for a routine conference.

The landlords in the meantime live in fear that the police could follow them up. The third volunteer stays on to offer his moral support since, as a Frenchman, he can mobilise international contacts and appeal to his embassy. Now he is under pressure. He is obliged to attend three 'informative talks' lasting between five and nine hours. He has to put up with isolation and verbal abuse. During this time, the landlord's daughter stays away from the apartment for fear that she could be raped.

Mai 1995: Return to Belgrade. Survival on next to nothing

Deliberations in Zurich turn on how things can proceed. One thing is especially hard to swallow. This is that earlier experience was not fully taken to heart, and this was that the later team was sent off into Kosovo only on tourist visas. These matters had brought them to this pass. The only thing to do now in order to demonstrate the seriousness of their mission is to go to Belgrade and there register the BPT as an NGO. This is much easier to digest for police authorities than the possibility of having harboured spies. A few weeks later, it is thought that this problem has been satisfactorily sorted out. This, however, is far from being the case. Detlef runs from one municipal office to another in order to register and soon realises that registration is going to be a long, wearisome business. Volker, having returned from Zurich, and who is 'holding the fort' in Prishtina, gets pretty clear indications from the police there that he is an undesirable intruder. Finally, Detlef gradually gives up in Belgrade.

This is farewell to Kosovo and a retreat to Belgrade. Here, life winds down somewhat. There is bookkeeping to be done and a data bank to set up. There is time to read and understand the constitution and to discover how a foreign NGO can settle in the country and how this is done. This is facilitated by founding an association whose members are local. Accordingly, Detlef sets off to find individuals who would be prepared to help in this regard. His conversations bring him into contact with notable people, persons from various walks of life in Serbia's varied society. More and more people declare themselves ready to support the Balkan Peace Team in the country. In the middle of this undertaking, Detlef's time runs out for him in the Balkans. It is now the end of May 1995.

In neighbouring Croatia, the military offensive which had called itself 'Flash' and had attacked Western Slavonia, is over, and volunteers from Otvorene Oci were underway as observers, while in Belgrade enthusiasm for official registration begins to wane. Shortly after Detlef, Volker's time with the Balkan Peace Team also runs out, and he is now followed by Vincent, the new man from the Netherlands who turns up in the middle of June. He is initiated into a crash course on how to find contacts, office management, bookkeeping and e-mail organisation, and subsequently left to his own devices. During the summer months, Frauke and Volker drop by to see how things are progressing. Jacques B. remains for three weeks in order to stand by Vincent during the coming visits he needs to make. And in mid-August, another volunteer joins them.

In the summer, too, the first potential founding members withdraw from the project. Vincent would have rather spent his time managing practical matters. He feels like a fish out of water with the job of putting flesh on the bones of the constitution, overtaxed and insecure when it comes to carrying on conversations with people in high places. In the autumn he decides that he's not the right person for the job. The support he receives from Daniel and Sabine at a distance are not sufficient to help him keep above water. Despite this, he manages to bring about a crucial change when, at the next General Assembly, he submits a more concise version of the association's constitution and one which ultimately leads to the registration of the association by

Vincent's successor at the beginning of 1996. *"This project is eating up volunteers"*, the co-ordinator warns his hearers in November 1995. The administrative work is frustrating, only marginally operable and the perspectives as far as Kosovo is concerned, rather obscure.

In stark contrast to the dramatic events having taken place in Croatia with that country's military offensive against Western Slavonia at the beginning of May and in the Krajina region in August, which bring about quick reaction and clear plans of action, work here in Yugoslavia appears to be constipated. There's no getting anywhere. With the threat of financial collapse just round the corner – the project is no longer solvent as the summer comes round – and there is a struggle to keep the Kosovo project afloat.

In Lyon and Paris in January and February respectively during 1995, work turns upon the processing of the experiences of the first team. Later, in Zurich in May, deliberations turn upon the management of the crisis in the second team, and, essentially, about what direction to take. No conclusion is reached. It is felt that there is a need for deeper analysis. To this end, an extra 'Kosovo Day' is inaugurated in Minden in July 1995 in order to get to grips with acquired experience there. In the following November at Amersfoort in Holland, a critical decision is taken about what direction to adopt. For the time being, Kosovo as target area takes a back seat. This is a conscious departure from earlier objectives; a 'change of orientation' as the minutes of the meeting diplomatically calls it. *"The assembly agrees to precisioning the approach and advocates that by working in/on all of Serbia, a more indirect, yet more realistic approach be taken, while Kosovo remains a special issue for the BPT".*

1996: New start in Belgrade. Smoothing out and widening contacts

At the same Amersfoort meeting, the Co-ordinating Committee commissioner, Mary from the Netherlands solidarity group, 'Tilburg Za Mir', is asked to step in as consultant for a few weeks, working with the team in Belgrade and later working on as a regular volunteer. Mary already has many contacts in the region, interest in the work of BPT and had generally made use of the opportunity to make contacts with people managing the Balkan Peace Team while its General Assembly was going on in Amersfoort.

A few weeks later, she is in Belgrade and renews her contacts from previous visits while working for Tilburg Za Mir. While doing this, she comes across a local activist, a woman called Uta whom she describes as "... *probably the most severe critic of BPT.*" They agree to meet and Mary makes use of Uta's experience with the BPT to later discuss how the team should operate in future. Being able to take the one-time critic seriously in this way, the Balkan Peace Team emerges with new credit from this exercise. Together with Uta and other acquaintances, Mary sets up an analysis of the strengths and weaknesses, possibilities and dangers facing the Team. In so doing, she *"learns a lot"* and submits a number of recommendations. In these is the distillation of what she has learned of the needs and wishes of all the other peace groups with which she has worked in the past.

In Belgrade, for example, there is the need to restore contacts and relationships, which have suffered in the last few months, cultivate them and so win back a good name. Dependable relationships with authorities must be developed or restored. As far as Kosovo is concerned, it is felt that one should still keep very much in the background. In other regions, among them Nis, groups ask for support. They want to know how e-mail operates, but also how they can represent themselves as NGOs and how they can work more efficiently. Mary's analysis concludes with the observation that it is these kinds of individual group contacts could also be put into operation in Kosovo.

Mary's work sees the beginning of a new phase within the Balkan Peace Team inasmuch as firm, supportable contacts can be established from now on. Her work lends a practical aspect to the endeavours of the Team in that she links on to the needs of her counterparts, her opposite number, so to speak, and also because of the fact that she has many valuable connections, mainly in Holland of course, but also other, international organisations which she make use of to the Team's advantage.

However, on the other hand, this kind of thing, although useful, does not correspond with the actual idea of the Balkan Peace Team, which could be stigmatized as - what might be called - 'imperialistic peacemakers'. With these sentiments in mind, the Co-ordinating Committee again questions its 'raison d'etre'.

Slowly but surely, regular contact leads to meetings and to deeper relationships. On an evening at the end of May, one or two members of the 'Albanian Youth Action' who are on a youth exchange programme from 'Pax Christi Netherlands and Flanders', and who are in Belgrade just at this time, stay overnight in the BPT apartment.

These young people speak of the needs and desires of the group so that Mary says later *"We also talked about dialogue and they said that they were ready to talk to Serbs living in Prishtina if the Serbs want to talk to them. We will have to see about this in July,"* that is, when Mary is back from Holland.

Autumn 1996: The Work of the Team acquires continuity

Since August, Katrin, the second volunteer, together with Mary, systematically go about widening and deepening contacts. One or two enquiries on the part of Otvorene Oci, for example, provide the perfect key to the door. With the reputation of having worked with a Croatian team at her back, she can introduce herself with ease to the corresponding NGOs, and others in Belgrade with what one might call a *"super visiting card"*.

The American, Ellen, joins the team at the beginning of November as a short-term adviser which does not appear to be much of an advantage to Katrin who in any case has not yet quite got used to things, but who can look back and say that she has learned a lot from the association. Two things, she maintains, have stuck in her mind: the first was to introduce *"...a point of view such as Ellen's which was to think within the framework of continuity, to imagine, that is, a time beyond my stay with the team."* This new concept had effects on the organisation of the office which, after formulating a common concept, was arranged in a more rational way. The success in this connection was reported as: *"We have now reduced our mountainous pile of papers to a file system with clear notebooks and labels. With a little time, anyone can now find what they are looking for. Local activists, on walking into our office, have asked if we could now come over and do their files as well."*

Thanks to the material help from Tilburg Za Mir, the general arrangement of offices in general improves, it is true, but it is accompanied nevertheless by a few complications: *"BPT-B(elgrade) now has a photocopying machine, a desk top computer and a laser printer. But we are only half way there. We do not have the computer programs for the printer, the copy machine fell in transit and smokes when we turn it on, and we have not found a way to access the computer. But it's a beginning."*

From August onwards, Katrin and Mary regularly drive to Prishtina for a few days in the month. Towards the end of the year, it occurs to them again that it would be a good idea to secure accommodation there, that is, a place to sleep, not an office. On one occasion they happen to meet the landlady who accommodated the exploration team in April 1995. She looks back with pleasure to that time, and offers the BPT an apartment, which is shortly to be vacated and which can be used for short stays and longer ones.

The second, important new perspective concerns content. Katrin again: *"What Ellen also brought into the programme was the suggestion to try and focus mainly on the groups in Belgrade and encourage an interest on their part for Kosovo. At the time she arrived, we were still strongly focussing our attention on groups here, groups there and trying to establish them. To build bridges between them was something really new."* Now, in the autumn, new ideas are afoot. *"Things happen,"* says Mary.

There is a new need among the groups in Belgrade, a need to make contact directly with the people in Prishtina, and a readiness to bring the question of human rights in Kosovo into public focus. The 'Women in Black' set things going with their silent public protests. *"Their vigil included a series of posters with facts about the human rights situation. It attracted small crowds of 15-30 people who seemed to read the material slowly and carefully before walking on. It was impossible to discern their opinions from this silent, but seemingly attentive reaction. But one Women in Black organizer later said she thought the attentiveness was a 'good sign', a change from previous reactions to difficult issues."*

One of the activists from Prishtina took part in of these 'Women in Black' meetings on one occasion and invited them to come over to Prishtina. Two of the women immediately said 'yes', and, accordingly, preparations were made in that town among the women's network for their arrival. For the first time, the 'diplomatic competence' of the Balkan Peace Team is put into action. At the women's forum of the LDK, they were asked to bring this idea of a visit forward and test reaction to it. The women in the network feared being dishonoured as 'Serbian favourites' should they take up the theme themselves. However, the Balkan Peace Team 'ambassador' can only report a positive reaction. The chairman of the 'LDK Women's Forum' is delighted with the idea that these 'Women in Black' are willing to make the journey to Prishtina.

Another member, this time of the 'Pancevo Peace Movement', has signalled interest in a direct encounter: *"He expressed an interest in accompanying BPT-Belgrade on one of its visits to Prishtina."* Mary and Katrin sound out the possibilities by tentatively exploring reactions among the 'Post Pessimists', a youth group in Prishtina sharing enthusiasm for graphic art and cartoons with the 'Pancevo people'.

Their procedure is a premeditated one:

"We spent a lot of time, finding groups who were, let's say, all the same age, who all had the same interest or had something in common. That was very tricky, because the groups in Prishtina are quite different from the groups in Serbia. But we found them in the end in Nis. But it takes some time to find out, because you have to know the people in order to know if they have a chance of liking each other. And if you know that some people are bound to like each other just because of their personalities, well, that's a major advantage. So we spent a lot of time searching that out. And then we spent a lot of time briefing both sides on the other side."

This skill in dealing with people was to pay off next year. In the meantime, the Balkan Peace Team is able to observe how the first contacts come about. An activist from Belgrade decides of her own accord to drive over to Prishtina and there establishes good contacts with Albanian activists.

"Personal visits like this appear to be the most valuable for building up understanding and BPT-Belgrade is encouraged by the fact that they are beginning to take place." An entry in the December report of the Balkan Peace Team comments.

Can it be, then, that direct human rights observation is possible after all? Mary and Katrin try to find out by enquiring at a number of organisations whether it would not be helpful for them to accompany their members into villages where violence is at work and discover that, *"No, such a thing is not practical."* Other international organisations wanting to go into the villages had been turned back by the police. Local activists, too, who are part of the Human Rights Council, for example, do not travel to the villages themselves, but rely on documentation provided by their highly diversified, local reporters. International observation of court procedures, such as that pertaining to Croatia as a standard process for observers in Split, for example, is impossible in Yugoslavia, since, apart from very close relatives in the cases of political procedures, no observers are allowed in the courts at all. Thus it is 'farewell' to something akin to the Otvorene model, so to speak, and the beginning of an independent one for the BPT-Belgrade.

"This year there has been focus on establishing contacts and on building up trust. In the future, we hope to move into developing a strategy and a concrete programme," the Team comments in looking back over 1996. In fact, things are already moving ahead; activities will very quickly develop which once had their roots in this year. At the same time, conflict in other arenas begins to accelerate in 1996. Here, too, the

Balkan Peace Team Belgrade is put on the spot. The subtle, discreet and patient building of bridges towards establishing dialogue must be balanced with reactions which, in their turn, ought to be increasingly quicker and more visible as they adapt to ever more dramatic, changing situations.

1996: Dayton – School Agreement – Liberation Army. The Conflict in Kosovo Now Acquires Momentum

The peace agreement, which takes place in Dayton in December 1995 and which ends the war in Bosnia, nevertheless ignores the situation in Kosovo. For the international community, Kosovo remains a domestic problem for Yugoslavia. While the Yugoslavian media exert themselves to present the situation in the region in ever rosier perspectives, and pressure on Albanian resistance leaders to communicate with their opposite numbers in Belgrade increases, resistance leaders for their part insist that the deplorable circumstances be publicly exposed and demand that negotiations be undertaken at international level. The tense human rights situation in Kosovo continues nevertheless, characterized above all by ill treatment, expulsion, torture and murder. The 'Council for the Defence of Human Rights and Freedoms' has already registered 13,226 cases in this context, and a further extension of this has been the assault of civilians in Kosovo.

On 22nd April 1996, five people were killed and another five injured in one single hour in three different places in armed attacks in Kosovo. A group which up to that time was unknown, calling itself the 'Kosovo Liberation Army', admits responsibility for the assaults. It is difficult to say at first who is behind this affair, and all kinds of conspiratorial theories are in the air. At the end of the year, there is a general consensus of opinion that it must have something to do with the Albanians.

Detlef, a temporary volunteer in the service of the Balkan Peace Team, who is looking for a substitute for the local members of the 'Balkan Peace Team FRY' (Federal Republic of Yugoslavia), says: *"The situation in Kosovo seemed to be more tense and risky than a year ago. Our presence as foreigners could become more and more difficult because of Western countries' global policy, seen as a betrayal by Albanians."*

However, in the second half of August, some movement is to be seen on the fronts that have hitherto ground to a state of immobility. Negotiations in fact have been initiated, and an agreement between Milosevic and Rugova, in other words, at the highest level, actually comes into being on 1st September. As a consequence of this, teachers and pupils can return to their school buildings. Just how this is to come about, however, is not debated. The result is that attacks on schools where the parallel system has so far been tradition, continue. This parallel system in the case of education and health care is particularly marked, and symbolizes non-co-operation. Instead of sending children to state schools and students to state universities whose legitimacy is no longer recognized, education is organized and financed independently by the Albanian community, and this, in part, under catastrophic conditions. Changes in this area, then, clearly indicate basic steps towards co-operation with each other. Notwithstanding, the agreement seems not to produce fruit and a year later, the situation can still be described as one of marking time.

In Serbia, on the other hand, the Dayton Agreement has brought relief in that sanctions, which had been placed on the country by the international community, are lifted. On the other hand, however, interior pressure rather increases, especially on the independent media. At the same time, the miserable state of affairs in the economic sector continues, aggravated by the exodus of 60,000 refugees and other displaced persons. In Eastern Slavonia, too, the Serbs are packing their bags. Officially, the area is still under the transitional governmental administration of the United Nations, but nobody can envisage a future for the region after their departure at the beginning of 1998. Distrust of Croatian authorities is too great.

A change takes place in the political situation when, in October 1996, the opposition party is partially successful in the elections. As a consequence of this, protests go on for months in Belgrade and in the cities of other parts of the country, mainly in Nis in the south. A regular struggle for power takes place between the opposition alliance, 'Zajedno' and Milosevic supporters. The Balkan Peace Team reports on the protests, supports the 'Women in Black' who, in the first few days of protest, characterize the demonstration scene. Pamphlets are printed and distributed which urge demonstrators not to indulge in violence. Students who have re-formed their operations are brought into contact with US colleagues and so on. Reactions to these protests in Kosovo are reserved. The Serbian opposition has no less nationalistically reacted to Kosovo than the government. In mid-February, the government withdraws the law, which had robbed the opposition of its election victory. In Belgrade and in thirteen other cities, the opposition takes over power. Students have established themselves as a new, independent political power in the country. Despite much provocation, the protests remain non-violent. Whether this signalises a change, the coming year will decide.

Sources

BPT no date, 4.94; 4.4.94; 5.4.94; 6.4.94; 7.4.94; 15.04.94; 20.4.94; 21.4.94; no date, ca 24.4.95; 24.4.94; 25.4.94; 20.8.94; 6.11.94; 23.11.94; 3.12.94, travel; 3.12.94, weekly; 5.12.94; 18.12.94; 21.12.94; 6.1.95; 20.7.95; 9.6.96; BPT Belgrade, 6.2.96, Hearts and Minds; 15.2.96; 5.96; 12.96; 9.6.97; BPT Biweekly 2.7.95; 11.-18.6.95; 16.8.95; 6.9.95; 5.3.96; 11.3.96; 27.5.96; 13.8.96; 4.9.96; 10/2.96; 11/1.96; 11/2.96; 12/1.96; BPT Biweekly Kosovo/a 8.2.95; 15.2.95; 1.3.95; 24.3.95; BPT CC minutes, 12.-14.1.95; 5.-8.5.95, 4, 6; Kosovo-Day, 16.7.95, 2; 16.-18.7.95, 10; 30.9.-1.10.95;BPT CC Daniel 10.1.96; Sabine M., 18.2.96; BPT GA minutes, 2.2.94; 15./16.10.94, 6, 15f.; 4.-5.11.95, 8f.; BPT IO 22.9.95; Interview Anton K. 1997; Frauke L. 1997; Jens K.; Katrin G. 1/1997; Mary F. 1997; Vincent P. 1997; Volker Q. 1997.

(2) Building Bridges: Dialogue projects (1997)

When Ellen departs in January, 1997, she leaves behind her another issue which is to bear fruit in the following month. In systematically pondering on what ways there could be of bringing Albanian and Serbian groups together, the team hits upon an idea. Katrin recalls, *"Many of the court cases are dealt with in Nis (southern Serbia) and here there are many Albanians in prison, and for the families who visit them it is difficult to find accommodation."* Would it not be possible for the 'Center for Non-Violent Conflict Resolution', a Serbian organisation, to serve as a kind of 'oasis' for Albanians who want to visit their relatives in prison? At first, the people at the centre are not so eagerly disposed to the idea. The Team informs them in detail about the situation in Kosovo, and in so doing it comes to light that, basically, there is interest in meeting people from the other side. On the other hand, there are many reservations. This original idea to transform the centre in Nis into a place of refuge is to trigger off enthusiasm, which will lead to the first dialogue encounters.

A workshop conducted with members of the centre by Jacques B. at the end of February on finding non-violent solutions to situations of conflict, deals with the problem of fear and discrimination. Katrin G., the volunteer organising the workshop, recalls:

"Then we asked the question: 'What is it that you fear most?' We assumed imitated roles. In my case, I played that of a nationalistic, Serbian landlady. This was played out by various pairs in different rooms and later compared, recounting then how we felt about it. For those activists from Nis who had played their own roles realized to their amazement that they could survive and put up with the very worst of verbal abuse. Even someone who rants in the most appalling way is pretty exhausted after about five of ten minutes. He simply runs out of abusive resources. This they found very encouraging."

The movement now seeks opportunity. The members of the Nis centre ask the Team to accompany them on the next phase. Suitable groups are to be chosen from Prishtina and contact established. At the same time, the Team is asked to organise a meeting and also to be present at it, at least in the initial stages. In Prishtina, Mary and Kristin then go about finding suitable partners for a dialogue, and from this develops a well thought-out programme of visits. This consists of official encounters, but also an unofficial meeting with members of such groups, for example, who are very much concerned about the possibility of their having contacts with Serbs and who do not want this to be common knowledge. This is particularly so in the case of a young man belonging to the 'Youth Action Group' who has suffered in this regard. His participation, for example, in a seminar promoting dialogue under the auspices of the 'Pax Christi' movement was stigmatised in a daily newspaper. If a group is not to lose its good reputation in the Albanian community, then discretion is the order of the day. The solution to this is simple: an invitation to an evening meal at which, 'by co-incidence', guests are present from Nis. The apartment in Prishtina belonging to the Balkan Peace Team is a suitable place for such unofficial encounters. It offers a private room to which one can withdraw, and also offers overnight accommodation. This situation provides an essential condition for the work of dialogue which now is about to unfold.

The weekend of the 19th-20th April 1997 is fixed as the time for the Serbian-Albanian meeting point to take place in Prishtina. Nis is only three hours away by bus from Prishtina and can in fact be regarded as a meeting within the neighbourhood. Three women from the Center for Non-Violent Conflict Resolution in Nis represent the Serbian side. There is to be a visit by two members of the 'Open Youth Club' for the first part of the programme and later the co-ordinator of the programme will be present. In the evening there is to be the 'joint project of cooking and eating spaghetti with two different sauces, along with a salad' in the Balkan Peace Team's apartment. Three members of the Prishtina 'Youth Action Group' exchange ideas on the activities of their respective groups with three women from Nis while slicing onions and preparing garlic. The visitors from Nis had already made friends with a group of women in Prishtina at a conference of 'Women in Black' a year previously and whom they want to visit on Sunday morning. In the afternoon, twelve members of the youth group, 'Post Pessimists', turn up to greet the visitors in their office.

Important matters in the garb of trivial conversation are brought up at these casual encounters. Issues of common interest are identified, such as ecology or women's rights. Ideas are aired as to what one can undertake together. An exhibition of pictures perhaps...? All this, however, is not the most important issue; it is not the essential, the 'nitty-gritty', so to speak, which makes these encounters of especial interest. The authors of a report on these first, tentative steps towards a full-scale dialogue have put it this way: *"In the course of the weekend, Swetlana B. said several times how very important it was to her to actually be in Prishtina, to meet and spend time with people there, to get to know them as 'normal' people and to see past the fictions of propaganda."* Their Albanian counterparts see the matter similarly: *"Members of Prishtina groups visibly relaxed in the course of the meetings and expressed that they were now looking forward to go to Nis and/or having further contact."*

At last, the fruits of last year's work and preparation are to hand. The team of women who have initiated the project are now experts on the Kosovo scene. Each month, they spend a week in Kosovo, and what they experience they relate to their partners in Belgrade. The 'Women in Black' who regularly report on Kosovo during their vigils, would like to be introduced to the contact-making process in Prishtina. At last these requests and other questions and enquiries! Their regular presence in Prishtina – albeit without registering themselves at the local police station, since this is a matter of indifference to their landlady - is a kind of lifebelt for their partners, a last straw of hope. The same is particularly true for those who work together with another ethic and who are exposed and vulnerable in their own societies.

Along with the Balkan Peace Team there are other active dialogue initiatives having to an extent the same target groups composed of students and young people generally. On these regular trips to Prishtina, the team gets to know the representative of a Norwegian church aid organisation, which has just opened an office in Prishtina. A representative keeps up youth contact in Kosovo with the former participants of a dialogue seminar called the 'Nansen Peace School' having earlier taken place at Lillehammer, Norway. Her 'post-graduates', three Albanians and two Serbs from Kosovo, meet each other from time to time. A subsequent seminar is to take place in Norway again in the summer. These are the people from the 'Nansen' group.

Again and again, Pax Christi Flanders, too, brings together members of both communities. Representatives of this organisation will again be in Kosovo in the spring of 1997 in order to bring Serbian and Albanian students from Prishtina and Belgrade together for a mutual seminar. Both Mary and Kristin know people belonging to this organisation. The circles mix with one another. Two of the participants, invited to an appointed seminar to take place in the summer this year in London and Northern Ireland stay the night in Belgrade on their way to their destinations. However, only one participant from Nis can actually undertake the journey. The other, from the Albanian Youth Action Group in Prishtina, has been refused a visa by the British Embassy for fear of his staying on with his sister who lives there, and who, probably, (at least in their opinion), wants to get out of the unbearable situation in Kosovo.

In March 1997, and after 17 months with us, Mary leaves the Balkan Peace Team. Her term of office was a long one and much has taken place during that time. She feels tired and 'burned out'.

Susanne who is rearing to go, takes her place. This is partly because of her good knowledge of languages and for this reason finds things easier. She can already see that the work in Belgrade and that Prishtina belong together as she drives for the first time to the latter. By the summer she is fully committed to the work and when the month of July comes round, she realizes that she will have to conduct the work of the office on her own, and she succeeds! We can say that she has 'arrived'. She carefully follows the work Katrin has been doing in promoting the mutual exchange of ideas between Nis and Prishtina, and learns that these have moved over to direct communication. This can be seen from the fact that, on next visiting the centre, plans have already been drawn up. At the end of the month, a reciprocal visit of the Post Pessimists is to take place. It is to last for three days and will include a tour of the mountains on the first day, a round visit of the Nis groups, and on the third day the possibility is provided for making use of the time together in whatever way they please. In June, there are ideas to arrange a similar plan for the second Albanian group. The actual programme will then reduce to one day during which the Post Pessimists spend in Nis. However, it turns out that the team finds satisfied hosts on the following day. Contacts will continue, the coordination is quite sure.

On the 'grapevine' we learn that there is some pressure from Prishtina on the Pessimists not to attend, but, despite this, contacts continue. The team which is frequently in Prishtina while members of the Post Pessimists or the Albanian Youth Action are in Nis, is apparently no longer necessary to serve as bridge. In August, a number of members of both sides drive to a U2 concert together in Sarajevo.

In the summer of 1997, there are dialogue meetings at every level. For the first time on Yugoslavian soil, a Serbian-Albanian dialogue takes place in Montenegro. The team is invited by a Belgrade organisation, the 'Belgrade Circle', to attend this meeting of intellectuals as observers. The Post Pessimists, who also have a group in Belgrade, are preparing for a meeting in Bulgaria in order to meet the Post Pessimists in Prishtina. Others are looking forward to a get-together in Hungary with Post Pessimists from all over former Yugoslavia. Other members from all the groups with which the team is currently working will be journeying this summer to various seminars arranged by Pax Christi.

Students Dialogue and Protest, Autumn, 1997

This year, in spring, Susanne and Katrin pursue a further possibility in setting up dialogue. They explore the interest in dialogue among Albanian students, and what which Belgrade students want to know. However, Serbian students only want these meetings to take place under the auspices of the international community. Susanne and Katrin discover that this is pretty important for the students and that, on the other hand, embassies asked would on no account take over the role of mediation. When it becomes clear that civil society groups or organisations such as the Balkan Peace Team will not be considered as mentors in the process, the team tries to find others who are interested. One thing is clear: dialogue is the central mandate area and anyone showing serious interest can act as a partner for BPT-FRY; no one is to be forced into anything.

In Kosovo there are interesting developments among the students. In May, Katrin and Susanne hear for the first time of a student union of the parallel system, and in July succeed in getting to know the people involved. Here, too, they come across people who are ready and willing to involve themselves in dialogue, particularly those few who have already taken part in seminars run by Pax Christi. They also learn that this organisation is preparing a meeting between Serbian and Albanian students. *"The 'Students' Union' said that they would be willing to meet any Serb student groups, as long as they were willing to accept the Students ' Union as an equal institution, as the representative of the Albanian University of Prishtina."* Natasha, one of the students' unionists says.

As far as the educational situation is concerned, Kosovo-Albanian students are deeply frustrated. Nothing has happened for a year in this sector. There are rumours of 'actions' taking place among the students sometime in the autumn. This frustration has already produced fantasies about the possibility of 'active resistance' without deeds arising from them so far. At the moment, these are still rumours, but Susanne and Katrin in their talks with other young people wonder what kind of reactions would be provoked among the Serbian public should the protests of Kosovo-Albanian students actually materialize.

In August, things in fact do just this and students begin to plan their actions. The Balkan Peace Team is invited to act in the capacity of consultant. Above all, the students don't want to be monopolized with their protest, which is concerned with students' matters. Ibrahim Rugova has, however, to give his approval. He will not give his 'approval' to the protest until 1st October so that the Serbian presidential candidature be running at that time will not be drawn into the action. The students are nervous. How can one react to provocation, whether this comes from the police or from the liberation army? Katrin and Susanne suggest that publicity be writ large in the affair, and are helpful in finding contacts. They offer the students the possibility to observe what goes on during the protests, and this is accepted with thanks. On the 1st October things will start.

From that moment on, the team begins to drum together all its contacts so as to inform them of what is going on. It discusses the issue with the German Embassy where the ambivalent attitude of the international community with regard to any kind of protest in Kosovo is a matter of discussion. On the one hand, there is concern about the possible response which such a protest might provoke from the Serbian side. On the other, the Albanians are encouraged to become more active.

In general, there is considerable understanding for bringing the educational issue back into the foreground. The central issue of education as a resistance theme for Albanians is discussed with members of a Serbian peace group located in Pancevo, and these are asked to come as observers to the protest. The peace organisation at Nis has in any case arranged for someone to be sent to Prishtina in order to 'demonstrate solidarity'. There are exchanges with the political officer at the US Embassy on how the protest will be received. He intends to drive over to Prishtina to see for himself. The editor of the Albanian newspaper, KOHA, which appears in Prishtina, fears escalation and the rapid conversion of local protest into a national 'issue' accompanied by corresponding symbols and demands for independence. That the students can control the affair themselves he considers highly unlikely.

The organisers of the protest, the independent students' union, in the meantime expect 16,000 students to take part in the proceedings. Many other organisations have offered their services. However, they want to remain the only organizers of their particular protest. Susanne and Katrin have now spoken to practically all the Serbian students they know. They can quite understand their colleagues on the Kosovo-Albanian side; on the other hand, they realise that every development in Kosovo could bring the right-wing candidate, Seselj, forward during the presidential elections in Serbia. Thus, the issue has a number of facets and perspectives coupled with both fear and hope.

As the turn of the month nears, the team invites observers from Serbia to attend events in Prishtina. In this, they begin with those people who have already shown interest in proceedings or those with whom they already have had direct contact. Two women turn up from the Nis centre. They are held up on the journey there and actually miss the demonstration. *"The following day we took Swetlana B. and Tamara O. along to meet members of the Albanian Student Union, and they were engaged in talking with them for hours. It proved to be very important for both sides. Swetlana and Tamara will come again to monitor the upcoming protests, and their visit to Prishtina has sparked a lot of discussions and some wider interest back in Nis."*

The Protest

"The first protest, on October 1st, was broken up by police using tear gas and truncheons. The chancellor of the Albanian University, as well as several leaders of the Students' Union, were briefly detained." This is the first terse summary of the dramatic events which concerned students' unhindered access to their institutes. By all accounts there were 15-20 thousand people who gathered together for a peaceful protest march. Previously, the police had said that they would not allow the march, but had given enquirers to understand that they would not take measures to stop it so long as it proceeded peacefully. However, then they blocked off the procession and resorted to violence against demonstrators. Several hundred people are injured during these assaults. Katrin and Susanne receive their 'portion' of tear gas and, on arriving back in Belgrade, learn the next day of the arrests which have taken place. They immediately ring the American Centre in Prishtina so that people there can keep an eye on those arrested, and then drive over to Prishtina to hear more of what has happened.

The students there are not going to allow themselves to be put off, and plan further moves. Thus, at the end of October, a second protest is announced, and again the Team is busy with observation.

At the first protest, diplomats were present, but hardly a member from the groups in Belgrade. This is now going to be changed. At the second protest, there is interest in coming along. The urgency to show oneself increases, and concern not to be seen in public diminishes. The majority of people come in order to experience the atmosphere and the situation for themselves. There are three people from the 'Centre for

Free Elections and Democracy' in Belgrade and Novi Pazar, one member from the human rights group in Leskovac and two from the centre in Nis, and a journalist working for the refugee circular, appearing in Belgrade called 'Odgovor'.

The second protest took place on 29th October 1997 and was a peaceful one. Again, about 15,000 people assemble to listen to addresses on the management of the school issue under oppressive conditions. No march is planned for this occasion. The masses then break up peacefully and pass as they do so the water canon and tear gas armoury of the police force which has just taken up position on a small hill. The mass meeting hardly receives attention in the local press. The students for their part announce further protests until such time as they can return to state buildings in peace. However, the general atmosphere is a mixed one. For many, the feeling is one of relief now that events have taken place without the accompaniment of violence. On the other hand, disappointment remains, because no change for the better can be registered. And just because it's a good thing when 'nothing happens', the folks who have journeyed here from Belgrade as observers as well as the team itself use the opportunity to further expand their contacts in Prishtina.

"Reactions to this trip were positive on all sides. The activists from outside Kosovo expressed satisfaction at having the chance to meet groups from Prishtina and to talk to individuals. It was clearly a moving experience for some of them, especially the younger ones who had never been to Prishtina, to get a feeling for the differences between the atmospheres there and in Belgrade. Many Albanian protesters and bystanders also expressed their pleasure at seeing people from Belgrade at the protest." The idea of using protests to further contacts between Kosovo and Serbia has been successful.

The Dialogue

Then, during these four weeks in October, something else occurs which is entirely unexpected, and something that makes great demands on the Team. Students from Belgrade meet student representatives in Prishtina, Serbian and well as Albanian. Katrin and Susanne are busy operating in the style of classical shuttle diplomacy plying back and forth using their acquired diplomatic techniques in establishing contacts between the two parties in order to trim them carefully for the first meeting.

These two women have gained the impulse to do this in Prishtina when they offered the students' union opportunity to gain contact with Serbian students. A possible partner in future discussion was one, Bastian, a person recommended to them by the 'Women in Black' and a member of the Belgrade student organisation. Susanne recalls here: *"Somehow we got hold of his telephone number and then we rang him and said: 'We know some people in Prishtina, would you like to talk to us about the possibility of a meeting or something...?' Well, he happened to be very enthusiastic, and then we met in a café and chatted with each other about how things could proceed."* The enthusiasm continued. Within a fortnight the whole thing had been worked out. The first protest of Kosovo-Albanian students had produced such pressure that one just had to move. However, there is that fear of operating too conspicuously under the public eye when a delegation of Belgrade students appears.

Another group registers its interest in a meeting. Serbian students in Prishtina want to get in touch with their Albanian colleagues. It's as absurd as it appears: students in the same city don't meet each other, but live separate lives as if they were living on different planets! The bridge-builders, Katrin and Susanne, from the Balkan Peace Team, provide the contacts in the first place. Serbian students in Prishtina are asked to participate in the preparations for the first meeting. Bastian for his part knows Prishtina and has contact there to Kosovo Albanian students, and is thereby one of the few who can range from 'planet to planet'. Other student representatives from various faculties and from the student parliament come to the preparations in Belgrade. Among these are two who have got to know Albanian students at a meeting arranged by the organisation, Pax Christi. Apparently, participation in its seminars helps to build bridges between the two ethnic groups when opportunity allows.

Shuttle diplomacy continues to flourish in Prishtina as Katrin and Susanne spend the next fourteen days in preparation, spending several hours practically every day in the office of the students' association.

Common experience between the students and the team members proves to be a catalyst in bringing them together in an atmosphere of trust which can now be used as a solid basis for dialogue. Information is offered on the student groups in Belgrade and their interest in coming together for talks. Both principal organisations on both sides are brought in direct contact with one another and much has to be made clear.

Susanne, looking back on past experience, points out the cliffs that have to be circumnavigated. These include the need to get to know the actual counterparts before talks as such begin. However, a lot remains uncertain almost to the end as to who, exactly, is going to take part in the talks. Standpoints, objectives and motives on all sides have to be clarified and points determined which ought properly be considered beforehand. What kind of character is the meeting to assume? Is there going to be some kind of declaration or not? Provisional results are pursued, but when everything has been clarified two days later, it is again something else. And, too, there is the need to bring mutual fears and prejudices into the open during discussion. For example: are we really welcome? For what purpose will the others use us? High above on the list are those matters, which it is perhaps better not to mention, since one cannot arrive at an agreement anyway. Sensibility must grow to realize what the emotive words are for the other group and vice versa. Then there must be the readiness to keep these out of the discussion. The themes about which one can talk are mainly those concerning education.

The Serbian students in Prishtina are even more circumspect. These are quite clearly fearful of a war in Kosovo. This motivates them to a discussion where the underlying conviction is something to the tune of: *"Let's have ten years of talking rather than war!"*

The day of the meeting finally approaches. Susanne and Katrin are in constant contact with Bastian who is busy organising the Belgrade delegation and these two discuss the last important details with him. At last, on 23rd October, the delegation sets off and when they arrive, Susanne and Katrin meet its members at a Prishtina hotel. Intensive exchanges take place during which Katrin and Susanne take stock of the situation on this evening and assure themselves that their guests from Belgrade have brought understanding and tolerance with them. The need to explain things is immense, even among Serbian students from both Prishtina and Belgrade. On this first evening in Prishtina, the Belgrade students meet their Serbian counterparts from Prishtina. They will leave the encounter with their Albanian partners until the following day.

Initially, only Belgrade students attend the meeting. They ask whether it is all right for Serbian Prishtina students also to come over on the next occasion. Then everything is ready. Belgrade and Prishtina students, Serbs in the one group and Albanians in the other, encounter one another in the offices of the Students' Union. The two women from the Balkan Peace Team take their leave at the door. For the next few hours, the disputants are alone. In the first ten minutes, each speaks his own language, and then changes over to Serbian, a gesture which has almost certainly been arranged beforehand. It is perhaps better after all that we are not allowed in, says Susanne and is for this reason not depressed by having been thrust out of the community. *"I think we would have had constant crises about something or other someone said."* So they just sit there like two midwives and wait. They are more than relieved when, after visiting a university building, they see the students stand up all crowded together under the roof of an institution and then, all together, go off for coffee. For this, the 'midwives' of BPT, are with them again and eagerly await signals. The atmosphere is good. Both sides have come together in goodwill and have not tried to provoke each other. Private meetings have been arranged. The dialogue is to go on. A mutual press conference is to underline this 'apolitical' meeting which has the features of an exchange of information.

There is a direct reaction from the LDK, and this is negative. In the press, Rugova attacks the students. The party, which is gathering strength as an Albanian, competitive parliamentary party in Kosovo, the PPK, reacts positively. Otherwise people say, *"Dialogue seven years ago, good; but now? It won't stay that way..."*. No one comes as an observer from the Serbian ranks to the next protest on the 29th October, and this disappoints the Albanians.

A few days after the meeting, two Serbian members of the Belgrade delegation organize a press conference. *"Most of it was absolutely in order,"* says Strabo, one of the two co-ordinators of the whole delegation trip later when he, Bastian, Susanne and Katrin sit down together and consider how they can get things moving again. *"...only at the end were things said which, unfortunately, were unacceptable for Albanians."* However, it is just these, which are writ large in next day's press reports. *"No, we're not going to talk to them again,"* the Albanian students counter. The fact indeed that one of them came out with a couple of things publicly which were unpleasant had not gone unnoticed by the team. Perhaps this can be dealt with later in the way of smoothing things out. The two Serbian co-ordinators send an e-mail to the Albanian students and try to explain what has happened. The team does not see this lapse in trust so dramatically, and confers with the Belgrade students as to what concrete steps can be taken next. At the private, personal level, the connections remain intact. The organisations don't meet again.

An inevitable setback? A hiccup in an otherwise professionally informative scenario? No, it is rather an indication of how vulnerable and sensitive such processes are. How small an irritation can be in tearing a bond that had just begun to form! Distrust can be created in one single stroke; trust grows when good experience repeats itself. The fact that dialogue between students living in such a polarised community can be attacked should not surprise anyone. Nor that, in the early stages, everyone creeps back into his shell. The history of the dialogue in this case might well have taken longer in other conditions, and if the Balkan Peace Team had taken up the threads again later. But here, alas, the process of dialogue has come to an end in the first round. The changing framework of conditions governing the situation does not allow room anymore for development.

The Dead-end in Serbia and in Kosovo.

Student protests express most clearly the growing criticism of passive resistance. This year, for example, the up to now uncontested authority enshrined in the person of Ibrahim Rugova as the leading figure for Kosovo Albanians declines appreciably.

Adem Demaci, who formerly headed a human rights organisation, now becomes the leader of the parliamentary party and a competitor to Rugova. The gap widens. One shock is the appearance of the deputy of the US foreign minister, Kornblum, in Prishtina. *"He made it unmistakably clear that the US consider the Kosovo problem to be solved within the boundaries of Serbia."* Rugova had always regarded America as a supporter of independence, a BPT report states. *"It is considered the heaviest defeat for Rugova in the last seven years."*

The view of the Balkan Peace Team in the autumn of 1997 is that the power vacuum is growing. Not only in Kosovo, but also in Serbia itself. There, people are exhausted and after the protests of the previous winter and pretty disappointed by the fact that things have not taken a turn for the better. Apathy prevails – especially among students. Milosevic' party loses its absolute majority in the Serbian parliamentary and presidential elections in September. At the deciding ballot for prime minister, the right-wing extremist, Seselj comes appallingly near to ascending the throne. This election has to be repeated in December, since neither candidate has the decisive majority. However, just how Seselj can be discouraged is something of a mystery to the activists in Belgrade, and creates an atmosphere of deep depression. Montenegro's candidate and Milosevic opponent, Dukanovic has arrived in the government and awakens fears of a collapse of Yugoslavia and the possibility of civil war. There are dark clouds over Serbia.

In the meantime, violence continues to escalate. Serbian policemen and alleged Albanian collaborators are shot down by members of the so-called 'Liberation Army'.

This state of affairs gives the Serbian police opportunity to take harsh measures, with the result that a hundred arrests take place; many of these are students and young people. Three of these die, two after being tortured. *"According to all our contacts, more and more people are starting to think in terms of violence as a 'solution' to the Kosovo problem,"* our half-yearly report states in alarm in the summer. They hear of Serbian families who secretly - and illegally - sell their land in order to leave Kosovo, despite the law, which prescribes that land, may not be sold to Albanians. A bleak outlook descends upon the year 1988.

Sources

BPT Belgrade 4.97; 9.6.97; 5.97; 7.97; 1.10.97;12.97; BPT Biweekly, 1/2.97; 2/1.97; 2/2.97; 1/3.97; 2/3.97; 1/4.97; 2/4.97; 1/5.97; 2/5.97; 1/6.97; 2/6.97; 1/7.97; 2/7.97, No. 32, 14.-31.7.97, Confidential; 2/8.97; 1/9.97; 2/9.97; 1/10.97; 2/10.97; 1/11.97; BPT CC Minutes, 1.-2.3.97; Interview Katrin G. 1/1997; Mary F. 1997; Susanne S. 1/1997. According to Clark 2003, 181, the Serbian student delegation observed the demonstration on 29.10.97.

(3) Solidarity, Support and a Channel for Information: The Team's Role during the Escalation of Violent Conflict until the beginning of the War (1998-9)

In November, 1997, the General Assembly of the Balkan Peace Team meets in the French town of Mulhouse in Alsace. The first round of the student dialogues with all its ups and downs has come to an end. Katrin is much applauded for the Team's part in what has been achieved. The profile of the BPT-FRY is now quite clear at last. The fact that the door of opportunity is already closing remains unmentioned, although the increase in armed attacks is registered with concern.

At the next meeting of the Co-ordinating Committee in February 1998, at Split on the Croatian Adriatic coast, the security of the team already plays a prominent part in the exchanges there. Various potential escalation scenarios are considered. New dialogue initiatives seem impossible. How can the team deal with the rapidly changing front situations?

A few days after this debate, a massacre occurs in Drenica and with it another threshold has been reached. The internal dynamics of escalation have reached international level. Kosovo is no longer an interior issue within the state of Yugoslavia. *"The work of the Balkan Peace Team in the Federal Republic of Yugoslavia in the summer and fall of 1998 has been dominated by the war in Kosovo and the resulting humanitarian crisis."* The half-yearly report coming out in December 1998, explains.

Looking back, the signs of the times are easily recognized. However, now, and especially during these last months, this was not the case. Information at this juncture is quite inadequate, diverse and contradictory. Despite this, however, certain assessments of future developments have to be filtered out from what comes in, and in this connection the options to act have to be identified and taken advantage of, and possible risks have to be assessed when they concern the safety of team members and that of local organisations and personnel.

Escalation

In November 1997, followers of the 'Kosovo Liberation Army' *"reveal themselves for the first time to the public at a funeral, armed and in uniform."* Up to 1st February 1998, the 'International Crisis Group', an international research team observing conflicts and which makes recommendations, reports that nine violent incidents have taken place having an ethnic background. What had actually happened is difficult to discover. *"Reports from different sources often agree on little more than the time and the place of some incident,"* the Crisis Group notes. Many people in Kosovo are attracted by the aura of armed resistance. Serbian forces increase their activities and civilians are being armed. Paramilitary groups from Serbia move into Kosovo. In mid-February, the 'International Helsinki Committee' calls the chairman of OSCE to action:

"The long-lasting status quo of peaceful and civil resistance of Albanians in Kosovo has ended. The situation seems to be sliding out of control and heading toward large-scale violence between Albanians and Serb police units. Every day, there are reports of more violent assaults and increased repression over Albanians in the form of Serbian reprisal expeditions. In addition, there are also increasing numbers of armed assaults against Serbian police and other repression-related targets, assumed to be carried out by the so-called Kosovo Liberation Army (KLA)".

The authors of note belong to the Helsinki Committee for Serbia, Kosovo and Montenegro. They know what they are talking about. They are demanding negotiation within an international framework which, similar to that in Dayton, can now quickly halt escalation in Kosovo.

At the meeting of the Balkan Peace Team in Split in February 1998, the representative of the Belgrade team outlines a similar assessment of the current political situation. In Belgrade, it appears that the political scene has frozen, whereas in Kosovo there appears to be considerable activity. In one or two weeks, that is to say, by the end of February, an *"urgent police action"* is expected, a demonstration of power by Milosevic.

In the period which follows, a number of varied probabilities could materialize: the first variant is that of police intervention with subsequent negotiation. The second form could be that of police action with subsequent escalation and the threat of a massacre of civilians. The third possibility, which is perhaps an unlikely possibility, is that of police action with subsequent escalation and the intervention of other countries such as Albania and Macedonia. The end of March, when elections are planned for a Kosovo Albanian underground parliament, is seen as the last date for the threat to be transformed into action. And finally, according to this assessment, there is the widespread view among Albanians that NATO will step in and save the situation. If this eventuality were thrown into question in speaking to Kosovo Albanians, one would not be believed. On the other hand, however, if this expected intervention is related to diplomats, one would be confronted with stony faces.

The idea of non-violent resistance finally loses its attraction in the winter of 1997/8. The intensification of non-violent protests has not strengthened resistance, but weakened it. It is now clear that Ibrahim Rugova's party no longer completely controls the political life of Kosovo Albanians. The violent reaction to protests on the part of Serbian police seems indicate the limits of non-violent resistance. The step-by-step procedure whereby aspects of the conflict can be controlled as in the case of education in schools seems to have failed. The Belgrade team belonging to BPT shares this evaluation. While, as before, Rugova continues to enjoy high standing among the population, he is apparently no longer in a position to correctly assess the situation. Apart from this, his confidence that the Americans would intervene to save the situation for the Kosovo Albanians has not been backed up by fact up to now.

That non-violence has not been able to work will just not sink in for those members supporting non-violence in the Balkan Peace Team. In the meeting in Split, they try to understand the sudden reversal of affairs, viz. that Kosovo finds itself in the middle of a violent conflict. Susanne, who as a team member, is able to report at first hand, draws the CC members' attention to the fact that people are already speaking of the possibility of war. Moreover, they speak in a way as though the shadow of war were the fulfilment of prophecy.

Up till August last year, stagnation was the order of the day. The student protests at first worked in a very positive way, because they were able to channel pent-up energy. Nothing came of these protests for several reasons, and the October protests received no attention from the media because no violence issued from them. The objectives, too, were vague. No group had been able to bring its counterpart to the negotiating table. As a result, the energy potential had dried up and had contributed to the fact that non-violence had failed. One could not count on student movements as reliable partners in solving problems of conflict without violence. Here, there was much more inclination towards a 'liberation army'.

Drenica and its consequences

A few days after the meeting in Split, the dreaded police action in fact took place when, on 28th February, Yugoslavian units stationed in the Drenica region murder the leader of the Liberation Army and numerous civilians. *"This turned out to be a turning point for public opinion in Kosovo,"* writes FRANKLIN DE VRIEZE from the Pax Christi Flanders group later.

But the non-violent protests are once more intensified. The Drenica massacre persuades students to include political demands to end suppression during their protests. At the end of March 1998, Prishtina, for example, sees the largest demonstration for the last ten years in which between 50,000 and 100,000 demonstrators take part. The protest proceeds peacefully in Prishtina while in other cities the police violently intervene. A week later, 10,000 women come together in Prishtina to demonstrate their solidarity with the women and children in the Drenica area. Every day in Prishtina, Albanians march in protest, and demonstrations and counter demonstrations alternate in the city. Clashes ensue between the two civilian communities, which increase in number as time goes on. For the students of the independent students' union, the last non-violent demonstration takes place on the 30th April, since no one can ensure control or discipline anymore. How can one propagate non-violent solution of conflicts anymore when it seems that nothing can stop an approaching war? The more the frustration of failure over the last eight years in the pursuance of a strategy propagated by Rugova, who is forced now more and more to take a back seat in the political arena, the more hope is placed on the Liberation Army in the hope of a solution to the region's problems.

"From February, 1998, until March 1999, the domestic and international political agenda was dominated by the fighting on the ground," writes DE VRIEZE. At first, the Liberation Army is on the offensive. More and more rural areas pass into its hands.

"While openly confronting Serbian police control, KLA declared 'liberated territories' within central Kosovo. After the war, KLA leader Hashim Thaci acknowledged attacks were sometimes aimed at provoking a Serbian response and endangering local population, since this would increase chances for foreign military involvement in the conflict." Background activity such as this was only learned of later.

International aid organisations and local women's organisations whose other work has more or less come to an end, now concern themselves with the civilian population. It is hardly possible to get into the area around Drenica. Aid organisations, which are active in areas beyond, speak of abandoned villages in which there are only one or two old people left. The number of refugees fleeing within the country's interior is rising rapidly. *"In some houses there are now almost 100 people. Most of the women's organisations BPT is in contact with are presently busy trying to help these people and their hosts with food, clothing, heating facilities (temperatures are freezing) and other humanitarian goods,"* the team reports during its daily information on the state of affairs in the spring.

The Liberation Army continues to advance during the summer months, and in July 1998, for the first time it conquers a town. On re-taking the town of Orahovac about one hundred people lose their lives. Then there is a reversal of the situation. At the end of July, a Serbian offensive captures every base belonging to the Liberation Army - *"frequently enough with catastrophic effects for the villagers,"* a BPT report announces. There are no reliable figures as to how many refugees were forced to leave their homes, but there is a general consensus of opinion that we have to do here with the fates of about hundred thousand people.

Montenegro does not follow Serbia into war. It does not wish to send its eligible servicemen into Kosovo, and allows refugees from western Kosovo to enter the country until closing its borders in the summer to a veritable flood of fugitives. At the end of August, and after a successful offensive, the Serbian parliament announces its victory, but the war goes on nevertheless.

Neither does this war spare the immediate surroundings of the Balkan Peace Team. Volunteers visiting the 'Centre for the Defence of Freedom and Human Rights' in Prishtina discover workers there who are very much concerned about the situation. Only a week before, policemen dressed in civilian clothes, had come to fetch one of their team members. No one had heard or seen anything of him since that date. All their enquiries had come to nothing.

The humanitarian catastrophe brings international aid organisations into Prishtina. This brings at least one advantage to the city in that *"the streets are somewhat safer"*, as one of the workers at the centre mentioned above observes. The UNHCR has set up a consultation room where various aid organisations can come together to deliberate on the current situation. At the end of September, the first convoys move into the affected areas in Kosovo, but later at once withdraw again on hearing that NATO threatens to attack the region from the air.

International Reaction and the Build-up of a Threatening Scenario

The fact is that violent escalation, and especially the scenes of civilian casualties and the plight of the refugees, actually achieves what non-violent resistance has so far failed to secure - that the international community intervene in favour of the Kosovo Albanians. After Drenica, international public opinion gradually becomes aware of what is happening. The World Security Council passes a resolution on 31st March 1998 in which violence on all sides is condemned and indicates that intervention on the part of the international community cannot be excluded. This is not received with much joy from one quarter. In April 1998, in a referendum on the matter, an overwhelming majority of Serbs speaks out against any kind of international mediation in the Kosovo conflict. However, pressure increases. The contact group, which has been in existence since the Bosnian war and which consists of the USA, Russia, France, Great Britain, Germany and Italy, decide on 24th April to apply sanctions against Serbia. Montenegro is excepted. The demand is for a dialogue to begin by the 9th May. It is to be the drawing up of a report on civilian victims and the appalling condition of refugees and others driven out of the country. In the summer and autumn, international mediation operations forge the plan together with all the potential pressure at its back, including the threat of arms.

In September, rumours of military intervention then turn into practical application. NATO presents an ultimatum. During this time, Milosevic is to observe the UN resolution, which requires the withdrawal of Serbian units. If this is not put into action, military intervention will follow. In order to avoid this, Milosevic agrees to remove his police units and also agrees to the sending of 2000 unarmed OSCE Observers who will monitor the withdrawal.

And in fact the Serbian police units do withdraw, and members of the Liberation Army then move into their positions. These then go about arresting Rugova's followers, especially those in the party who had insisted that people should not trust the Liberation Army that couldn't protect them after all. The aid organisations who are no longer held up by Serbian police controls, now return to their tasks, but instead of harassment from the police they are now faced with the unpredictable violence of the Kosovo Albanian Liberation Army as they make their way to help victims of civil strife. In October of this year the team comes into contact with the technical personnel of the OSCE preparing for the commencement of the observation mission. Altogether, there will be over 1000 people comprised of local workers, who, according to the NGO's representative responsible for the arrangement, will be employed as translators and administrative workers and where work is already in progress. Will there be a chance after all to break the round of violence?

Private Dialogues: Keeping up Contact

What is to become of the dialogue? At the beginning of 1998, it seemed to those looking on that this was a viable option. "Use every opportunity to enter into dialogue", the International Crisis Group urges in its statement issued in mid-February. *"Non-government organisations and UN agencies should continue to explore every avenue that can bring people of the two communities together."* However, it may well be too late now to make new contacts. At least this is the view of the Balkan Peace Team. As far as the furtherance of dialogue is concerned, the BPT had decided in February to maintain contact with those people and organisations already established and to continue to work with them. This meant that there would be no more contact seeking with Serbian or Albanian groups. That doesn't seem possible anymore at the moment. Students from Belgrade and those from Nis continue to take part in the observation of demonstrations.

The Drenica massacre has unsettled both ethnic communities, including of course those, too, who have put out feelers towards the other social group. The business of processing this experience varies. In Nis there is no unanimous opinion that contacts should be upheld at the private level, despite everything. In situations such as these, people become less liberally minded, and more *"narrow minded"*. This, anyway, is the view of the new volunteer who asks himself whether, after all, there are really no more themes on which it is possible to debate.

The dialogue process does not dry up completely, however. It chooses rather to transfer its attention to the private sphere, to that of creating encounters between individuals belonging to both ethnic groups. This inclination, especially in the current situation where the respective groups are at loggerheads with each other, is a particularly salutary one. Katrin, in interview at this time remarks: *"It is like this: people speak to each other at the unofficial level in quite a different way than they would at the official one. In speaking at the unofficial level they are inclined to give reasons for their official stance. In this way, strangely enough, much more tolerance and understanding is created."* This then leads to situations like the following: *"Two women from the Nis centre were guests at the invitation of an Albanian who wanted to get to know them. For our part, the Balkan Peace Team had invited two Serbian students so that they could get to know the two women from Nis. The Albanian host came, too. This was not a planned affair, but nevertheless resulted in a very positive development, but the first ten minutes or so were a little tense as we sat at the table."*

In the critical summer months, the Team kept a very low profile, especially in Prishtina, knowing well that contacts, particularly for Albanians, could be associated with risk. Notwithstanding, connections are sustained, particularly between women's groups in both Belgrade and Prishtina in order to further promote dialogue and keep the channels of information and communication open. Groups who were formerly active in the process of dialogue can now no longer continue to meet and are somewhat circumspect about the pressure exerted on them, and about what the future might hold, but are nevertheless supported by the team.

Here, one realizes how important the tasks are which uncover rumour and rectify exaggeration. This is a strategy chosen by the team, too, in acquainting Serbian students in the faculty of law, for example, with some of the facts associated with police violence against young Albanians. The students don't swallow this piecemeal, of course, and reserve their opinions. However, the firm, but polite insistence on the Team's behalf that it is an unprejudiced, independent body in its judgements, allows it to impart information to students who, albeit only accept the data grudgingly.

The team takes a walk with one the members of the dialogue group in a part of Prishtina which is apparently unsafe for Serbs. These are small steps in order to break down fear and the anxiousness about being separated in the town. On this walk they come across an Albanian who critically appraises their presence, but then nevertheless accompanies them, because he takes them for journalists. He shows them the houses in which refugees live. In the distance one can hear the noises of artillery fire howling through the valley. The Albanian asks them to coffee at his house, which is served to them by the woman of the house. They drink coffee together in the courtyard and listen to stories about a refugee who is now living with the family. They hear how the police come in the middle of the night and how this man is beaten up and then released. *"Our friend was uncomfortable and especially nervous at being invited into an Albanian household. He told us later how his heart had pounded in his chest the whole time. But he seemed to have heard the stories and taken them seri-*

ously." These are examples of individual encounters. There is no room for more, but opportunities are sought and used. Perhaps the leeway allowed to us will expand again.

Using Knowledge Which Provides Decision-makers with Information

Things start coming to a head in the winter of 1997-8. Up to February, the Team feels fairly secure, since, for the most part, battles take place in the countryside and they are not expected to migrate to Prishtina.

The team's contacts will warn them before about the possible evacuation of Prishtina and - in any case - the American Consulate in Prishtina will provide refuge should things come to the worst. Despite this consideration, Susanne has had feelings of panic even before events in Drenica and writes in these terms to the support group at the Balkan Peace Team. She says: *"What do we do here if war comes?"* Accordingly, the Team sits down to consider emergency operations. Those driving to Prishtina are to mention their intentions in the consulate in Belgrade and are to ring the Team on their arrival. Further, they are to have their name entered in the international organisations who are to be informed should there be a call to evacuate the city. They do not drive to Prishtina via Drenica, because of police controls on the way there, whereas in Prishtina itself there is never a need to register at the police station since the Team is tolerated in this shadow area.

What role can the team play in this situation? When the Co-ordinating Committee meets in Split, on 19th February 1998, the Team asks itself whether other activities are not now necessary? Examples of such activity would be more work on publicity and more work in the lobby. Resources are limited here, however. The team feels that the member organisations could be become active, since this would seem a good time for such activity, but these have hardly much more potential than publicity work through the circulation of articles. There is a large NGO conference coming up, otherwise there is not much going on. The general level of information among the public at large is assessed as 'minimal'. Just what concrete demands there are for the acquisition of information for the team is a question difficult to answer.

The team now sees itself primarily in the role of an information channel. It can't do much in this line itself. It changes its report coverage to include events after Drenica. After it has got over the shock, the team decides to spend more time in Prishtina in order to be more of a presence there, to live out the situation and give less attention to the activities of organisations. After Drenica, the team issues reports on the situation several times a day.

The situation visibly escalates towards April. The objective is also to relay information to the consulate in Belgrade. Contacts are closest, apparently, with the German and US American consulates, and in this Katrin remarks: *"By now we have acquired quite a large degree of authority or credibility at consulates with whom we have closest contacts. We have even had small instructions or contracts from an embassy regarding groups, for example, which are to be sponsored by an embassy or requests for this or that subject to be clarified. If it's at all possible and if it's within the range of our work, then we oblige them."* The reason is simple. As a result of the confidence the team enjoys as far as its contacts are concerned, the team picks up information which an embassy would never receive. The team´s informants *"don't have to sell themselves to us at all and can speak to us relatively honestly. And that's the kind of access to information a consulate or other kinds of representatives of large organisations just don't have."* As a result of the increased need for information in general as far as the international side is concerned, the team has much less time for talks with its counterparts in Belgrade. It is precisely here that ignorance of what is going on in Prishtina is most marked and where, incidentally, information is most needed.

Presenting diplomats with information is a top priority, and this is certainly a worthwhile objective for the team. Here, Susanne has a word or two to say: *"When they have to make correct decisions, they need good information, and if we can contribute to that, then I find that both good and important."* The decisive channels for this are the consulates from where their information can flow right up to Contact Group level, although of course they have *"their policy"* as Katrin calls it. The team´s informants are Albanian and Serbian students in Prishtina, aid organisation helpers who supply Drenica with relief and workers at the Humanitarian Law Centre.

"Do you hope to be able to reduce escalation through your contribution?" The answer which Susanne gives to this question with a 'gentle sigh' in an interview on 28th April, 1998, is one which indicates the limits of impact that a project like the Balkan Peace Team can have on the situation as a whole:

> *"Not that I can imagine, I mean that would be slightly foolish of me to assert that we have. The level at which we work is on the long term and is very small. The great historical events will just take their course whether*

we're here or not. In other words, in matters of whether war will come or whether we'll find ourselves in the middle of a big wave of terrorism or some such thing – as far as these things are concerned we have not the slightest influence on them. None at all."

A Bridge of Information and Contact: A new (old) Role in autumn, 1998

The coming of international aid organisations and the OSCE mission in October changes many things. Here, the Balkan Peace Team has a special job. It has nothing to distribute, but it is very familiar with the circumstances. And because it is composed of foreigners itself, it can easily establish contacts with international organisations. This transforms it into a bridge of information and contact similar to that of the function of Otvorene Oci when this team played this role in Western Slavonia and in the Krajina region. It is a bridge which links not only the international with the local, but also the large, well-established local bodies with the new, smaller bodies, that is to say those groups, that are familiar with the special features of a place and are themselves known to the inhabitants. Misunderstanding and mistrust on the part of local people on the scene as far as foreigners are concerned is evenly balanced by ignorance of local people on the part of international representatives who have no idea about local populations.

In this connection, the Balkan Peace Team served as intermediaries between the local scene in Prishtina and the international NGOs. As a result of their contacts with embassies, questions concerning visas, for example, and the financing possibilities of projects can be explained. The number of international organisations located in Prishtina continues to grow right into December from six to forty-five. With this large number of foreigners having infiltrated the city, the atmosphere in the town is more relaxed in the autumn. Its streets are free from tension and the BPT no longer has to tread so carefully. Now it can risk holding public meetings and publish articles.

It is clear to the team that that is all one can do at present. This, however, is not true for the broader scene of peace activists who are again thinking of a large non-violent intervention in Kosovo. And, in fact, in the autumn when the peace groups, Beati di Costruttore di Pace and American Peace Workers who have already gained previous contact and experience in the region play their role in sounding out the options for a non-violent intervention on a massive scale. Among other things, the Balkan Peace Team is asked for an assessment of the current situation. The representative of the

Peace Workers, along with recommendations for Belgrade and Prishtina, receive a critical assessment on how, at demonstrations, the peace worker actions during the last year had possibly endangered their contacts with people in Prishtina. They were also informed about how the land lies with non-violent student movements and what their commitment is at the moment.

The team is not willing to support the possible intervention of thousands of volunteers. Policemen control the streets, the villages are all but inaccessible, and the reactions of opposition, and the activities of paramilitary groups on both sides are difficult to prognosticate. The enquirer would do better to ask the local people. Now if that's not turning things upside down? Here is a project whose object it is to appear on the scene with suggestions of non-violent intervention in the local community saying 'No, thank you' to non-violent intervention! The episode, however, makes it clear that the Balkan Peace Team in the meantime has come to recognize its own limitations and, no less, has learned what conditions are necessary for non-violent intervention. One cannot say how and under what conditions non-violent intervention will meet with success, but one can say with a fair degree of certainty under what condition it will or will not be a success when the organiser has in some way to take responsibility for the lives of activists taking part in the action. Yet the question remains in retrospect for a number of participants as to whether this is not the moment which has been allowed to pass too quickly. As far as the current situation is concerned, however, the BPT places its hopes on the internal contestants, not least those in Serbia on whom responsibility for significant decision depends.

Solidarity in the Dangers of Autumn, 1998. The Balkan Peace Team remains in Belgrade despite the Threat of NATO Bombardment

From the early summer onwards there have been actions against the threat of war. The independent Students' Union in Serbia initiates an anti-war campaign which condemns war in Kosovo with the help of leaflets and posters and which tries to get the public on its side, a movement which, according their own reports, meets with much positive approval. Despite all this, for their Kosovo Albanian colleagues, these actions are disappointing, since they never get into Kosovo and do have no Serbian allies there. There are policemen, for example, who refuse to do duty in Kosovo and parents who have sons who have been called up for military service and who want to fetch them personally from Kosovo.

The 'Women in Black' continue to regularly appear at demonstrations against war. They run into trouble when right-wing, Seselj, the deputy prime minister of Serbia accuses them of working in the interests of foreign powers. In this atmosphere of ultimatum at a time when embassies are withdrawing their personnel, the threat of NATO bombardment is literally 'in the air'; rumour, hysteria, the hoarding of provisions and fear of foreigners is beginning to spread. The 'Helsinki Committee for Human Rights' in Serbia, the 'Belgrade Circle' and the 'Women in Black' are referred to by name and threatened should NATO in fact drop bombs.

The Balkan Peace Team notes in its report: *"In response to this threat, BPT spent the next few days visiting each of the organisations, plus the 'Humanitarian Law Center', offering whatever assistance would be appropriate for increasing their security."* The threat is received in varying ways by the different organisations. When the Balkan Peace Team makes enquiries about reactions to this, it appears that the 'Women in Black' have something quite different in mind. For example, one activist storms into the office quite beside herself with indignation, and furiously asks why Kosovo should not be at the centre of attention during the protest, and why there is only a protest against the NATO threat of bombardment. She had worked for seven years against the nationalists only now to find herself possibly on their side at a demonstration! She fears that in this way the students of the anti-war campaign will give their true objectives away, and that their activities will be interpreted as support for the government and not as a declaration against further violence. The threat against her own organisation is taken more or less with a pinch of salt.

The chairman of the 'Helsinki Committee' for his part does not wish to underestimate threats of this kind by dismissing the possibility that anything could happen. The threats from NATO, on the one hand, don't impress him unduly. Nevertheless, people ring in and ask where the bombs could fall in the assumption that they as an organisation, ostensibly supported from abroad, would almost certainly know! The next day a bomb threat reaches the committee. The team comes across a chairman who views this impartially and thanks them for coming.

The workers at the 'Humanitarian Law Centre' have not yet come across any intimidation, perhaps because their particular institute doesn't air its views publicly. The worker at the 'Belgrade Circle', however, reacted quite differently and stayed regularly in his office overnight together with friends and colleagues, and avoids his own apartment which is situated in a remote place. Many activists are nervous, he says, and are leaving the country. The speed with which certain international organisations leave Belgrade annoys him. The team members, too, receive signals from their respective consulates. Hubert is to listen to news on short-wave radio and remain in contact with his consulate, and also be ready to leave at short notice. A day or so later, news arrives together with an injunction to leave immediately. Hubert departs for Budapest in order to lengthen his visa, and then re-enters the country.

A certain sick humour makes the rounds in view of the tense situation. The team organizes a party to which former volunteers from Otvorene Oci, internationals that it knows and who are still there, activists from Belgrade, students from the same city, and from Prishtina. To be able to laugh and hold normal conversations relaxes the atmosphere and raises spirits after a week of tension and fear. Finally, the situation takes a change for the better with Milosevic' willingness to yield, and with the withdrawal of Serbian forces along with the assurance of an OSCE mission. But for how long?

The Curtain Falls: New Escalations in the Winter of 1998/99

"Many people are fearful, and some even work on the assumption, that war is likely to return in the spring, if not before." Thus, the BPT's December report's prognosis. There are rumours which report that the Liberation Army simply clear its opponents out of the way. One aid worker working with an international organisation recounts Albanians having found refuge in a Serbian village after the Liberation Army had driven them out of their homes because they had refused to comply with orders to defend themselves with weapons. In December, fighting actually does break out again between the Liberation Army and Serbian forces. More and more special police units and military forces are sent into Kosovo.

A pessimistic outlook is not only to be found in the areas of conflict. The German Bundestag (Second Parliamentary Chamber) has already agreed to a NATO intervention without UN mandate on 8th October 1998. On 15th January 1999, at a massacre in Racak, 45 Albanians lose their lives and this marks another milestone in recent developments. So far, it is not clear whether this affected civilians or armed combatants. However, it succeeds in bringing Europeans and US Americans together to make one more effort at reaching a solution of the problem by diplomatic means. The result of their exertions is the coming together for discussion of Serbs and Albanians at Rambouillet in France.

A desperate attempt is undertaken by students in Prishtina to bridge the ever-widening gap among Albanians. Fifty-one students go on hunger strike, demanding moderate political leadership, and at the same time calling upon the separatist rebels to seek political common ground. An independent Kosovo is their objective, too. Their strike begins on 28th January and is broken off four days later after they have received confirmation of a meeting between the leaders of the moderates and the rebels. Thousands of students support the cause of the hunger strikers who declare their readiness to further undergo their strike should nothing come of the negotiations. However, other Albanians try to break up student action by using violence, intimidation and attempts at bribery. One young woman with whom the team spoke at the beginning of January was subjected to abusive language while having a pistol levelled at her head while being urged to produce a list of those on strike. The degree of violence within Albanian society has assumed appalling proportions.

At the beginning of February 1999, Prishtina is in the grip of fear. As the team arrive in the town at 7 pm, there is hardly anyone on the streets, and only members of international organisation sit in the open restaurants. Members of the team hear from both Serbian and Albanian partners how life has considerably changed for the worst over the last few months. This is mainly because hand grenades and bombs are arbitrarily thrown into cafés and into the crowd at markets. On the day of their arrival, a Serbian café had been the target of such an attack, and in the night following, three Albanians and a young woman were killed as a bomb goes off in a small grocery shop. Despite all this, a growing expectation lies over the city. Independence seems something, which can't be avoided. There are two words which one needs to learn in the Albanian language: 'mother' and 'independence'.

For the Serbs in Prishtina it's quite a different matter. One student puts it as follows: *"Everyone says they are staying here and that they will never leave, but they are all buying homes and flats somewhere else."* There is even a problem affecting the Balkan Peace Team inasmuch that as a Serb one shouldn't be seen with its members for fear of being ostracized by friends. As a Serb, she learns, one doesn't even need to think about applying to international organisations, whereas Albanians are simply appointed. The feeling of isolation has received another impetus.

From mid-February to mid-March there is a period of transition. On 16th February 1999, negotiations begin at Rambouillet near Paris between Serbs and Albanians which, only after a few days end in deadlock and are to be continued on 15th March.

In this time, the team find themselves in Prishtina again. Here, there is speculation about the deployment of NATO troops which, it is felt, is the only means of resolving the situation. Otherwise, the OSCE observers could serve as good hostages and nothing would be done until the Serbs decide to undertake a major offensive and resort to atrocities. The press officer acting for the OSCE, on the other hand, draws a positive conclusion from the work of the observers' commission, and makes both sides responsible for the escalation in violence. She is, moreover, very interested in the initiatives associated with the Balkan Peace Team and the insights resulting from its activities, insights, that is, which the mission itself cannot acquire. An appointment is made for another meeting in March.

This never materializes. On 17th March, negotiations in Rambouillet collapse completely. The Serbian-Yugoslavian delegation dismisses a suggestion that foreign troops should be stationed in the country and refuses to sign an agreement to that effect. Richard Holbrooke, the 'Architect from Dayton', abortively tries to bring Milosevic into line with the proposals on 19th March. A few days later, on 24th March, NATO begins its air attacks on Yugoslavia. In Kosovo, Serbian militia and police commit appalling atrocities with the effect that hundreds of thousands of people flee the country.

The Balkan Peace Team Leaves Belgrade and Kosovo

There is hope for a political solution: such is the basis of the work of the BPT after all. In the report of March-April, 1999, we read:

"The activities in this report were carried out as normal projects and contacts for the team until we came to the decision that it was right to leave the country." The week before the beginning of the bombardment has something strangely unreal about it. They hear views from political quarters on all sides that declare escalation to be inevitable. The members of BPT see people on the streets of Belgrade to whom everything appears to be a matter of indifference. This, time, so the general opinion, the probability of an attack is more likely. There's more at stake.

On Saturday evening, 21st March, the team begins to think seriously of leaving. The list of warning signals has been extended to include intimidation and threats to team members as well as other international parties on the street, demonstrations against foreigners, the closing of the embassy and concern about the welfare provided by family members and friends. Reports broadcast by the BBC on Tuesday evening of the following week are alarming. There has been no agreement between Holbrooke and Milosevic, and Yugoslavia has declared an immanent state of war. In a later broadcast, the BBC reports of cut telephone lines to countries abroad and at the same time mobile telephone lines are blocked as well as regular inland connections. The team had not expected this to happen. *"The possibility of not being able to communicate by telephone or e-mail made us quite anxious. We made our final decision on Wednesday morning when we heard that B-92, an independent Belgrade radio station, had been shut down by the authorities claiming a technical irregularity."* Seeing that communication abroad is no longer possible, coupled with the fact that there is no longer possibility of communicating with information sources either, the team decides that the time has come to depart. Just a few hours before the air raid on Belgrade, team members are to be found sitting in a bus on their way to Zagreb before departing from there for Split. *"The thought of leaving many friends who could not themselves leave was a painful and difficult decision."*

In a report written at the end of April, the team has collected views from those whom they had to leave behind. One of these is from Novi Sad: *"...they didn't bomb Novi Sad yesterday night (but, they did the first night), but, tonight, I think they'll bomb again, because we hit their two planes over Fruska Gora.....now, that it started, I don't think it'll be over soon...it'll last till they don't get what they want....I'm very, very angry and so are my friends (they attacked MY town!..)"*

In Kosovo, one hears people say, *"NATO in the sky and Milosevic on earth."* Evita from the 'Centre for the Protection of Women and Children' in Prishtina has been placed on the search list pf the Serbian security forces. She remains in hiding in the city for three months while they try to find her.

Sources

BPT Belgrade 5.98, 3, 4-6, 11, 15, 17;12.98; BPT Biweekly 2/2.98; 2/9.98; 1/10.98; 2/10.98; BPT Monthly Report 12.98-12.2.99; 12.2.-10.3.99; 10.-31.3.99;15.6.-15.7.99; de Vrieze 2002, 291f.; ICG 17.2.98; International Helsinki Federation for Human Rights, press release 12.2.98; Interview Hubert P. 1998; Katrin G. 2/1998; Susanne S. 2/1998; Loquai 2000, 25; Müller, personal records 20.-22.2.98; Nasa Borba, 15.6.98; Ronnefeldt 2001, 88; Schmid 1999, 281f.

(4) Are There Still Points of Connection? The Transition from BPT-FRY to the Youth Centre in Dragash

The Balkan Team 'in Exile' (April to September, 1999)

Neither peace organisations nor NATO bombs can prevent excesses in violence wrought by Serbian forces on the people of Kosovo in the spring of 1999. They succeed in making life such a horror that hundreds of thousands of people seek refuge outside the country's borders.

At an international seminar in the summer of 1999, Daniel M. is self-critical on the subject of the peace movement's failure to have properly dealt with this so clearly prognosticated war. The Balkan Peace Team was also in his sights as a model for the prevention of war, he notes, at the same time adding that *"We need to continue to work on the possibilities that peace teams offer,"* noting, too, however, that, as before, offers from pacifists in situations such as these are limited.

One thing which the Balkan Peace Team can do after its evacuation from Belgrade is to present the people in Serbia and Kosovo in another, clearer light than that presented in the media at this time. They want their listeners to be aware of the fact that news is still coming from opposition groups in Yugoslavia. Accordingly, the team tours 20 towns and cities in Germany, the Netherlands and Great Britain where they hold lectures.

At the end of April, there is still no sign of a quick end to the war. The team doesn't want to stay any longer in Western Europe, but wants to get back to its partners and friends, many of whom have had to flee. It wants to know how they have fared, and what they have experienced and how they see the future. After this nightmare, is there a chance at all for alternatives to violence? A delicate question indeed and one which must be carefully and tactfully presented.

In Macedonia the team quickly find contact. At the OSCE office they run into an acquaintance whom they knew in Prishtina and who helps them to find a number of others they are looking for. Once, in Tetovo while eating ice cream, they come across another woman who used to be a member of the Post Pessimists in Prishtina. Later, from an Internet café in Skopje, they are easily able to contact many others pretty quickly. All of those whom they subsequently meet have their own story, how they were either forced by the police or paramilitary units to flee or how they were obliged to give way to the pressure of fear and violence. The police had badly ill-treated one friend who had managed by the skin of his teeth and much luck to get over the border. Another mourned the passing of his mother who had died a refugee in Montenegro. *"How can I forgive the Serbs for letting my mother die alone without her family so far from her home?"* he asks. Only shortly before, these people who speak of their fear and humiliation were themselves activists and organisers who had helped others. But, despite all this, and in the middle of this tragedy, volunteers still find people who are again trying to treat the wounds inflicted on society and eventually heal them. Some of them still subscribe to the well-organised, powerful social structures which, during the period of resistance, enabled them to stand together. These people are trying to transmit another picture to the world of Kosovo Albanians than that of helpless victims of refugees typical of those seen in the media at the moment.

Hungary is the second country of refuge where the team looks for former contacts and friends and finds them there. Here, support is organized for Serbian conscientious objectors who have fled from Serbia.

After returning to Western Europe, the team is confirmed in the fact that it wishes to continue its presence in the region and from there support the Serbian and Kosovo Albanian communities in their reorganisation. At the moment, longer perspectives for its work are not a consideration, and so there can only be a rough outline of what their activities could be to promote dialogue, offer alternatives to violence, to help in building up society, and to make reports of human rights. It is also not clear at the present time when the team can return to Belgrade and Kosovo, a situation that also affects other projects.

For Belgrade in particular, things look pretty bleak. The information Mary has received since the end of April from her Serbian contacts leads her to a somewhat pessimistic prognosis. *"The situation for any kind of activism in Serbia proper looks very grim, people seem to get more and more de-motivated by the day, and I am really not sure if there is a place for BPT anymore - in 2-3 years perhaps, if at all."*

An activist belonging to the 'Women in Black' is later able to support this view. *"When the bombings started, we felt there was nothing more we could do; all public demonstrations were banned. The NATO-intervention ruined the whole of society. We felt we had to start from the beginning. We don't know any longer how to talk about democracy, human rights, civil society and so on."*

For a long time, the Balkan Peace Team members cannot quite imagine not being able to return to Serbia anymore. For the whole of the following year, the exploration of post-war Serbia is high on the list of priorities, but nothing comes of the plans. There's neither money nor people at hand for the task. The apartment there is held on to for a time until the owner declares the contract for null and valid in the summer of 1999. In the following December, the office furniture etc. is removed and finally finds a use for the organisation, 'Women in Black'. What is still of any worth is placed into a plastic sack and taken to Prishtina. The Balkan Peace Team finally arrives as a team at a place where it had always wanted to be - in Kosovo, and only there.

Here, there is enough to do and here, too, war activities are mobilizing energy again. It is not only at this place that the Balkan Peace Team acquires publicity. Because of its operation in a war area, it finds that the International Office can hardly keep up with incoming requests enquiries, but the Quaker movement there sees the BPT as a suitable channel in order to place its own volunteers.

"In Kosovo," maintains one former volunteer in April, *"the situation is even grimmer, there is no NGO scene left, of course, but at least there is some hope that things will change and some kind of political solution will be found. If that is the case, then a BPT role could be trying to see if we can make Kosovo society slightly democratic. This because I assume that Kosovo leadership will turn out to be possibly military and certainly very undemocratic."*

The War is over – return to a changed Kosovo

The turning point comes in the first weeks of June when the Yugoslavian leadership agrees to comply with international demands. Yugoslavian troops withdraw, followed by Russian and NATO forces belonging to a UN transitional administration (UNMIK) and those responsible for civil affairs. The disarmament of the Liberation Army is also to follow, but the suspicion remains that not all weapons have been handed in. Refugees return surprisingly quickly to a Kosovo that has been extensively plundered and destroyed. Despite the promise of protection on the part of the NATO, Serbs and Roma now begin to flee in their thousands.

On 26th of June 1999, the team again visits Prishtina which now appears to be *"fairly normal"*. On penetrating into the town, however, one comes across military patrols, plundered shops and abandoned cafés. There is a general observation circulating here among Albanians at the moment: *"Maybe I will be able some day to forgive them, but I will never forget what they did."* Is there any hope here of reconciliation? At the beginning of July and on visiting the place for a second time, much of the tension has disappeared, and life reappears in the city. There are already as many as 84 NGOs registered in the city. *"It was hard for us to believe that the peace agreement had only been signed a few weeks before,"* the travel report maintains, but also notes that security is still a precarious affair: *"It was not uncommon to see one or two burning houses from our apartment building."* In the matter of revenge on the Serbs and Roma for what they have done, opinions are divided among the population. They either feel that the public at large are still very restrained in their need to carry out acts of revenge or they feel appalled about the way their own people have behaved.

The Centre for the Protection of Women and Children in Prishtina is open again, and it is here that the team once more find Evita who has managed to survive the searches for her conducted by security forces over the last three months. She talks about the horrors she has experienced. The other helpers are still in Tetovo in Macedonia, but are expected back at the beginning of July. The Balkan Peace Team accelerates its plans to return to the area, and during this summer finds an apartment in Prishtina. It is still open as to what opportunity there will be for reconciliation – if at all. The signs are not very encouraging.

It has already come to the notice of members of the Balkan Peace Team on their trips into countries in May to which refugees have sought asylum that partners in conversation with them from political circles in Prishtina are remarkably reserved when it comes to making political observations. No one can be tempted to say anything beyond the most general comments and, 'as long as the bombs fall', no one can talk about negotiation. We learn that a quarrel has flared up between the legitimate leadership, the exiled Albanians and leaders of the Liberation Army and the LDK under Ibrahim Rugova. They appear to have become entangled in a fractionist struggle, which has led to general political paralysis. In this situation, the Kosovo Albanians find themselves in a position of having no political structure. All of them, however, are at one as far as the objective of an independent Kosovo is concerned which, after the interim government, can be finally achieved. But this, too, is still an open issue!

In this society there is no place for reconciliation. Moderates immediately come under fire from their own people. Mixed, ethnic groups are a rarity, since there is a general consensus of opinion that reconciliation on a broad basis is something that must take a back seat. This pressure from within also affects the Post Pessimists as one of their members seeks to represent the view that ways must be sought to found a multiethnic Kosovo. For this view he is attacked publicly in a newspaper. The BPT learns that after much alarmed discussion within this particular group, the member is urged to give in his resignation.

The Council for the Defence of Human Rights and Freedoms celebrates its tenth anniversary in December, 1999 at a conference with the motto: *"The best way to protect your own human rights and freedoms is to protect the human rights and freedoms of others."* Serbian guests from the Humanitarian Law Centre and from the Helsinki Committee in Belgrade are also invited. This, too, is possible. 'Radio Contact' is another organisation, which runs counter to the flow of general conviction, and in the real sense of the word 'comes under fire' for doing so. Threatening phone calls are common, and the office is broken into and its contents ravaged on several occasions. A shell explodes in the apartment next door. No one is injured, but everyone is worried about whether this attack was directed at him.

Along with the suppression of tolerance in general, arson, plunder and actual expulsion continue. Surviving Serbs live in isolated enclaves in the north of the country, in the south east and in Mitrovica. The fact that 37,000 armed KFOR troops cannot secure order and so stop ethnically motivated violence and organised crime undermines confidence among minorities and confuses and frustrates the Albanian people into the bargain. DE VRIEZE puts this down to the failure to build up an effective police and justice system. The erection of a UN civilian police system only slowly comes into being. By September, of the planned 3000 policemen, only 1000 are actually on duty and most of these in Prishtina. KFOR advises people in September not to go onto the roads between one village and other after nine o' clock in the evening, having in mind as it does so organised crime, car theft and prostitution.

The building up of political structures is also something, which only progresses very slowly. The United Nations has organised a transitional government which is at first boycotted by Rugova, but is one in which Serbs, Muslims and Turks (but not Roma) are represented. The 'Common Transitional Administrative Structure' as the temporary UN administration is called, is established on 15th December 1999, and is represented by many people from all walks of life in Kosovo. Twenty ministries are each administered by one local and one international director. At the same time, the parallel institutions are dissolved which include the governing bodies under Thaci and those under the president, Rugova.

New Entry Points and New Starts. Variations of Peace Building in Post-war Kosovo

Before the war, the ways of dialogue initiatives such as those from Pax Christi, the Norwegian group, Nansen and that of the Balkan Peace Team often crossed with each other. Even in March 1999, just before the evacuation, the activities of the other groups were more and more integrated in its planning programmes. In the summer of 1999, the Pax Christi co-ordinators drive with the team through Kosovo and try to revive old contacts. The idea of a dialogue with Serbs meets with *"a generally cold reception"* on the part of the Albanians. The Nansen dialogue group in Prishtina doesn't seem to want to go with its activities.

A seminar conducted by the Richardson Institute from Great Britain which announces chances for dialogue in the autumn then comes to the conclusion that, from the perspective of the Albanian, direct talks between Belgrade and Prishtina will not be on the agenda, and only as far as regional matters are concerned, will Serbs be welcomed as participants in discussions.

In September 1999, the Balkan Peace Team meets in Amersfoort, Holland, and many ideas are put forward. For the most part they concern the possibilities of dialogue in general and also the work of the localities having a mixed population. Here, an interview project is looking into reports of people from both sides within the society having mutually helped one another. The work in Serbia is not altogether abandoned. The former Belgrade Balkan Peace Team now decides to discard this title and henceforth refer to itself as BPT-(Kosovo). Even though it does not appear to be the case at the moment, this gesture symbolizes a departure from work in Serbia and a concentration of attention in Kosovo.

At this meeting, too, there is another farewell, although it does not immediately strike one as such. If dialogue is no longer welcome or desired, then work must be directed elsewhere. *"More project oriented work seems to be needed."* However, this somewhat neutral remark contains powerful explosive. The idea of a community centre with emphasis on youth work as its main preoccupation is now considered. It should be located at a place outside the city having an ethnically mixed population and preferably in an area with few international organisations. This marks a departure from former dialogue work up to now with its interlinking activities.

Other initiatives keep to their former concepts. In Mitrovica, for example, the Nansen group are to work on the construction of dialogue groups after the year 2000. Pax

Christi Flanders and The Netherlands for its part is going to continue its seminar work in Northern Ireland, this time working with members of various communities in Kosovo, while the BPT follows a new route which will lead to the youth centre in Dragash.

The Youth Centre in Dragash

In October, four possible options are considered very carefully as to where the project should be located. It should be a place where one is desired and one not doubling up on similar activities, and it should be a place where service offers are poorly developed. Dragash seems to be the most suitable alternative. It lies in the south of Prizren, in the economically poorest region of Kosovo, with its centre, Dragash. It lies in a beautiful countryside, but is not easily accessible, and about three hours journey by car from Prishtina. Here, many Slavic Moslems have their abode and make up about half of the inhabitants, while the other half are Albanians. As the war raged, Albanians fled to Croatia or Albania and have now returned to Kosovo. Here, the ravages of war are not too serious and, contrary to many other parts of the region, refugees returned to find their homes intact. In this remote area, the people are used to working and living together as in the past.

Nevertheless, there are tensions, tensions that existed even before the war and recently there have been reports of shelling, a case of kidnapping and also violence in the market place. The centre is to be established here with the purpose of bringing youth together. The needs of youth here according to an enquiry are: computer skills, the need to learn English and to indulge in other activities such as sport, art and crafts. Then there is the task of finding a room to organize and so fulfil the needs of these young people, a place, which is acceptable, and one where they can build up relationships based on mutual trust. It is calculated that within two or three years the team can then withdraw from the project. Because this kind of project is relatively new, the security side of the project and the structure required relative to the needs in the place appear to be reasonably easy to deal with, and one should get on with the job as soon as possible.

In the debate ensuing at the General Assembly in November, it becomes clear that this more socially orientated project is viewed quite differently than work directed at keeping the peace. Perhaps this is a matter of perspective. In the USA, for example, youth work counts as political work, but in Europe more as social work. Then there is something that was critically decisive on this occasion: The team sees no other alternative than to carry on working with this one concrete project. In the general consensus of opinion, however, and with one or two reservations, it is felt that the project should be given the assembly's blessing.

The project will make demands on the Balkan Peace Team, especially in the financial area. The team is to be increased to five people for a start and then there are the additional costs of a four-wheel-drive vehicle, telephones, premises for the centre which will have to be rented, computers, printers and teaching material, etc.

The turn of the year 1999 to 2000 is a period of transition. The last documents are gathered together so that they can be submitted, and money can be collected. The new volunteers are trained and prepared. They want to see the place in the second half of the following February, settle in, work with the teaching material, and get used to the building and its potential (school buildings and computer). Should more money be available, the current facilities can then be expanded. At the beginning, it is felt that instruction should take place in groups ethnically separated from one another. In this way, initiatives will unfold during the work and so provide ideas on how to proceed with mixed groups.

As in the past, the team will hold on to its apartment in Prishtina. From here the network of contacts with other groups can continue to be cultivated. From this quarter we learn of dialogue initiatives which are still being undertaken, and in this connection come to know of the plans of a European Students' Association that is to undertake a mixed delegation to Cyprus and Northern Ireland – in other words also into separate societies. In the case of holding special talks, the team places its apartment at general disposal, but notes that the participation of Serbs is increasingly hampered by the security situation, one which is too precarious for open activity.

Two bomb explosions, too, shake Dragash. According to reports from the OSCE, approximately 1000 'Gorani' or Slavic Moslems leave the region. Despite this, lessons in English begin in April 2000. In the first week, no member of the Gorani come along. Apparently, they have not been informed about the offer. This is then rectified, and in the second week seven Moslems turn up. After the team has visited a number of villages inhabited by this ethnic group, more arrive in the third week. In the third week, too, lessons have to be transferred to the senior school, a place in which the Gorani don't feel particularly comfortable. Not only instruction in the language is given, but also co-operation, and the promotion of peace is alluded to. In the middle term, the team plans to go a bit further than mere instruction and make other offers. In this connection, it wishes to establish a forum in which the various groups are represented who, later, can decide upon the centre's affairs. At the moment there is support for this within the Albanian community.

Violence, Readiness to Enter into Dialogue and Changes in Constellation. Kosovo and Serbia in the Year 2000

Violence in Kosovo simply does not come to an end. At the same time, those in public office are urged again and again not to resort to its use. To this end, the US Institute for Peace brings all the important leaders in the political field together as well as those working at community level, both Serbs and Albanians. These are invited to the United States in July for talks. There, they draw up a 'Pact Against Violence'. This occurs again in the spring of 2001 after the next local elections. It becomes clear that, to an increasing degree, Kosovo will have one day to stand on its own feet. More and more international organisations are leaving the region, and it is often the case that the people of the region are not prepared for independent administration.

When, in September of that year, Vojislav Kostunica wins election to the presidential office against Milosevic, Kosovo nevertheless remains indifferent to the event. Here, feelings are taut, because final self-determination remains a matter, which is not yet clearly resolved, and frustration is rife as a result. The first local elections for this reason are set for October 28th, 2000, and this, it is hoped, will lead to some kind of resolution. Before the elections there is an increase in violence during which journalists and political activists within Rugova's party are the targets of attack. Although the LDK wins the day, international administrators are nevertheless unwilling to hand over key positions to the winners.

Calling itself the 'Kosovo Action for Civic Initiatives' in Prishtina, a local organisation takes up the issue of minority groups. In September, it proposes what has been referred to as a *"proposal which was exceptionally concrete in describing rights for minority groups..."* Then, in December the same year, Zoran Djindjic wins the parliamentary elections to become the Serbian prime minister. This changes the attitude of the international community towards Yugoslavia. It now seeks active partnership. This month, too, brings the leaders of the Kosovo Albanians and Serbs face to face at a conference in Princeton University. Openings for negotiation are revealed at this meeting, but whether these will develop into a means where violence can be restrained and controlled is another matter. In February, 2001, observers come to the conclusion that violence has long since no longer been a matter of acts of revenge on the part of single individuals, but that it appears to be something which is organized, co-ordinated and carefully targeted.

Dragash, Summer 2000

The waves of tension even reach the little town of Dragash. Here, in this microcosm far away from anywhere, the second semester is being planned with four classes running until December. In the meantime, a room has been found which has been donated to the team. The more familiar the volunteers are with their surroundings, the better they can express themselves in the language and the more they learn of existing problems. The young Albanians, who are receptive and open-minded as far as the other side goes, are nevertheless placed under huge pressure not to display this feature. On the few occasions when a young Albanian has stood on the street to speak to a 'Gorani' student, he or she is immediately taken to task for it by their own respective community. In this, the division in Albanian society plays a role. It seems to penetrate every aspect of life. Rugova's followers, for example, fear revenge from those following Thaci when the former declare themselves open to the Moslem community.

This state of affairs has its consequences for the team's work. The youth centre, which is now taking form, is a good place to meet for young people – that is while it is in the hands of internationals. One of these young folks put it quite simply:

> *"If it's your initiative, from internationals I mean, I wouldn't have any problems in coming...We know what needs to be done and how to work with the Gorans...I could come and be with them and if they [Taci's followers] ask me -Why are you going there with those Gorans?- I can always say: it's not me who had the idea, it's the internationals...I'm only going there because I can learn English and use the computer...I would feel safe then in coming, because they cannot do anything to me."*

How, then, is it going to be possible for the local community to set up and run its own centre one day? A tricky question indeed.

On the other hand, a Catholic priest in Bince tackles the problem directly. He openly speaks of the necessity for reconciliation. Now and face to face. Every Sunday without fail, people come from elsewhere to hear him, even from Prishtina. During the war, a Serbian general saw to it that he and a few Albanians who had taken refuge in his church came to no harm. *"Kushner and Thaci say it's too early for reconciliation, but I think we have to start now, otherwise we will never get there"*. This is the priest's motto which has been referred to into the team's report.

During the autumn of 2000 the youth centre is opened, in the first instance for six months with a view to extending this time. The Balkan Peace Team maintains the project while other organisations co-operate in the work of running it. One of these is 'Forum for Civil Peace Service', an organisation in the service of peacebuilding from Germany and the 'Children's Relief Association', which is also based in Germany. Weekend workshops making socks and constructing kites constitute the first, official, ethnically mixed working groups, albeit separated by sex into two activity groups. When the United Nations' children's aid association, UNICEF, declares its willingness to assist the financing of the youth centre in October, a lot of energy and enthusiasm goes into the acquisition of computers and in preparing for their installation. Local people are to be employed to help in setting up language and computer courses.

The idea of also setting up a forum in order to clarify with locals what they want to do with their centre is taken up by the OSCE and KFOR whose representatives meet village elders and administrators. Several offers are made in the youth centre for mixed ethnic groups, and the team receives considerable support for it. For example, without the assistance of an Albanian community head, the team would never have acquired a building for their intended activities. The aid organisation, Children's Relief Association took over the job of its renovation. The members of the peace organisation mentioned above already spend half their time in the centre.

At the moment, the basis for the creation of relationships between the two societies is being laid, but those taking part have still to show that they can make it work. These new activities awaken interest between the communities, but also different generations, too, find a new way to get on with each other. This is the way one volunteer described the actual peacebuilding principle operative at the youth centre and in her work in February 2001.

In spring, 2001, the Balkan Peace Team resigns from its office as maintenance body for the running of the youth centre when the volunteers together give up their work at the Balkan Peace Team. The Dragash project provides for it to be eventually passed into the hands of another governing body and for this reason the members of BPT are at one in placing it under the administration of someone they can trust to produce the necessary means and material to run the place over the long term. How this eventually comes about and in the end leads to the closure of the Balkan Peace Team will be described in the following chapter. The members of the team, together with other committees concerned with the project, strive as one to see to it that the transfer of the Dragash project to another governing body runs smoothly and without a hitch.

The Transfer

One of the volunteers would like to carry on working at the youth centre and places himself at out disposal during the project transfer. The team is on the spot with several other organisations during these deliberations. For the team, the most important thing is that its principles and ideals are upheld. These are non-violence, impartiality and here also the wish that the principle of maximum participation on the part of the local community shall continue to be cultivated. In February and March corresponding negotiations take place at which local representatives of the communities and women's organisations also participate.

The idea here to bring both ethnic communities together in one project constitutes what is special about this operation and that which distinguishes it from other, outwardly similar projects for which service functions are the prominent feature. If, in such cases, groups mix with one another, then this is something of side effect, but not the object of the undertaking. For the Dragash project, the active mixture of ethnic groups is the kingpin of the concept. In March/April, 2001, the youth centre passes into other hands. Thus, two-and-a-half years later, at the end of 2003, one could read the following on the Internet page of the Forum Civil Peace Service: "The multi-ethical youth centre was founded by the Balkan Peace Team in 2000. In April, 2001, the Forum Civil Peace Service together with the 'German Society for Technical Co-operation' took over the project."

Sources

Broken Rifle 2000; BPT 12.99; 17.11.2000; BPT Monthly Report 10.-31.3.99; 4-5.99; 15.6.-15.7.99; BPT CC minutes 28.-30.5.99; 10.-12.9.99; 11.-12.2.2000; 2.-5.5.2000; 8.-10.9.2000; 9.-11.2.01; BPT CC Mary F., 20.4.99; BPT GA minutes, 20.-21.11.99; 12.2.2000; 23.-25.3.01; BPT-K, 10.99; 26.9.2000, 3.7.2000, 17.11.2000, 3.2001; Ferizi 2003, 2; Forum Ziviler Friedensdienst, 31.12.03; de Vrieze 2002, 292-296, 298f., 300; Ronnefeldt 2001, 88.

(5) The End of the BPT: Passing the Legacy on to Équipes de paix dans les Balkans

In November 2000, the General Assembly draws up plans for the coming year and, among these, is a common exploration trip to Kosovo together with the French branch of the BPT, Équipes de Paix dans les Balkans. Everything appears to be normal.

On the 9th January 2001, however, the team writes a stiff letter to the Co-ordinating Committee containing the tidings that, *"We are seriously considering withdrawing our commitment to the field."* The grounds for this lie the fact that the team after returning from the Christmas holidays finds that it is at the end of its financial resources. It has no more money on its account. One of the amounts due to be transferred has again got stuck somewhere in transfer. Another has apparently not been demanded by the team. The consequence of this is that the installation of computers financed by UNICEF has to be put off again, but there is also the fact that the interviews announced for employing new people become questionable if one cannot assure candidates that they will regularly receive their salaries.

"We are sorry if we sound so bitter, but we think it's time for all of us to take responsibility for our actions. What are we trying to achieve here? A long term commitment to the local population and lay the foundation for them to be able to take over in a few years, knowing that what we promise we can do... or are we going to go on improvising?" Volunteers call for an organisation, which supports them in their doings.

"To have a presence in the field you also need a structure behind you that works with you, not against you, and is able to take quick action and react promptly. In the course of the years, BPT has gone through many crises because of this (the Croatian experience is just one example). BPT might be under the impression that because the organisation has 'survived' all those bad moments, things are fine the way they are and we can go on pretending that nothing really happened. This attitude will only lead us straight into the next crisis. What keeps us in the field is the commitment we all have to the people here, the project, and to each other, but this cannot be sustained for long either if we don't perceive that we are backed by, and part of a solid reality, as BPT should be."

The employees at the International Office are both surprised and to an extent 'paralysed' by the announcement that the team is declaring its resignation. For them, the first reports from many members of the Co-ordinating Committee are shocking. Their thoughts turn on the issue of ending the project, not how it could go on.

Two days later, on the 11th January 2001, the team as a whole resigns. The first reactions to this, which do not promise a quick solution to the problem, confirm the team in this decision. The Balkan Peace Team– a project without a team – is there in which volunteers promise to shut down the offices in Prishtina and Dragash properly. For this, some of the volunteers would not quit immediately, but remain on duty until the end of February. In this connection, a domino effect takes place which limits the options for action of the Co-ordinating Committee before it can organize itself and react to the crisis. Without a team, tasks must come to an end, and so in this way the whole machinery comes to a halt. On the 12th January, the co-ordinator switches in to the e-mail discussion: *"It seems as if all the team members are withdrawing from the work in the field and I can understand their frustrations with BPT structures and processes. I think that it is imperative that BPT re-examines its way of working. But I am very sad to see that it is happening like this."*

He develops two scenarios by which the project can be closed. Two days later, those responsible for finances and members of the Sub-groups meet in Minden. The activities of the project are stopped and a task-stop instrucion is issued. The team proposes that the Dragash youth project be placed in other hands of other organisations on the spot, and commences with special talks with people from these organisations. At the beginning of February a routine conference of the Co-ordinating Committee takes place in Paris. Here, it becomes clear that none of the member organisations can do more than hitherto to keep the BPT afloat. This in any case has nothing to do with alleviating structural weaknesses as everyone appreciates.

Parallel with all this, the General Assembly is planned for the end of March and will decide on the fate of the whole project, Balkan Peace Team. The recommendations of the Co-ordinating Committee tend towards not managing the Dragash project any longer, but, if such is possible, rather to give into the hands of another organisation. The preparations for this are to be undertaken by two volunteers by the end of March at the latest. Up to that point there is to be exploration in Kosovo in order to find out where there is a need still outstanding for a team based on the BPT model. The principal employees at the International Office are to be given notice by the end of April, and the members of the Co-ordinating Committee will give in their resignations at the General Assembly. This is the state of affairs when the meeting takes place on 23rd March 2001. Energy has to be mustered to make a new beginning, since there will be no *"business as usual"* as the invitation makes clear. *"Either BPT will change its structure radically or it will close down."* What, then, are the options?

Knowledge of the structural weaknesses on accompanying the team has made it impossible for the explorers to sound out options for a team, which will work with all communities. They present the need for volunteer co-operation working directly in local organisations. This is the concept adopted by the Équipes de Paix dans les Balkans, the French branch of the Balkan Peace Team.

It becomes clear at the General Assembly in Bonn in March, 2001 that the member organisations are not willing to consider themselves as a source for the dispatch of further volunteers to other organisations. This is being done by a sufficient number of other organisations. The model of the Balkan Peace Team with its own mandate, contract and work with communities has been the attractive thing about it so far. The woman responsible for having made investigations then brings the long discussion to a head: *"It was a good idea. There is still a need for dialogue work. BPT needs a new structure. There is no energy for this. Close BPT down. Re-assess!"* And that, finally, is the decision made.

The rest is a matter of clearing up and passing on authority. The backlog of work still needing attention is then completed during the course of the year. An evaluation and assessment weekend in October serves to consider that which has been achieved and that still extant as also the weaknesses in the construction of the organisation. Finally, on the 12th October 2001, the Balkan Peace Team is dissolved.

The Search for Reasons

The work of the Balkan Peace Team remains incomplete. Its collapse can now be clearly seen from start to finish. From the point of view of the team itself, the project organisations must have presented a pitiful scene: structures hardly capable of making decisions; insufficient money for suitable furnishings; no reliable source of funds sufficient to allow the team to play a responsible role compared with other partners. It is not the work which presents a problem, but the constant struggle against one's own organisation. The team's outcry at the beginning of January 2001, when it was realised that there was no more money in the coffers then marked the end of the road.

The joint exit two days later underlined the fact that there was no faith left in the idea of prospective change. Reaction to the team's decision was also significant. The decision was accepted without demur. The initiative, too, as to how one is to deal with the project lies with the team and not with the organisation. The prospect of sending a new team with a different profile turns up merely as an airy possibility. A need arising during March in Kosovo simply doesn't get the chance to be taken seriously as a serious option to put a new team to the test. The structural weaknesses of the project organisation are all too evident. What are these weaknesses which have proved to be its undoing?

The Adjustment of Structures to Procedures Does Not Succeed

There are attempts to help oneself. Since the General Assembly in 1999, the International Office has been demanding clearer structures in the matter of decision in emergency situations and for those responsible in general. Assessments of internal evaluations throw up questions with regard to structure this year, too. A Sub-group of the Co-ordinating Committee attempts to work out clearer areas of responsibility and receives instructions to lay down modifications by November 2000. The team insists that immediate, drastic changes be made: if Sub-groups fail to function, why not admit to this and organise things differently? The only concrete option resulting from the work of the Sub-group, however, is the recommendation in November that more emphasis should be laid on winning over single individuals for co-operation. It is clear to everyone that this is merely a small step in a process of reform, and many doubt whether the problem can be tackled quickly enough and radically enough, and whether the team and its demands are fully met and dealt with in such a way. While it is true that the position of a 'Field Co-ordinator' is now set up and worked out, the Co-ordinating Committee will never put it into action.

In February 2001, one is confronted with the same set of problems as a year before. Again, there is no treasurer, for example, and the Co-ordinating Committee is understaffed as well as a support group for the office. From the point of view of the employed people in the International Office, Oskar K. and Ellen B., the structures are improving slowly, but the withdrawal of the team has brought this process to an end.

Thinning out of Personnel and a Crisis of Confidence between Committees

Again and again problems devolve upon one single issue, that of there not being enough qualified people with sufficient time to spend dealing adequately with work as it occurs. Rather, the opposite is the case.

There are in fact too few people to fill the posts available in the Co-ordinating Committee and Sub-groups, and the filling of such posts has always created big problems. Long serving members would like to leave, but are faced with considerable problems in finding suitable people to follow them in their organisations. The sharing of positions is one way of dealing with the problem. Other positions remain free, and vacant functions remain unoccupied. The commitment of organisations is another matter, which depends on personal connections. As long as individuals link an organisation with the Balkan Peace Team, then everything functions, but once this connection loosens for some reason, then the BPT suffers a corresponding loss of connectedness. Tamara P., from the Federation for Social Defence, a person who for years has belonged to the inner circle of BPT associates, recognises this fact. Indeed, she is rather surprised that the project has functioned at all so far in view of the fact that *"...the human infrastructure of CC people and the individuals and groups supporting them and BPT in the background had been 'used up' in terms of exhaustion and changes of personal priorities while we did not manage to find alternatives early enough to have new CC members introduced into the particular practices, to principles and people of BPT work."* From this the acute problem can be seen when, *"... so when the project had to undergo major changes, starting with the change of the region, away from Croatia already, and when, at the same time, important CC people decided to withdraw for various personal reasons, it was not very surprising to me that crisis situations were more crucial to the project. The latest very big change in my perception, changing the kind of project we run, might have been too much to be managed by the human infrastructure of the project."*

When the grasp on personal resources, on positions of authority within the organisation and on experience begins to weaken, leadership tends, unrecognised, to edge into other committees. In the International Office, for example, which, after 1998, and since then has been now and again occupied by people in an honorary capacity, Ellen B. and Oskar K. both of whom work part-time in their positions, have found themselves working in a sort of vacuum because those responsible for particular decisions have not been identified. From the point of view of the legal position, the executive committee of the association are responsible, and from the political, the Coordinating Committee, and these two in the International Office do the work!

And then finally, the evergreen of finances and financing. The Balkan Peace Team is a finance-problem-solution-project. Or, to put it into the words of one volunteer faced with such issues in the last team: *"There has never been a generation of volunteers which has not been confronted with a profound financial crisis affecting the organisation as a whole,"* and this despite international fund-raising. The scarcity of money, a matter that is not structurally solvable, binds the project organisation at important points. In the first place in furnishing the team with enough material, but also in the area of training and in the area of well-planned advertisement whereby suitable volunteers are attracted to the work of the organisation.

In a similar way, teamwork suffers, because one doesn't know whether the work that has been planned can be financed. Again and again this leaves volunteers insecure, and on the last occasion this occurred in 1999, it was a case of what they would do after leaving Belgrade. Every plan is tinged with the reservation of whether or not it can be carried through because of financial insecurity.

Infrastructure suffers, too, because nowhere near enough personnel can be installed to deal with the work coming in at the International Office. In 1998, internal evaluation had to be postponed because everyone was obliged to adjust himself or herself to overcoming a serious financial setback, a situation caused by the cancellation of a large EU application.

In the spring of the year 2000, for example, the exploratory trip to Serbia had to be cancelled because of lack of money. The consequence was that the work of setting up a 'model' for the Balkan Peace Team options to sound out the situation on both sides was hindered. It could have been, of course, that the result of such an enquiry would have been negative, but there is no answer to this anymore. The constant need to scrimp and scrape for necessary financial assistance constitutes an enormous drain on energy over the long term, even when the burden is borne by many shoulders.

The Dynamics of the Year 2000

And notwithstanding all this: not all the structural weaknesses are new. The Balkan Peace Team lives with crisis and does not make much of it. The volunteers, at one time a large team with five people who go to work with three beginners and great enthusiasm in January are surprised and frustrated right at the beginning of their operation. They are shocked by the conditions governing the financial framework, frustrated by their limited possibilities and made insecure by the fact that the organisation apparently does not react with the appropriate energy necessary in such a situation. They demand the expected conditions of work and straight away start to work out fund-raising strategies. A lively exchange of e-mails develops from which the crisis strategies of members of other committees of BPT become clear. One has to get used to the fact that an assured income will never reach beyond the next three months, Daniel says in an attempt to soften the situation. *"It's not the first time that volunteers are stressed with discussions about finance in the Co-ordinating Committee,"* says the co-ordinator. *"As far as the BPT is concerned, that's not a crisis, but the normal state of affairs,"* adding the comment that it's all *"very unfortunate, but true."*

One of the former treasurers admits that this is not a situation to which one should accustom oneself, but at the same time it makes one aware of an important point which always dogs such pioneer projects: *"The reason why we have come so far with this project is that during it we have never been held up by a need for material, computers, data, communication or anything else."* He is still optimistic, but *"there would be a reason to give up if I didn't see a chance of improving the BPT over the long term and the possibility of dealing with problems with which we're constantly confronted. But I don't see this at all!"* The team doesn't share his long-term optimism.

It is here that the volunteer must possess a basic trust in the organisation, otherwise the critical balance between team and project organisation begins to lose its footing and collapse. A representative of the volunteers in the Co-ordinating Committee refers to this balance. He describes the financial crisis, which had affected 'his' volunteer generation a few years earlier. His picture of the capacity of the organisation changed at that point when for the first time he began to meet people on a personal basis at a conference who were trying to keep the team operating on the spot. His personal recommendation was that members of a team should personally try to get to know as many others in the organisation as possible, since, he feels, personal acquaintance is essential in creating necessary mutual confidence and trust.

"One of the reasons for the demise of the team in Split was its loss of trust in the Subgroup and the CC. I really hope that a similar process is not underway now in Prishtina because, if it is, and it continues, we might as well all give up. BPT teams have always been isolated to a large degree. There have been times when their relationships with the CC have been problematic but, at least to me, it seems that there

has always been a basic level of mutual trust." Prophetical words. During May in Prishtina, there is a clash between one of the volunteers and the co-ordinator. In what followed, part of the problems could be sorted out, but the basis of trust had been seriously impaired. Looking back, one of those involved saw the encounter as pretty damaging, and comments, *"That was a collision with an iceberg; everything that happened afterwards was just a matter of sinking slowly."*

This process is exacerbated by the fact that communication lines are disrupted too by the team itself. The team has been in arrears with its report since the summer. This means, in effect, that the Balkan Peace Team is not in a position to inform interested parties, possible donors and the public at large on the continuance of its work. Since these internal reports are not forthcoming, neither the Co-ordinating Committee nor the International Office know actually what is going on in the team. The team for its part rightly complains of awkward and wearisome procedures. It fears presenting itself as an unreliable partner to donor organisations and local partners. However, resorting to a procedure which somehow circumnavigates its structures leads straight into a cul de sac. The year 2000 is full of such organisational hitches and correspondingly results poor co-operation.

Changed Surroundings and "the Mission" of the Balkan Peace Team

In the course of this year another cause for dissension which arises within the BPT. This time it concerns content. Does a youth centre, for example, fit in with the concept of the Balkan Peace Team? This is most clearly formulated by the critic, Jens K. from MAN in February, 2001. He wishes to find an alternative to the Dragash Project and does not want to see the BPT dissolved. It is evident that self-interest plays a role here, since the Èquipes de Paix dans les Balkans desires to keep BPT.

But there is more to it than that. He claims that the Balkan Peace Team had concerned itself far too much with practical matters, and had not bothered sufficiently to implement political strategy or analyse a changing situation. Youth centres are something for other organisations. In this, his assessment was in accord with that of representatives of 'Stichting', the Netherlands finance organisation for the BPT, the International Fellowship of Reconciliation and the WRI.

Charles, from the International Fellowship of Reconciliation, adds that, along with a youth centre, there are other areas and themes to tackle for the Balkan Peace Team. The investigations of March 2001 show signs of that kind of work where the Balkan

Peace Team has experience and to which it could attach itself. One of these, for example, is work, which seeks opportunities for dialogue. Frauke reports that, as before, there is a need for dialogue in the Balkans. There are many people there who are already trained, but no follow-up. It would cost the BPT a good deal of energy to follow up this situation. She went on to say that there were people she had met who told her they had Serbian contacts, but that they didn't want to contact them at the moment. The team could service as a channel of information, opinions and the exchange of ideas.

The team in Dragash feels quite differently. It sees itself as a body acting directly of its own accord. How the new reacts to the old and what counts – all this is the subject of much thorough discussion in the spring of 2000. However, it is not discussed by everyone, and later becomes inflamed on a topic, which is really a subsidiary matter, namely, what is to go into the team's status report. This discussion reveals much about the conception of oneself assumed by those who are the champions of BPT, and about the new ideas which the team has brought along.

Just how much the team understands itself to be its own, sole performer here is very clearly seen in the draft of the report: *"With its permanent base in Prishtina, its expanded team membership and the implementation of its peace-building mandate through specific projects, the Kosovo/a team is creating a new framework for the organisation...."* It also describes how much at home it feels: *"Through its two projects, the team hopes to continue to listen to and work with all communities in the region, so as to contribute meaningfully and responsibly to the construction of cross-community tolerance as well as to the preparation of a foundation for a more peaceful future."*

This is a new start for the team and a break with the old. But: *"What is so new about it?"* is the question of the co-ordinator, pointing at the history of the project. There is no end to new starts in the history of BPT, from the human rights work to dialogue, from concentration on Kosovo up to bringing together Serbian and Albanian groups. It is assumed that after a phase with concrete projects, there will again be forms of work for new teams. To listen to the opinions of local participants constitutes a basic element in orientating the work of the team. To meet people, link them to others and to report on these activities are essential working methods. What is wrong with those that demand structural change? The Balkan Peace Team has several times had to adapt itself to changed conditions. In a phase in which former dialogue work appears to be impossibility, and on the advice of local partners, one now seizes upon a concrete project. Adaptation to changed political conditions and to follow the suggestions of local activists is nothing new to the Balkan Peace Team. There is only one new element and that is a concrete project to carry through as an executive body. The dialogue on this between the team and in this case between the Sub-groups does not take place but ends with an unfinished discussion between International Office and Team. In an e-mail of the same day, the team announces that in the next few weeks it will put its energy into the practical work at Dragash, and no longer shape it according to the report, *"regardless of what the structures...decide about matter, and what the focus of the report should be."*

Apparently, the team has understood things in such a way that it feels that it fulfils the mandate of the Balkan Peace Team with its own activities and projects, and that it places less emphasis on supporting local initiatives and building up new networks among them. If, however, one's own projects are to be shouldered, then the result is a much greater responsibility for the organisation. Evidently, the organisation has not accepted nor appreciated this view on the team's part. Both sections of the organisation have kept to their own, different way of looking at things with the consequence that both have delivered less than what the other needs and what is felt to be its right to receive.

The French arm of the Balkan Peace Team takes up the task of carrying on dialogue applying its own accents and using its own resources. Here, too, it has taken a long time until structures have developed, concepts are clarified and the organisation is able to act according to its plans.

The Équipes de Paix dans les Balkans Follow as Successors

In the case of the French groups, it is MAN, which is powerful in the matter of preparing and sending its own volunteers. This is a strong point in France, a challenge that in this country has no tradition of sending volunteers abroad. This also means that they have no status, no legal framework in which volunteers may move. However, since the abolition of military service on the 28th October 1997, something at last is moving towards the initiation of a new law, and the Kosovo-team of the BPT is to be the first field of operation for the French team.

At the same time, the French parliament is trying to put through a law pertaining to voluntary service of this kind, a proposed law that is taking its time being passed due to the many consultations it has to go through. Another innovation is that of a platform of organisations has been set up in the meantime which is to represent the interests of civil peace services. In June 1998, MAN has come so far that it is ready to take the plunge. Even though the proposal mentioned above is not yet law, they want to proceed right away with a pilot project. One wants to show how it can be done. However, this is a controversial point with other groups at MAN. The one party says that we should wait for the parliamentary proposal to become law, while the other maintains that they may merely become the dogsbody of a government with such interventions whose reservations could well lie much deeper. Yes, it will bring about changes, say those who will drive the project on and not allow it to be stopped. When the law relating to volunteer work is finally passed in France in January 2000, it couldn't have come early enough.

The law also allows peace operations. MAN has been busy in getting this through as a codicil to the law while members of the Green Party have committed themselves to help in getting it through. MAN also has prior support from its merger with other European peace services, which quickly deliver information from their respective countries.

As a result of its own project, the position of MAN in the Balkan Peace Team has now changed. Now, at last, the organisation can really show what it can do and so prove its competence. It is pursuing another approach for work in the field than that of the dialogue, in other words, what BPT-FRY is doing. MAN is so proud to be recognized as a source of reference for Kosovo within France. Members of parliament listen to its members in the Foreign Office and when they return from their excursions into Kosovo. Although their anti-military attitude does not fit in with their parliamentary concepts, they are nevertheless asked for their opinions as unloved experts. In this way, MAN has worked itself into attaining the status of experts and in this way placing itself in the first circle of its country's political life which, as yet, no other member organisation of the Balkan Peace Team has succeeded in reaching. As far as the work in Kosovo is concerned which is just beginning to take form there in the years 1996/7, the people at MAN do not feel that it is comprehensive enough, and maintain that the process of working on conflict must be accompanied by direct mediation. Mediation is the long-term path to be trodden in the work of the team, and for this training is of the utmost importance.

Just how these abstract concepts will actually boil down to terms of realistic work only the future will show. Nevertheless, the substantial acceptance of a stronger commitment on the part of MAN in the Balkan Peace Team since the end of 1997 definitely means a new "enthronement", so to speak, and one which helps to dispel the fear and reservations which up to that point had characterized co-operation. MAN has moved up to a position where it alone has represented the French groups in the Co-ordinating Committee. MAN concerned itself with the development of the pilot project in the summer of 1998. Just how large the demand is for qualified personnel is reflected in an enquiry as to whether the movement could place fifty participants at the disposal of an OSCE mission in October 1998. Unfortunately, MAN had to decline.

What now actually hinders implementation is the situation itself. The escalation of the conflict in early 1999 has made any kind of operation impossible. One member of MAN is stationed at the OSCE Mission in Prizren. The movement itself gets wind of the general atmosphere in Paris in February, 1999 at the negotiations carried on between Serbs and Albanians at Rambouillet 'just round the corner' so to speak. A meeting of 20,000 Albanians *"where no one wants to talk about non-violence"* is a sobering experience for MAN activists who attended the meeting.

There is another problem, too, and that is the recruitment of volunteers. At the beginning of 1999, there is enough money for their training and this is also thoroughly prepared. But only two people turn up. The question then is whether these two should be accepted or whether it would be better to seek more participants for training. It is also difficult to organise the money for the Balkan Peace Team as a whole since it is not located in France. But, despite this, another team is to be started in September 1999. This, however, proves to be an illusion, and it is not only the war, which intervenes.

What, precisely, has this other team to do there? It has not proved easy for the Kosovo-team to find a point of connection again in the meantime. In November 1999, the Balkan Peace Team General Assembly would like to get beyond general declarations of intention. Jens K. from MAN receives the commission to bring forward a concrete project suggestion at the next meeting in February 2000. For the meantime at least, there is a structure, which facilitates the employment of volunteers.

On the 6th December 1999, three members of MAN found a new association, 'Équipes de paix dans les Balkan'. It understands itself to be a branch of the Balkan Peace Team, and serves as an instrument to give French volunteers a legally regulated status in their deployment. The EPB which now abbreviates the French branch, concerns itself with the selection and training of volunteers, the preparation and subsequent study of the operation, the selection of partner organisations with which the volunteers will work on the spot, and the whole practical side of actually sending them off to the scene of activity. And further, the organisation has to submit a project suggestion if something is to come of the planned co-operation with the Balkan Peace Team. In the meantime it is spring, 2000, and the connections are lost again. MAN cannot after all always attend the Balkan Peace Team meetings. In this way they miss the opportunity to vote on issues along with others. At the beginning of 2000, a lot still hangs in the air, and extra meetings must be arranged in order to know how far the French branch has got on in the meantime.

It is in this spring of 2000 that Jens K. and Alphonse M. for EPB develop their concept for work in the town of Mitrovica, the divided city in the north of Kosovo. It is just here in a place where there is considerable tension and a high potential of violence that volunteers who work in various organisations could, they feel, help to create and enlarge room for contact between the communities. This is a different point of departure than that taken up to now by the BPT. Volunteers up to that point had not been settled plans directly with individual organisations, because in such a situation they cannot any longer work as a team nor have the opportunity to be impartial.

On first enquiries, only a few Kosovo Albanian organisations have shown interest in keeping up contact with the Serbian side or are interested in re-contacting their Serbian counterparts. The two representatives of Équipes who talk about the concept with Daniel M. and Ellen B. from the Balkan Peace Team at the beginning of April, see no danger of one-sidedness, while the other two are probably reminded of the experiences of the first Kosovo team. They nevertheless agree that, in the first exploratory phase, the concept should be tested. At the Balkan Peace Team on the other hand, one is not so convinced of the proposal, not least because a similar proposal had fallen through last autumn. At a meeting of the Balkan Peace Team in May in Prishtina, the French proposal was heavily debated. Since no written proposals were submitted, nothing could be decided.

The Équipe has problems in the meantime in getting volunteers together. The first training programme takes place in May 2000. It is not specifically equipped as preparation for volunteer employment. Of the twelve participants, no one is either suitable or interested enough in being deployed in Kosovo – and once more the start of the project has to be postponed. By the next meeting of the Balkan Peace Team in September 2000, the necessary volunteers are still not at hand, and by November there is no money for the pilot project. New training is fixed for the first half of 2001 and a new exploration of Mitrovica for February, 2001. The project start is not calculated to commence before the autumn or winter of 2001. However, in the meantime the Équipe has been able to strengthen its structures. They have been able to increase the number of employees in order to systematically build up contacts with potential promoters, partners and volunteers.

In February 2001, the problem is to be found in quite a different place. Now, just when the Mitrovica project is at last in sight, the BPT itself is at an end. This is an extremely frustrating situation for Équipe. Jens K. fights for the preservation of this *"multi-country project"*. At least he doesn't want to give up the co-operative liaison with organisations and lose out on the common experience, even if the BPT cannot re-form its ranks. When it becomes clear that the other organisations cannot join a move to keep the BPT moving, Jens K. offers the Équipe as a new point from which to crystallize matters. *"EPB has momentum right now and this is an opportunity for other organisations to work together."* Now they have volunteers and money and are eager to get going without further delay.

On the subsequent exploration in Kosovo, it appears that there is certainly interest in employing volunteers at organisations. Whether this, then, is also the politically relevant work imagined by the volunteers is another matter. At the General Assembly it appears that member organisations have not regarded the Balkan Peace Team as a deployment agency for volunteers, but that they have found the idea of teamwork a decisive one. This is the point for Équipe at which things will go along further on their own, because it is just this for which it stands for, i.e. as a deployment organisation in the context of other organisations in Europe with which they can share their experiences. When none of the others continue to co-operate, then one does not need the organisation anymore. On the other hand, one regards oneself as part of the Balkan Peace Team tradition and would like to testify to this by keeping the name: BPT France!

In autumn, 2001, the first volunteers take up their work in Mitrovica. When, on the 12th October 2001, at the last General Assembly of the Balkan Peace Team on which occasion the dissolution of the BPT takes place, they realize that 'Équipes de Paix dans les Balkans' is carrying on the work of the Balkan Peace Team. The Netherlands is supporting organisations for the BPT transfer the remaining funds to the EPB on its closure.

The Équipes de Paix dans les Balkans arrive in Mitrovica in the summer of 2003 where they seek opportunities to establish dialogue. After a long run-up to this moment, the Équipe is now organised and established. A circular, 'A bridge over the Ibar', reports three times a year on the situation in Mitrovica and on the project's progress. In December, 2003, Xavier S. reviews the situation in general and comes to the conclusion that: *"The establishment of a lasting peace in the Balkans requires, without any doubt, that there should be no let-up in the efforts of the international community and of NGOs."* He was present in 1993 in London when the Balkan Peace Team was launched. He knows what he's talking about.

Sources

BPT 30.4.2000; 19.1.01; 3.01; BPT CC minutes, 19.-21.2.99; 28.-30.5.99; 5.-7.5.2000; 8.-10.9.2000; 19.11.2000; 12.2.2000; 13.2.2000; 9.-11.2.01; BPT CC Daniel M., 3.3.2000; Edgar E., 6.3.2000; Martin K. 12.1.01; Sebastian K., 4.3.2000; BPT France Newsletter No 4, 2002; BPT GA minutes 20.-21.11.98; 20.-21.11.99; 12.2.2000; 18.-19.11.2000; 23.-25.3.01; 12.10.01; BPT IO 20.1.2000; 4.3.2000; 13.3.2000; 12.1.01; BPT-K 2.3.2000, Team; 2.3.2000, website; 7.3.2000; 13.3.2000; 9.1.01; 10.1.01; 11.1.01; 12.1.01; BSV Tamara P. 2.2.01; EPB, 9.4.2000, Minutes; Meeting EPB-BPT; Hämmerle 2000; Report Martin K., Member of CC in 2001, 4.2003; Information Jens K., 19.8.2003; Interview Jens K 1998; MAN 31.1.2000 v. Thomas und Nicolas MAN / French CPS; Non-violent Peaceforce Feasibility Study 2002; Official Founding of Équipes apparently on 12.2.2000, s. BPT GA minutes, 12.10.01; Schweitzer, Clark 2002; WRI Execmins 19.-21.5.2000.

Chapter 4 Interaction in the Balkan Peace Team

(1) Lack of Money restricts Initiative: Fund-raising in the Balkan Peace Team

The Balkan Peace Team's international coalition has a great dream, but the essential, day-to-day activities of the Team look very different from this vision. Its work consists of finding suitable volunteers, training and preparing them for their duties, fitting out the teams on the spot so that they are capable of doing the job and accompanying them on their operations. This requires money. How many people can work as full-time employees in the International Office and how many volunteers can be accepted and trained depends on money. How big the teams can be, how many teams can go into action, and whether every team can be equipped with computers, fax machines, cars and an acceptable apartment depends on money. Money also determines whether, in some cases, experts can be appointed to undertake certain jobs, and whether the chances which are often in the region can be used in new projects. The Balkan Peace Team in all its existence has never experienced a day on which the financial possibilities allow it to realize its political potential, neither at the desirable level nor even indeed that which it considers necessary. In view of this, therefore, it is clear that it has never been able to exhaust its potentialities. What could have been possible if......? This must remain speculation.

In 1994, the Balkan Peace Team manages to acquire a total of about 208,000 deutschmarks and in fact goes over into 1995 with a surplus after expenses have been deducted. However, this surplus first comes into being at the very end of the year. In May, on the other hand, there is a deficit of 60,000 DM to reach the budget target. As a consequence, tough priorities have to be set. Rather save on the equipment of the teams, which, in Croatia, have now set themselves up in Zagreb and Split than return them to work in one office again. And if this doesn't work, then rather dispense with a team in Croatia than relinquish the opportunity of starting up a new team in Kosovo. And so on. It becomes very clear how the financial limits of the Balkan Peace Team's budget on strategy and policies cramp its style when it comes to the possibilities for action on the scene. The surplus at the end of the year was therefore a consequence of tightening the financial belt during it. The Balkan Peace Team is stuck fast in this treadmill and will never be able to leave it.

Strictly speaking, the member organisations are responsible for fund-raising. However, just 2% of what is taken in during the year 1994 accounts for direct membership contributions. Another 14% comes from volunteers who themselves organise support circles or obtain money from organisations which place volunteers at our disposal. Fifteen per cent comes from individuals, while another 24% comes from the sponsorship of the BSV for the project in which it provides a capacity for personnel. This is the co-ordinating unit financed by public programmes for providing work for the unemployed. By far the largest source of means is provided by donations and accounts for some 45%. These come for the most part this year from Germany and Sweden, but the percentage varies from time to time.

On the debit side we have to reckon with 166,000 DM, a sum which has to cover the main position at the International Office and administration which, in fact, accounts almost for forty percent. The team in Croatia requires 35%, and the Kosovo team, which only really gets underway in November, just under a tenth. Money required for material, investments, training and project co-ordination account for the remaining 15%.

Ambitious targets are set up for 1995. Up to ten volunteers are to be included in the teams sent off, and in this way it is hoped that expansion in Kosovo can be attained and at the same time create personnel stabilisation in Croatia. The budget rises to 368,000 DM. Almost half of this must come from sources which are not yet identified at the time the General Assembly met to decide the next budget at the end of 1994. The surplus spoken of before which had just been accomplished, now has a moment or two to 'breathe' as it were.

Already in January 1995, the co-ordinator had warned that there is only a little of the applied for money left. He receives all the sums that flow together, but he has no general view of the activities of member organisations in various countries. And fund-raising is not one of his tasks. In the middle of July, the project is overtaken by an inability to pay. Then, two applications, which had long been pending, were approved. Nevertheless, *"with costs growing and low fund-raising activity, BPT faces the danger of bankruptcy as early as September!"* the co-ordinator warns, his eye fixed on the budget for the next few months,.

At the beginning of July, the team writes: *"The financial business has gotten us all down a little, though. We felt a bit strapped, restricted. These past two months has for the first time seen us hesitate to take steps we thought were necessary due to lack of funds."* The year 1995 – is there something wrong here? Yes indeed; it's the time when the team is in Western Slavonia organising the observation of human rights, setting up and linking various offices and writing reports, which receive wide acclaim. The signs of a new military offensive in the Krajina region are coming in thick and fast. While the teams are busy keeping a watch on possible human rights infringement, linking up with others and making a name for themselves in setting up their reports, the co-ordination team members and the co-ordinator himself are working overtime to find any money anywhere to keep the project going.

Of the projected 98,000 DM for the work of the team, only 32,000 - can finally be raised. However, this summer sees the first successful concept for raising money. The most successful applications are those, which pass through the International Office, a department that should not actually be concerned with raising money. These are the support groups coming into being in the Netherlands and Switzerland. The International Office is responsible for fundraising. The key to a modest and temporary success lies in the ability of certain individuals from member organisations to make their access to certain donors available for the Balkan Peace Team. The figures, the applications for projects and all the formal work is taken over by the International Office. Added to this, the BPT own one or two special treasures which as the Heinrich-Böll Foundation which continuously promotes its activities in the first three years. Another is the 'Diakonie' (Social Service Agency of the Evangelical Church in Germany) which has undertaken to insure the Team and the volunteers working for it. There are individuals, too, who, so to speak, *"stand by the Balkan Peace Team in its worst hours"*. The well-trodden paths of finding money, over and above the appeals to member organisations, is upheld. *"All financial responsibility for the project lies with the members."* The Co-ordinating Committee underlines this connection in autumn, 1995, at the same time drawing attention to the fact that there are, in all, eleven bodies responsible.

It is here that the problem is presented in all its keenness. The member organisations are already tied down, and each organisation can point to its own contributions with which its assists the Balkan Peace Team towards its upkeep. Some of these are, for example, the periods of work which its representatives undergo in order to guide and control the BPT; the applications which they prepare for it; the charity concerts they organise, the volunteers, and so on and so forth. And it is also recognized that the Balkan Peace Team can oblige its members to do so. That is the point where *"everyone says, 'I can do this, and this and this' and the point at which everyone knows that this is not enough."* Thus, one of the participants.

Despite the rescue in 1995, success is only temporary. Grants and applications only last for a year in the main. For this reason, new donors must constantly be found and so the future always remains insecure.

More than DM 400,000. - is to come in 1996. Again, the 'summer dip cycle' has reappeared with the threat of not being able to pay by the autumn. A supreme effort like nothing before it is now initiated. First of all, a letter of emergency is compiled and sent by the Balkan Peace Team, but this brings little response. Several member organisations send out an impassioned call on behalf of the BPT, activate donors and contribute further monies of their own. The pattern of the rescue repeats itself at the last minute. Just as the crisis meeting takes place in September to decide on closure, on that very day, approvals come in for long since submitted applications. For a long time now, economy measures have been reducing the amount of money needed for survival. The original plan for increasing International Office personnel is waived. Expenses amounting to DM 285,000 - can just be covered. In the meantime, they are distributed to cover around half the funds needed for the two teams and to account for administrative, co-ordination, training and investment costs.

On changing the co-ordination in the International Office, responsibility for fund-raising is taken from here and once more placed in the hands of the Co-ordinating Committee. In February 1997, on seeing the current state of the household financial budget, the Co-ordinating Committee decides to introduce economy measures. The International Office once more receives the main responsibility for writing applications. Mid 1997, sees the income so horrendously in arrears and so far behind what was originally anticipated that, at the General Assembly in June, the threat of closure is announced.

The essential problem is one which concerns structure, and is seen as lacking someone who is mainly or exclusively responsible for fund-raising. The interaction of the international fund-raising operations, which had begun to develop last year, has somehow disappeared. Since, above all, the applications have not produced the expected results, the Balkan Peace Team struggles on into 1997. Even in December of that year, a 'council of war' is held in order to consider income and, if this is necessary, to introduce drastic measures to prevent things from getting worse. Managing the crisis this year assumes the features of a chronic situation where, in a whole series of sittings, control of incoming revenues is secured right away with the consequence that an enormous amount of energy is consumed in the process. There is an 'end of the world' atmosphere among the teams. However, there is some hope for the coming year, since a large application at the EU might be pending. According to the coordinator there, verbal approval has already been given by the department.

From 1998 onwards, the Balkan Peace Team now seeks to disentangle itself from the problems of short-term planning and fund-raising by implementing a three-year plan. At the beginning of this year, money is sufficient for two months, but donors in ministries and foundations who have hitherto supplied funds, now indicate that they will change their promotion strategies. This means, in other words, that some of them do not want to continue to be regular donors. The large EU application from which one had put so much store to enable us to work into the summer comes to nothing, and the widely cast net of applications at ministries in the Netherlands and Germany, at foundations in Great Britain, the Netherlands and the United States fall upon stony ground.

An urgent review of total funds is made in August. The issues of bare survival and closure loom upon the horizon. There are councils of war, emergency sittings, and it becomes clear that massive curtailment in the budget is necessary. In this situation there is a treasurer for the first time and someone who is directly responsible for finances. Financial support is then forthcoming with the inflow of new funds; the threat of closure of the project by the end of October can be circumvented. Altogether, 271,000 DM can be acquired, so that the end of the year finds the organisation with a deficit of 21,000 DM. Despite this, a survey of the financial situation as a whole becomes increasingly more difficult to assess, since the bills and expenses submitted by the teams reveal large gaps. Even a year later, there is still no final balance in sight where one can see what has been calculated for the teams in the previous year.

It is planned to send another team into Kosovo in winter, 1998, and this envisages finding new sources to supply the 200,000 DM needed initially and, in order to realize all the aspirations of the new plan, about 420,000 DM will be required in all.

The year 1999 begins reasonably well when the first credits can be redeemed. Then the war starts in Kosovo, which forces the team to think anew. The question now is whether the team's activities, which are in excess of that budgeted, will be financed at all is a debatable one. While it is true that it is a little easier for peace organisations to come upon funds and other sources of money during wartime, but even so, before the money is available there has to be careful enquiry into its eventual use. This is pretty disappointing for the team, which feels that it has been left in the lurch at a time when it is urgently necessary to act. There has never been a generation of volunteers in the Balkan Peace Team where this frustration has not been felt. This year, about a quarter of the income comes from private sources, making a total of 279,000 DM. A fifth of this total has been brought together by member organisations, 16% via applications to governments and 11% as grants from organisations.

The pattern of payment changes from year to year and cannot be anticipated. One thing is working better and this is the continuous writing of applications and the mutual reception of information. Although on this occasion that achieved is behind that planned, one can say that by the autumn of 1999 that one can look back on a year without acute monetary crises, and that one has learned a lesson from the previous year which was not to rely on accomplishing too much when the large applications are too few. In future, it is determined to place more reliance on the smaller donations and on individual donors.

A new problem comes into view at the end of this year, and that is the attempt to reconstruct the team's financial entries for the previous year. This results in the nightmarish realisation that the final balances have been wrongly entered since 1996. As a consequence, everything has to be newly entered and all entries carefully controlled. After all, the credibility of the team as a non-profit making public body with its corresponding tax relief depends on proper bookkeeping. Moreover, the integrity of the Balkan Peace Team as a professional organisation is also at stake. Right up to the end of the Balkan Peace Team and beyond, this challenge accounts for a great deal of energy in the coordination of the International Offices until correct financial balance sheets can be submitted to the tax office.

Total expenses for the large new team in Kosovo for 2000 is assessed at 366,000 DM. A third of the budget must be recruited from somewhere. Added to this are the expenses incurred for the Dragash project youth centre. Its yearly requirement will amount to something like half a million marks when it is fully built out. The project begins in March 2000, and will be extended bit by bit, so that only a small amount of the total costs come into consideration at the moment. From autumn, 2000, onwards the approvals for this project begin to come in.

As the Balkan Peace Team closes, it finds itself in the same position as it experienced eighteen months previously, in other words, money will last for another two months and later, as the result of feverish fund-raising in the meantime, it will just manage to balance things out. In addition to this, a list is drawn up which is to be updated when money is to be expected. This will detail who applies for how much and from whom. Just how critical the actual time of money-flow is, is now something realized by everyone. A balance is sought between contributions issuing from applications, and between donations and contributions from sources associated with member organisations. There is to be a clear allocation of function, so that everyone knows who can make decisions on priorities where there are bottlenecks in the flow of money.

As always, saving is urged at the beginning of the year 2000. In May of that year, money will last until the end of July, but this is not enough to pay for an exploration of Serbia or provide pocket money for the team. Despite these facts, the summer is surmounted without a crisis, and in the autumn it seems that the BPT is no longer in a position where fund-raising will be a matter of swinging from one crisis to another. But since current bookkeeping still can't keep up with events, no general survey of the situation is possible in winter 2000/2001. On the one hand, there are indications that fund-raising for the Dragash project is making good progress. On the other, looking at the administrative costs, those incurred for co-ordination and for the office in Prishtina, things look rather bleaker. However, before this can be investigated further, the Balkan Peace Team goes into dissolution.

Looking into the financial situation, taken as a whole, is like looking into an abyss. This is partly due to domestic policy, because the BPT first has to learn how to turn a penny while involved in the multiplicity of its international contacts. It had first to learn that constant fund-raising is one of its main priorities. Even in the phases of relative success, it has failed to pull itself out of the quagmire of virtual poverty. This same dearth is experienced by member organisations, too. The WRI and the Federation for Social Defence experience the same, serious financial crises, and this regularly to some extent during the same period of time.

For the Balkan Peace Team, applications made at funding institutions become an essential instrument in the matter of raising funds, but this, too, runs against tight limitations. For what purpose, one may ask, do donor agencies give money? As far as the activities, which are offered by the Balkan Peace Team, these have to fall through many a sieve of regulations. 'Success', for example, is one of these yardsticks; another is 'Measure'. How can one pigeonhole the support of local activists in terms of 'success'? Or, for that matter, the dialogue and information work in Kosovo? Certainly, effects can be supposed, researched and set down. This essay is one such attempt. At the same time it becomes clear how insecure and vulnerable all such attempts must be. Other peculiarities characteristic of funding institutions, whether these be foundations, governmental programmes or other financing organisations, make it difficult for the Balkan Peace Team to survive.

One of these hindrances is that there is generally no money provided for the co-ordination and organisation of support work. If at all, then on the spot. But just how the people are to get there and how they can be prepared for their tasks, and how they can be politically and personally accompanied - this doesn't interest them. The setting up of the infrastructure is the task of BPT, so the concept. But how is that possible when the infrastructure itself can only be kept intact by external means? Funding institutions are, moreover – and this is another of their peculiarities – shy creatures. Hardly any of them enter into a permanent relationship with an organisation promoted by them. Here, exceptions tend to prove the rule. Finally, promoters of this kind generally fall prey to fashionable tendencies. This means that one must forever be presenting one's own work in different terms, or during those periods where one falls on bad times or is active in the 'wrong' region. In other words: who's interested in the Balkans when Rwanda is in turmoil?

The Balkan Peace Team manages to survive mainly because it is always willing to compromise on its own standards. It relinquishes the need for necessary equipment and materials for its teams, for volunteers and for another portion in the International Office. The price for all this is high.

A Fond Dream: The Balkan Peace Team with Sufficient Means and Money

The Balkan Peace Team has never managed to sound out its own possibilities. For this, the financial pinch has been just too great. Having said so much, however, we can still imagine what directions the organisation would have taken had it not been shackled in the ways spoken of above, and had, instead, enjoyed the freedoms of greater financial resources. It is possible, for example, that teams would have been numerically stronger, technically better equipped as far as possessing computers, cars, offices and general accommodation is concerned. Would there have been other offices in other places perhaps? This question is most often discussed in connection with concrete projects and generally rejected because the Balkan Peace Team lays emphasis on flexible teams. Notwithstanding all this, it is quite possible that the BPT, had it possessed the necessary resources, could have developed a small network of regional offices.

Such an expansion would have demanded that the Balkan Peace Team improve its capacity to enlist volunteers, train them and accompany them. With the maxim in mind, *"The whole project suffers when a part is neglected"*, many of those taking part in the final assessment were thinking of the bottleneck occurring in the International Office. Here, it could be imagined, a further specialisation and promotion of professionalism could have taken place. With a little more money in hand, the International Office could have sensibly employed more people in the areas of publicity, volunteer accompaniment and fund raising. Less administrative work would have been left, too, to the Co-ordinating Committee. This organ could have been allowed to concentrate more intensively on political guidance, and perhaps even on a conceivable assessment. When needed, we could have brought in more outside expertise according to the adage: *"Try to find people who know - if you don't know yourself".* It is also conceivable that there would have been more time and energy to reflect upon those elements indicative of the future for which, in the past, there was never the time, and so in this way be in a position to orientate our concepts and ourselves. One of these would have been the possibility to continue the Dragash project and, presumably, brought it to satisfactory maturity.

The strengthening of structures in the financial and personnel sectors would have had several positive side effects. The stress referred to in the chapters above, resulting from an ever-present paucity of means and money would in this way have been eliminated. New initiatives could have been started with adequate resources. This was so often simply not possible. The situation is summed up in the caveat: *"Don't start anything new before you've got the resources for it."*

This does not necessarily mean that the Balkan Peace Team would still exist today. All these eventualities set down here are the history of the organisation. With accessible resources of money, investment could have been made in these directions. We can also imagine that the range of its activities could have been expanded, extended and intensified. Whether or not wholly new projects could have been developed of course remains speculation and cannot be considered here. On the other hand, when considered, an astonishingly long list of probable activities presents itself, if reflected in the light of a solid foundation of basic financing or in that of a reliable partnership or in the light of one or several donor organisations which could have made these things possible.

Sources

BPT 31.12.95, 19; 12.96; 12.97; 31.1.98; no date, September 98; 6.9.98; 15.9.98; 26.11.98; 9.12.99; 17.1.2000; 25.1.2000; 9.6.2000; 10.2.01; BPT GA minutes, 15.-16.10.94; 4.-5.11.95; 14.-16.11.97; BPT IO, no date, 1994, Profit; 21.3.2000; BPT CC/GA minutes, 13.-14.6.98; BPT CC minutes, 2.-4.5.94, 1, 13; 12.-14.1.95; 16.-18.7.95; 30.9.-1.10.95; 14.-15.9.96; 1.-2.3.97; 20.-22.2.98; 4.-6.9.98; 28.-30.5.99, 5, 9; 10.-12.9.99; 19.11.99; 13.2.2000; 5.-7.5.2000; 8.-10.9.2000,10; Otog Zg Biweekly 2/6.95, Confidential; Information Oskar K. 8.5. 2003; Interview Charles O. 1997; Friedhelm D. 2/1998; Schweitzer, Clark, 2002, 48f.

(2) Leadership and Orientation: Who will determine the Direction of the Balkan Peace Team?

High expectations are directed to the Balkan Peace Team that, after all, has assembled 13 organisations from Europe and the United States to work together on a common project involving a network, which almost spans the world. [A list of these appears at the end of Chapter I (2)]. One volunteer expresses this fact succinctly: *"We are the peace movement's expression, and that's why we should be more of a campaigning organisation."* Since the Balkan Peace Team does not belong to any particular political way of thinking, it is able to make radical suggestions as to the solution of conflicts occurring in the region. As a result of the work of volunteers, the member organisations would have been able to mobilize their potential in order to unify and consolidate their commitment in the Balkans. However, instead of this, they participated a little in the efforts of the BPT in order not to be obliged to get too involved in the conflict. Seen thus, the Balkan Peace Team as whole is a failure.

Whether this point of view coincides with that of the member organisations within the Balkan Peace Team can be doubted. The most interesting thing about the Balkan Peace Team is that the question as to who determines its course is one that cannot so easily be answered. Who may formulate expectations? Who may reject them? The points of view which find their expression in this chapter are those collected during conversations taking place individually during research in the years 1997 and 1998. From these it becomes clearer who does not feel responsible for the course the BPT takes. The member organisations belong to this category, which in a 'coalition project' and, at first sight, seems to be a paradox.

Policy-making with the Balkan Peace Team: The Member Organisations

The 'World Peace and Relief Team', for example, is a small, 'one-man, one-woman organisation' which runs on a purely honorary basis. It has no interest at all in further developing the project actively itself, but would like nevertheless to support it financially from its own small potential. After a few years, this organisation virtually withdraws its membership – as do others, too – which never turn up at meetings or otherwise give evidence of their existence. In the year 2000, the Balkan Peace Team strikes the two 'Geneva' groups from its list of member organisations after having tried in vain to establish contact with them.

But the active member organisations, too, take good care not to give the Balkan Peace team any guidelines. The general director of the Federation for Social Defence emphasises that, *"The Balkan Peace Team always insists that it should manage things itself and for this reason the BSV keeps out of its way."* The representative of the International Fellowship of Reconciliation who, as its deputy leader, takes part in the General Assembly in November 1997, does not have any definite guidelines which she has to implement. Rather, it is all a matter of the points of view, which are allowed to come to the surface during the process of general, internal discussion. The strongest commitment comes from the International Peace Brigades who, in 1995, voiced criticism of the BPT in that it felt that the Balkan Peace Team was not sufficiently impartial. This debate was conducted for the most part between the Team and this organisation and therefore did not affect other member organisations directly.

The question arises as to what advantage the member organisations see in such a coalition; what binds them to the project? Member organisations can profit from the Balkan Peace Team in several ways. In the first place, it gives them opportunity to gather practical experience together on site in crisis areas. They leave the theoretical world of debate on alternatives to military intervention to an assessment of the practical problems of working directly with the fact of conflict and with the means to hand. Here, they find out what conditions pertain, what chances there are and where the limits are set, as well as the range of their operations. Along with the credibility, which they have acquired through practical experience, it is also an immense opportunity for them to learn from their experience and, at the same time, widen their sphere of competence. Above all, in Austria, France and Germany, experience with the Balkan Peace Team can be used by member organisations to help in stimulating initiatives like the peace services to make a breakthrough. In this respect, the points of departure on such lines are varied. In Germany, for example, experience gained from the work of training later flows into the further development of training programmes for peacebuilding. In France, this experience is used to provide a lever in influencing legislation to bring about a volunteer law that makes operations such as this possible.

The Balkan Peace Team further serves as a justification, which might be summed up in this way: *"Look here! This is what we're doing in the Balkans."* A certain 'deputy capacity', so to speak, takes place when the Federation for Social Defence no longer sees itself anymore, say, as an organisation having its own way in the Balkans, but regards the BPT as such. However, even here, different organisations react differently. For those in the WRI, for example, engagement in the interests of the Balkan Peace Team is seen as the most important project in connection with the Balkans. Along with the Balkan Peace Team, Eirene International, a Christian service for peace also supports the initiative, 'Students Help to Live'. For the Austrian Peace Services, on the other hand, the BPT is only one of a whole list of peace projects in the Balkans. Another advantage is that one's own project in the Balkans gains direct access to information flowing out of the crisis region. This is an advantage that is more and more appreciated by member organisations.

How do the experiences gained by the Balkan Peace Team flow back into the organisations? The transfer depends on those participating persons who work with the BPT and at the same time with the member organisations in decision-making committees or at least have access to these. In many member organisations reports to the respective executive committees are regularly submitted. On the other hand, more intensive discussions or even decision-making ones with regard to strategic positions are, for example, no longer taking place within the Federation of Social Defence, since its representative in the BPT has ceased being a member of the BSV executive committee.

Difficult Orientation in the No-man's land of Working on Conflict

At the Balkan Peace Team, one must be a member of the Co-ordinating Committee in order to participate in decisions affecting daily activities and, accordingly, those concerned with learning processes. At the General Assembly, representatives of member organisations confirm by and large what has been planned and what is envisaged by the Co-ordinating Committee and, increasingly, what is mooted in the Sub-groups on Croatia and Kosovo and in the teams. This does not detract from the value of these meetings. They constitute one of the rather few opportunities offered where team members can actually come into contact with representatives of member organisations. At them, the rare opportunity to exchange experiences can take place face to face. Then, the diversity of the Balkan Peace Team comes together once or twice a year. Again, at these meetings, it so happens that, again and again, debates on content take place, but decisions are rarely taken. On these occasions, work is confirmed, but not determined.

Here, too, exchange between organisations also occurs, organisations which, despite their variety, are nevertheless very similar, and which are intent on finding a model in non-violent alternatives which is applicable everywhere. After a time they find that it is important to promote and support civil actors, and that the needs of local activists provide vital orientation. There are recurring opportunities to act non-violently, even when this is not the complete solution to a problem. In this way, such initiatives are steps in the right direction. One acquires greater clarity about the way solutions to conflict function, and about one's own role in this process. It is both important and possible to demonstrate a feeling of solidarity, to organise means of observation, and eventually to hinder violent incidents as well as to report back to one's own organisation to the effect that things are not exactly in order, even though there's no actual fierce fighting going on. These make up the vital experience of member organisations.

From the practical point of view, the Balkan Peace Team experiences and processes that which, at the end of the 90's, was understood as the promotion of peace alliances in the framework of peacebuilding and conflict resolution. As a pioneer in this area, the Balkan Peace Team has collected experience which has not yet found its way into books or training programmes as invaluable, consolidated human experience which can be passed on to others. This fact places the Balkan Peace Team before considerable theoretical problems. It has to move into new areas and in so doing hopes that the mistakes it makes, and inevitably will make, are recognized and corrected in time. The experience above touching upon police questioning in Prishtina at Easter, 1995, for example, is certainly the most serious warning and, in this case, the quick withdrawal on that occasion was the correct reaction to the situation. Those trespassing in no-man's-land do well to take note of landmarks. The principles governing the work of the Balkan Peace Team are independence, the support of local initiatives instead of their own – to mention only the most important. However, sometimes these principles get in each other's way; sometimes it's the one that is of foremost consideration and sometimes the other.

Of all the members of the Co-ordinating Committee it is perhaps Daniel from the WRI who most consistently follows a concept and acts from this. Just how this guides his conduct and orientation in Kosovo has already been described in Chapter 3 (1). He belongs to the most reliable people supplying feedback to team reports of their activities and so demonstrates important orientation. However, we can't speak of yet of an agreed set of rules, and the consequence of this is that teams receive the most varied advice and assessments. The most important counterpart to orientation in no-man's-land is one where teams are equipped with the basic ability to guide themselves.

Be Your Own Guide, please: On the Myth of Self-guided Teams

When it comes to the execution of practical work on scene, tension develops between the teams as 'experts' and those working on behalf of the Co-ordinating Committee who make the decisions. This tension requires trust between the parties, which can only come about by personal contact. This trust has to develop anew from team to team, if the co-operation is to be made possible over a distance. The gulf between the team and 'the rest' of the Balkan Peace Team corresponds to the isolation on location. This is felt by volunteers from the very first team, and they expect strong leadership. But this, too, is ambivalent. One volunteer has put it into so many words: *"More direct focussing would have been better, but the attempt on the part of the Co-ordinating Committee to control matters more tightly would have found opposition in the team."* As far as the members of the co-ordinating teams is concerned, the first team sent to Croatia is that which is the most self-guided team, and without which the project as a whole would not have developed as it did. This experience corresponds best with the expectations of the Co-ordinating Committee in the matter of self-guidance and, in fact, lays the foundation of what is expected from those who follow.

This is all very well, but the expectations of the teams in the business of self-guidance nevertheless collide with its desire for guidance from the Co-ordinating Committee. There are differences among the teams in dealing with the lack of leadership by the CC. Some are in a position to manage them. How do they find the priorities and criteria?

There are indications here, which have come to light from interviews with volunteers working for the Balkan Peace team in the years between 1994 and 1998. These reveal that a significant problem area such as that of evictions provide good, clear orientation. Requests from activists on 'the home front' generally have precedence, otherwise on the day in question the most important task is taken up. The making of reports on human rights is also very important to define and put into practice. Much more difficult, however, is the whole area of linking up connections and the development of the civil society.

The interests of team members also contribute to the job of setting up differing priorities. These have to be dealt with in the team. In addition, the talents of volunteers also enter the scene. Some are good at making contact, for example, while others are good at research and putting together stimulating reports.

What it's all about – that's something the new volunteers learn from the older ones when they are introduced to the job. Here, too, the procedures must first be developed; there is no certain, readily recalled knowledge. The first Croatian team practices handing-over routines. The idea is to establish an introductory period of rest of four weeks in which the newcomers can spend their time reading up on the literature, getting to know people, going off with the older group, and with learning the language. One aspect which is important during this phase is that the contacts made remain intact, so that these can be successfully co-ordinated into current activities.

The second great challenge is the large team changeover in Croatia at the beginning of 1996. The team had prepared itself for this event, but its success did not remain entirely in its hands. There must also be a well-timed placement which, if it is to function properly, must provide an adequate transition period where the 'old' and the 'new' can gear up with one another. This is something, too, which frequently goes awry. In Kosovo things are different anyway, since the building up of a team doesn't come off at all at first.

The third significant experience with radical change of this nature in Croatia was the team crisis of 1997. On this occasion, the Balkan Peace Team intervened with the despatch of a short-term consultant who is active in team development and who used her positive experience gained with another team in Kosovo. This resulted in a better evaluation of the introduction regarding volunteers in 1998. The orientation and introductory phase is marked by changing structural conditions, so that it is not surprising that volunteers very often experience things in very different ways.

Of the 18 volunteers in the Croatian team who receive introduction between 1994 and 1998, twelve falling within the framework of the accompanying project are asked to give their opinions. They recount their own experiences, the experiences of others, and about those of participants for whom they have organized introductions. What is particularly striking is how they tend to be harshly critical of their own performance in introducing others to their tasks. This doesn't always tally with the assessment made of them by those going through the introductory course.

Nine volunteers have given an opinion on their own introduction. Five of these found that their introduction was good, because enough time was allowed them to arrive and get settled in to their new environment, or because the form of introduction chosen for them suited, even in the case where those volunteers who carried out the introduction judged things differently. The four others had as good as no introduction or an inadequate one, that is to say, one which had succeeded in allowing them to settle in and make contacts, but which had not supplied them with sufficient basic knowledge in order to know what the work was aimed at. Again and again, volunteers have undertaken the task to specifically improve the introductory period for those coming after them and have also invested a lot of energy in this project.

Taking along trainees to meetings and allowing them to settle into the complex network of contacts is certainly a basic element in their training. On top of this, there are attempts to make formalised units obligatory, such as the use of the filing system, the computer and the introduction of newcomers into the political context. A further starting point for them is that which unites team transition with team development.

In Split at the beginning of 1997, work was re-structured by the introduction of analysing instruments and regular sittings to reflect on progress and plan strategy. This helps the newcomers considerably in settling in with their work. This impulse, which originates from the proposal of a volunteer, is supported in this phase by a consultant who has been sent by the Balkan Peace team for a while. She also assists in the development of strategy and in the re-construction of contacts. To judge from the effects it has had, this has been a pretty successful beginning. The Zagreb team is afterwards in a position to carry out an analysis for an ordered exit; the Split team writes a remarkable report about the situation of the return of refugees (see Chapter 2 (6). The Kosovo team had already benefited from a consultant's advice. As far as the strategic orientation of the team's work is concerned, team transitions are therefore rather problematic when they fail to succeed. Not only do experience and contacts suffer and break up, but the general perspectives of the work as well.

When the Balkan Peace Team as a whole discusses and decides on the orientation of its work, the maintenance of teamwork takes up a central role. As criteria for decisions on what courses to follow, the co-ordinator counts firmly on certain issues: those of commitments at the scene have priority for example; the stabilisation, expansion or the needs of existing teams are to be categorised as more important than new projects. All this is frequently enough placed under that which is viewed as necessary, considering the tight financial framework already alluded to, and not to mention those things which might also be desirable. The Co-ordinating Committee has developed this conservative strategy of constancy, a matter which has also been confirmed by the General Assembly. The first team develops its norms and orientation from practice. The Co-ordinating Committee confirms this orientation by saying: *"You're in the field [and you know what you're doing...]"*

As far as their daily decisions are concerned, volunteers are left to their own devices and for many that is good for them. Others would also like a theoretical basis for their practical work. Yet others experience the coalition at times when it is more active and consequently more visible, whether this is due to enquiries or when direct help is to be given in a specific case. In general, one can say that the response is diverse. While teams in Croatia increasingly expect and demand more leadership, development in the Kosovo team works the other way round.

The latter begin with a high degree of expectation from leadership and then, as time goes on, develop a very high degree of independence. The construction requires from volunteers that they develop a high degree of personal organisation, initiative, common sense and an insight into local possibilities and contexts or gain this during their work. Impulse is expected from them, since only they know the local set-up, plus the fact that they also have connection to local advisors. This is something of a two-edged sword for volunteers. They want both autonomy and orientation. They want to possess the freedom to act, and that is what this project offers them as no other in fact can. Added to this is that the context of the work is also unstable.

In 1995, the volunteers in Croatia experience the first rapid change in their work. Critical reports from a member organisation come in about their work and this in turn persuades the volunteers to demand discussion of their mandate in spring, 1996. This then comes about at the beginning of February 1996, at a sitting of the Co-ordinating Committee.

While we are speaking here of the experiences of the past, little is being done to focus on the future, one of those participating remarks. In the course of the year, all the volunteers taking part terminate their services with the Balkan Peace Team. Essentially, one must keep discovering exactly what the content and limits of the mandate are and, at the same time, what new emphases occur in a changing situation of conflict. *"The 'sexy' conflict is over,"* they say, the teams note at the beginning of 1997 and come to the conclusion that, *"consequently, the role of the Otvorene Oci has changed radically as to what must be considered and how strategy is to be planned."* At this time, the volunteers in their offices prescribe the direction of their work corresponding to their interests and to agreements made. They also reject the role accorded to them of being 'experts' and write:

> *"Knowing the theoretical structure and reasons for BPT, you as experienced peace activists have a lot to offer us through your input and advice as individuals and organisations. However, all too often we feel that we are here alone in the field to be the 'experts.' This leads us to 'creative improvising' during the best of times and 'desperate floundering' in the worst. In essence, we depend on you to share your knowledge with us - whether through direct correspondence and training endeavours or access to your publications, etc. We on our part should be trying to ask for specific trainings, needs, guidance, etc."*

These basic enquiries are taken up inasmuch as they form part of the strategy discussion, which is initiated in 1997. For the immediate feedback needs of the team, there are always the well-trodden paths of discussion with individuals in the Sub-groups, and from time to time debate at the General Assembly. In the autumn and winter, the capacity for strategy development in the teams is increased by the presence of advisors and the independent activities carried out by team members. General debate, as well as that concerning basic issues, is recognised as both desirable and necessary, but fails to be organised.

In the Network of Relationships with Local Partners: Networks at All Levels.

Together with the team and the Co-ordinating Committee, the influence of local partners can also be noticed as playing a part in the destiny of the Balkan Peace Team, even if somewhat indirectly and not always transparent for everyone. Relationships with local organisations in Zagreb, in Split, in Kosovo and those in Belgrade are all very different the from one another.

One of the most important is that between the Antiwar Campaign in Zagreb and the WRI. When the Zagreb group cannot confirm that the teams are not doing a good job, then this is cause for serious concern for Daniel M. from the campaigners. Since the Zagreb people encounter him in the Executive Committee of the International War Resisters, there is ample opportunity at informal encounters for sounding out situations of this nature.

It is suggested to the teams, too, that they look for such people as a source of reference in their sphere of activities. These should be people who can give an account of their work and people whom they can trust. In Kosovo, this is frequently difficult and sometimes even impossible. However, if successful, the work of the teams can then be firmly established locally. In this way, leadership is determined by surroundings, which, from volunteer to volunteer, can range all the way from the punk scene to that of diplomatic circles.

A second line of feedback between the Balkan Peace Team and its local partners is that of evaluation trips through which a representative of the Co-ordinating Committee can gain information from partner organisations as to their opinion about the team's work on several occasions. The results of these then flow back to the Co-ordinating Committee as internal information, and from there decisions can be made on the recruiting of volunteers or on changes in policy. Here, partners can voice their criticism of individual volunteers and can demand greater personal initiative on behalf of the team. On these occasions, principles and concepts can be analysed and also confirm good work.

This is not direct influence on the Balkan Peace Team by its partners. The latter has its own additional attachments to people who must continuously remain in contact with the region and with the BPT. Otherwise those associations which provide a common basis of trust as far as mutual assessment or evaluation, weighing up the pros and cons of a situation, and decisions taken on what direction to follow would be lost. The gradual relinquishment of that which has served for a long time is not only a loss of collective knowledge. It also threatens – at least potentially – to become a loss of that firm establishment created in local networks. Quite early on, the teams sense this danger and, at the beginning of 1997, after an introductory process for future members of the Co-ordinating Committee, demand: *"With the departure of several key CC individuals, we are concerned about the need for new people in the CC, their integration process, and the effects that this will have on our work here in the field. Just like the training for a new field volunteer, we believe that any new CC members should have an as comprehensive initiation as possible into the working group. This is particularly important for any new Sub-group members."*

New Structures and Strategic Orientation: At the End – Open Questions

The year 1997 is a difficult year for orientating teamwork. Major changes within the Croatian teams and changes of direction necessary in a post-war society make the persistent theme of introduction and orientation particularly acute. At this stage, the idea of implementing a co-ordinator on the spot is born. This new post is to assist the teams in the matter of orientation, and also to help bridge the distance, since this person is much nearer to the teams than the International Office in Minden, Germany. In this critical phase of crisis, the idea is discussed, and all hopes are pinned on this new concept as well as all the frustrations with the already existing structures. In fact, the idea is virtually finished off during discussion, because the support created by short-term advisers who are arriving at this time enable them to take initiative to act again.

However, the Balkan Peace Team itself is trying to get away from the ad hoc arrangement and, in this, the three-year plan is to assist it. It is accepted in 1997. In the first place, it provides for individual obligation on the part of the member organisations to commit themselves for a further three years' work with the Balkan Peace Team. The driving force stemming from the financial situation has already been referred to. Added to this, there is also an intrinsic need for orientation.

And there is the ever-open question as to when the Balkan Peace Team mission can be regarded as fulfilled. In Split in 1998, the criteria for finishing the work are discussed with former volunteers. The organisation as a whole is to undergo an internal evaluation. To this end, local partners, active as well as former volunteers, the member organisations, individuals in the Co-ordinating Committee, together with the results of accompanying research, are the various perspectives to be taken into consideration during the enquiry. In May, 1999, the results of a pretty thin response flowing back from various sources indicate the need for action in the matter of structures. A general debate on strategic orientation has not come about: the financial crisis, the escalation in Kosovo and the ensuing war have wholly captured general attention.

Work however proceeds on certain elements of the strategy debate, especially as the need for strategic orientation is something, which is irrefutable. The new project in Dragash, for example, requires a planned, well thought-out foundation, since it is here that the Balkan Peace Team has for the first time directly involved itself in a large project organisation having a correspondingly large team to manage things.

In November 2000, a debate is opened in which the guiding themes of 'Goals and Principles' set up in the early years are now subjected to critical examination. At this point, all the questions which have accrued over the last few years now present themselves: the necessity of a new orientation in the post-war situation; the need for limitation and clarification of the mandate, and the question: Is one to be considered as a coalition or a project? During this discussion, the Balkan Peace Team recognises itself as an organisation, which provides for volunteers to be sent into crisis regions and thereby intends at the same time to transform conflicts. What this assumption actually means remains open-ended. Before an answer can be given, the Balkan Peace Team folds.

Sources

BPT no date, ca 3.95; 5.99, Evaluation; BPT CC minutes, 20.-22.2.98, 6; 10.-12.9.99; 19.11.2000; BPT CC/GA minutes, 13.-14.6.98, 1, 14f.; BPT CC Edgar E., 6.3.2000; BPT Field 17.2.97; BPT GA minutes, 19.-21.11.98, 8; 20.-21.11.99; 12.2.2000; 18.-19.11.2000; Büttner, 3.11.97; Interview Albert P. 1/1997; 2/1998; Anselm F. 1997; Charles O. 1997; Chris N. 1997; Claire P. 1998; Daniel M. 1/1997; Diana M. 1998; Ernst V. 1997; Felix P. 1998; Frances E. 1998; Friedhelm D. 2/1998; Hanna L. 1997; Jacques B. 1998; Katrin G. 1/1997;Laura Z. 1998; Mary F. 1997; Nadine O. 1997; Nicole M. 1997; Rosa T. 1997; Sara F. 1998; Simone V. 1997; Tobias K. 1/1997; Valeska C., 2/1998; Verena J., 1/1997; Volker Q. 1997; Xaver A. 1997; OtOc 11.-13.12.95.

(3) How is Co-operation Organised? Co-ordination and Task-sharing

In autumn, 1994, the Balkan Peace Team receives its 'International Office' (IO), situated in the small town of Minden in Westphalia, together with its first appointed co-ordinator. The announcement, *"High expectations, low salary"* fails to put him off. On the contrary, he finds the idea stimulating. Looking back, he refers to himself as the *"man of the moment"* who gives form to what he saw as a *"gigantic vacuum"*. His talent for organisation, a quality which, at the selection committee, was something placed rather low on the scale of qualifications required, finally proved itself to be a key factor.

Up to that time the project was directed by a co-founder who co-ordinated activities *"from my room in Cologne"*. The room in which the project began to unfold, the 'vacuum' was shared by the co-ordinator and the Co-ordinating Committee. They then developed a scheme of sharing of tasks whose main responsibilities were changed from time to time according to where the greatest need lay at that moment for the paid personnel. If, in those early days, the agreement was that the job of co-ordination should undertake everything which is not otherwise delegated, then 1995 was the year when it only accorded one priority: to raise funds, funds and more funds!

1994-1996: From the Myth of Equality to Departmentalised Project Organisation

The picture that participants have of the beginnings is one where *"everyone has done everything. 'Everyone' in those days... was just five people responsible for the organisation's main functions.... This was the Co-ordinating Committee and those who virtually brought the project into being and who, in the first phase, had to develop the project."* This attitude is one that has rubbed off on the concept of itself as an organisation and is underpinned by the conviction that *"we are all equal in our view and in our practice – from the co-ordinator via the volunteers to the CC members."* This view does not correspond to reality, because there have been co-ordination structures and selective distribution of work since 1993. Team members and members of the Co-ordinating Committee have different roles and different tasks to fulfil which, at least to some extent, have been set down in black and white. They can never be thought of as equal. The claim that all those participating have the same rank camouflages the fact that there are hierarchies and also a 'division of labour'. Really, it is only the self-imposed myth among members in the terms described above which adamantly refuses to accept the reality of the situation.

With the deployment of teams in Croatia, and the first team beginnings in Kosovo, the project as a whole has experienced a dynamic phase of growth. From one meeting to another, the Co-ordinating Committee - like a government - develops new courses of direction and procedures, which have a lasting effect. Responsibilities and operations are regulated, and, as a result of this, new forms of co-operation are developed which, at the end of 1995, finally coalesce into new structures. Taking leave of the myth that everyone is equal is felt to be a loss. *"It had a lot of wonderful aspects about it and in fact bore fruit, but, finally, it failed."*

On the other hand, what has happened was a necessary process of differentiation, which finally produced the distribution of work and an intensified co-ordination. *"At the beginning we had a Co-ordinating Committee, a team, an office, really quite primitive and then at the end, we had for certain about twenty internal abbreviations for clearly defined structures, all of which had their respective authorised powers."*

Three levels then take form and are appropriated to different committees. The General Assembly and the Co-ordinating Committee are the upper, formal and also the essential capacities in decision making. Sub-groups are formed to undertake the complex of tasks affecting training, personnel, and finances. Croatia and Kosovo also have their own sub-committees. Together with the International Office, these are the levels at which ideas are put into practice. The third level is constituted from in the first place one, then two and finally three team offices in Croatia, Serbia and Kosovo. Later, a Sub-group is formed for dealing with publicity work and, from time to time, another liaison comes into existence as a connecting point between the International Office and the Co-ordinating Committee; the basis structure of the organisation is completed by 1995. This phase of differentiation runs through the Balkan Peace Team within the first two years and, with it, certain advantages.

The communication channels are so organized that enquiries can be answered within a reasonable time. A simple example from daily activities suffices to show how this was achieved in the early days when electronic communication such as e-mail and fax, standby online and SMS were not the privilege of everyone to possess. *"The teams make an urgent enquiry on Wednesday, say, and this arrives per e-mail on Thursday morning. Unfortunately in this case, that's a public holiday in Germany and the co-ordinator is off duty. It is then read on Friday morning and forwarded. The last people in the Co-ordinating Committee receive it perhaps on Monday, Tuesday, Wednesday and thereafter answer it. In the meantime, 12 to 14 days have passed until the team has answer to its emergency enquiry, and that just won't do.*" If another round of urgent questions follows the first, then the chaos is complete. *"Sometimes they receive the third reply before even having read the second question!"*

The Co-ordinating Committee, which meets up to six times a year, and nevertheless is tardy in keeping abreast with decisions, is, as a result of the new distribution of tasks, noticeably relieved. Now, with only four meetings, which each last for two days, there is, room at them to discuss matters of content, such as the development of strategy for example. The distribution of work is a relief for everyone. Instead of *"eighty e-mails per month, there are now only fifteen"* to deal with, but these are those that individuals can really tackle properly.

With the new structure, the International Office receives a new task. It is able to bundle together information, which is then discussed in the various Sub-groups. The 'IO News', which is a short list regularly informing its readers of what is being carried on where becomes *"the only common knowledge"* when there are no meetings. The IO News sets norms in that it announces the results of coordinating processes which are afterwards valid so long as they do not arouse protest elsewhere. On top of this, each meeting, be it CC or GA, starts with a review and confirmation of decisions made in the meantime by this procedure. The co-ordinator in the International Office is to be the watchdog over procedures and communication. He is allowed to intervene when it is noticed that the same question is being dealt with in two parallel groups. The International Office becomes the collective memory of commonly agreed upon decisions. In 1996, formalisation becomes part of many new papers so that those new to the organisation can familiarize themselves with what has been agreed upon.

Despite this, there still remains enough room for misunderstanding. Despite the wide, general agreement on values, this international project comes up against quite different organisational cultures and personally accepted norms of conduct and thinking which then cross swords in the International Office as the co-ordinator knows only too well: *"I would say that during the general run of daily routine, the cultural differences between, say, French Catholics, Mennonites from the Netherlands, German alternatives and American 'who knows what other people' are already so large that they lead to misunderstanding, to different ways of looking at things and to wrong as-*

sumptions about the motives of the other, and this is a day-to-day phenomenon."* The general, workaday lingua franca of English in its Italian, Swiss, French, German, Irish, American, Netherlands and British variations – to mention only the most common – is enough to lead to *"the most vehement linguistic misunderstandings"*. When we also take into consideration the fact that e-mails as a medium of communication is not the most desirable by which nuances of expression can be conveyed, then it will be clear what challenges are inherent in keeping this interplay of cultures free from friction. The co-ordinator however adds that, *"the Balkan Peace Team is the only organisation I know where getting on with each other was such that, so to speak, everyone could have a say...."*

The Weight of Too Much Work and the Assumption of Responsibility

Even after the careful differentiation of structures, committees and communication routines have been established, there is still a basic problem at hand, which weighs heavily on the International Office and Co-ordinating Committee. The six to eight people active in the latter still assist in dealing with administrative work, because the financial situation will not run to the employment of more qualified personnel in the International Office. It comes about therefore that professional people and those in honorary positions belonging to other organisation find themselves saddled with a long list of tasks to do for the Balkan Peace Team. In connection with introduction of sub-committees, the number of members in the Co-ordinating Committee is augmented. At the same time, there is a determined effort to employ women, an undertaking which bears fruit. At the end of 1996, there are for the first time more women in the Co-ordinating Committee than men, and where one co-ordinator recalls, *"indeed one can say that a 'womanly presence' has returned to the place,"* and adds, *"something which is certainly noticeable to those outside."*

The heavy workload is thereby not reduced. What once assisted the International Peace Brigades, that is, the recruitment of former volunteers for work on the project is something that fails on several occasions for the Balkan Peace team. Those who don't work in intimate connection with the structures with others, gradually get out of touch, can no longer keep up with the flow of information, and finally lose the feeling for that which is currently relevant. Keeping up contacts means, in effect, running after information, and in the structures, too, people can only keep up with things through experience and in contact with an organisation allied to that idea, and also equipped with organisational support. *"Without this, it's pretty difficult"*, a volunteer concludes who himself had worked for three consecutive years as the only independent individual member in the Co-ordinating Committee.

Over the years, some members of the Co-ordinating Committee find themselves cut adrift from their institutional bearings when they leave office positions given them during their employment with member organisations. Others represent their organisations as honorary employees in their free time.

Finally, however, volunteers gradually grow into their responsibilities. Sebastian K. is one example of this. He worked for six months during 1996 as a volunteer with the International Office in Minden. He underwent training and visited the offices in Croatia. In this way he was able to gain an idea of what the work of the teams was about. The Balkan Peace Team remained an abstraction for him for all this time until, at a General Assembly, he was able to personally encounter in *"flesh and blood"* what had hitherto been mere names on e-mails, *"and that was a good thing"*, he said. After his active period in the office, he then slipped into the filing data as a 'former volunteer', which cuts him off from the flow of information and so sees no chance anymore of being able to play an active role within the organisation. His proposals to the International Office find no reciprocation. He is just about to lose contact when there is an enquiry from a member of the Co-ordinating Committee. *"I'm going to leave; do you want to take over my job?"* It concerns the co-ordination of training programmes. After brief reflection, Sebsatian K. accepts the offer and agrees to be elected on to the Co-ordinating Committee, since it isn't possible to look after such an undertaking without being part of the structure. Later, he undertakes other responsibilities, as treasurer, for example, and jumps in to help elsewhere when urgent need arises.

Other former volunteers place themselves at the Team's disposal over the years as trainers or are employed as explorers. One such former volunteer, who is still in Croatia, puts himself at the disposal of the North-Croatian team in the spring of 1998. He evaluates how work there is to be continued. Another, volunteer supports the teams as an advisor. Others still – above all a number from the Netherlands – work in the supporting groups of the Balkan Peace Team. Detailed, purposeful co-operational work is possible and allows the project to continue to exist over this long period of time. However, the question in the forefront of these events is how the work can be passed through the needle's eye of the International Office.

1997-1998: Co-ordinating Committee - Self-management is Requested

The summer of 1996 brings the hope for a short time of being able to appropriately stock up on the workforce of the International Office. Extraordinary favourable financial conditions would continue to allow the co-ordinator, who has been working there up to now, to be paid on an hourly basis. The position is then to be occupied by another via a further work deployment measure. Added to this, a volunteer can be employed for the office. The plan falls through because the co-operation envisaged is not realised. The overload continues.

The succeeding co-ordinator sees herself as a the executor of decisions made, and has to adjust herself to an expanded structure in which she realises that she has little leeway as far as fulfilling her ambitions for re-design are concerned. She is responsible for looking after the teams, and for special tasks she has partners to whom she can appeal for help and who, according to her estimation, are more or less reliable. A criterion by which she can judge is, for her, whether and how she can be relieved wholly or in part of extra work. Individual tasks such as minutes of meetings she can deliver as well as simplify the work of dealing with financial balance sheets. As before, here, many areas of work are welded into one. Principal areas of attention vary according to what has priority at this moment. The limits of her working capacity are, according to her, neither regarded nor appreciated. She finds that the work of decision-making is ineffective. *"There is always the tendency not to make a decision, that one discusses everything, that one turns everything over and over again, and that every decision must be reached in consensus."*

For the members of the Co-ordinating Committee, the problem lies elsewhere. The IO News ceases publication in 1997. For the CC members, the Sub-groups are no longer effective, because, they say, the flow of information is no longer reliable and contact between the International Office and Sub-groups no longer functions. Since, therefore, one no longer gets to know what has happened in the meantime, personal meetings and encounters as the only place where information can be exchanged becomes more important – and the need to talk correspondingly greater there.

That work which has not been covered by the International Office lands for the most part at the feet of members of the Co-ordinating Committee. People as a rule see service in at least another Sub-group and have several areas of responsibility. One member, for example, in the winter of 1997, has the following schedule: On the whole, he works between five and ten hours per week on average for the Balkan Peace Team.

Sometimes, in the case of special crises or where there are special tasks to be performed on behalf of the whole organisation, such as the coming assessment, the preparation of a concept for debate on structure or at a sitting of the Co-ordinating Committee, all his time is dedicated to the affairs of the Balkan Peace team. He is not contented with this situation. The Co-ordinating Committee is too little concerned with the vital job of guiding the ship because it is too much bound up with its other responsibilities. The division of labour is only rudimentary and only works here and there and now and again. Tasks, which are accorded to others, are not fulfilled. Progress in some areas is set against regression in others. Interfaces are foggy.

Here, there is a 'black hole' wherein all those things in particular vanish on those occasions where people say: *"Not me!"* In the forefront is material, things like cars, for example. In the matter of collecting money, everyone, on the one hand, promises an amount, and yet, on the other, everyone knows that it will not be enough. In the matter, too, of contacts with interested parties, interfaces are again obscure. Someone who undertakes things which no one else wants to do is Claire: *"On the outside we are always the big show; we are a good coalition here, but it needs a lot of pushing and trying to get things organized."*

What there is to organize and how difficult it actually is to realise a distribution of work that functions reciprocally and interconnectedly is supplied by a glance at a meeting taking place in January 1998. It concerns the Balkan Peace Team, Netherlands, at a regular sitting. For roughly three hours, the four members present go through the tasks pending. Two of these are former volunteers; another is a member of the Co-ordinating Committee. Two people are absent due to illness. The one is a member of the 'Stichting Nederland steunt Balkan Peace Team', the Dutch money collecting point, while the other, as honorary assistant, concerns himself with a circular for the Balkan Peace Team.

The tasks fulfilled since last time are recapitulated. Some have already been dealt with, while some are still open. Today, those at the table are concerned with the performance of the Balkan Peace Team in the media. Up-to-date articles are lacking, and it is difficult to write them. One reason for this is that team reports are in part confidential, and another is that they are to an extent too specialised, and as such do not present themselves as suitable material for publication. As a first step, articles at hand are translated. In future, a colleague in the Co-ordinating Committee is to be asked whether he can produce articles. The team members are not responsible for writing articles. *"They already have enough to write,"* say those who, from their own experience, should know. The group here, too, cannot tackle an article, because it is not in possession of the facts, and not au fait with developments to date on the work of the teams and the situation generally. This can only be done by someone in the Co-ordinating Committee who knows what is going on and who is near enough to the teams and their work. In other words, there is no forthcoming solution to the problem, but only a start. We proceed with publicity. The most recent circular is at the home of the sick colleague; the address distributor is also at this address, as well as the translation job, so that nothing can be done in that direction at the moment.

What's new from the teams and from the International Office? Not everybody has had a chance yet to read all the reports. The coordinator in the International Office is brooding over the bill for an old contract, which has to be processed again. *"Everything else threatens to be left undone"*, she warns in a fax. The training planned to take place in the USA has been cancelled, interested applications to International Office have not been answered. Applications were made to members of this group in Holland, which cannot be answered because the information has been out of date for some time. Equally invalid, because they are out of date, is information regarding the financial situation, so that new applications to ministries and foundations, cannot be carried out in time either.

In March, an assessment is planned, and selection meeting at which those interested in working as volunteers for the Balkan Peace Team can decide for themselves whether this is the place for them. There are only two applications for this at the moment and so the situation is critical; in less than eight weeks things will begin. Without applicants' documents and details being sent on time, there will be no assessment. Then there will be no training and, subsequently, no future volunteers. For a moment or two there is a pause in which no one knows what to do. Then, gradually, ideas are forthcoming. It is decided that one member of the group should travel to Minden – with the 'Interregio' express, a matter of less than four hours – in order to get to grips with the application papers. The day appointed for the journey to Minden is in February with the consequence that a whole stack of information enquiries waiting can be dealt with after all.

These passing insights make the weaknesses and the strengths of the Balkan Peace Team at this time pretty clear. Many ends can't be tied up, and should really be carefully tied up, if the many participating positions are to work in accord with one another. Very much later, when the newsletter is brought to life again in the International Office, the co-ordinators reflect on this re-integrated issue as follows:

> *"It seems that one of the biggest difficulties in producing the newsletter is coordinating the timing of various steps. Starting with the writing of articles, editing them, layout, choosing pictures and graphics, printing, packaging and mailing it. If we do not have a clear, scheduled procedure that is acceptable and followed by the various participants in the production process, the newsletter will continue to be a very stressful operation with many delays. From the editing to the final mailing took 6 weeks. This could be shortened greatly in the future with a workable timeline."*

What is said of the process of producing the Newsletter is a prime example of much of the self-organized co-operation in the international project, Balkan Peace Team. The art of re-organisation time and time again, and in so doing in the best case to optimally employ the respective, comparable advantages of so many different participants, is one of its strengths.

1998-2001: Re-organisation and Small Steps towards New Responsibility

In summer, 1998, the Balkan Peace Team is confronted once again with change in the International Office. It turns out that there will be no suitable successor on the basis of a publicly supported position. In the meantime, members jump in to help manage the secretary's office and deal with finances. From February 1999, a solution is found in which the Balkan Peace Team manages to occupy the International Office with the help of its own resources and without the need to employ external personnel anymore. Employed on a part-time basis, but in fact doing the work of two, full-time jobs, Oskar K. and Ellen B. undertake the job of re-organising the International Office.

In February 1999, they take up the tradition of IO News, this time, however, as a kind of report on activity before the sittings of the Co-ordinating Committee or before that of the General Assembly respectively. In this, they critically review the capacity to decide in general and the sense of responsibility in particular. Both are submitted to scrutiny. There is a double structure in which the executive body of the association, registered as 'The Balkan Peace Team' has legal responsibility, but must cede political decision to the Co-ordinating Committee. The co-ordinators in the International Office have no power of attorney and are not authorized to act in the name of the

Balkan Peace Team. This disadvantage has to be got out of the way. At one of the next sittings, another decision-making procedure will be laid down which must take account of the fact that there is always less money at hand than expected for what has been planned, and that therefore priorities must be set. These small moves help to establish clear rules for action, and at the same time, provide more transparency.

During re-organisation, it comes to notice that there are documents with contradictory interpretations for concrete questions. In clearing the office, documents appear whose status is not clear. This newly developing memory with regard to institutional matters in re-organising the International Office stimulates the need for a clarification of 'policy papers' at the end of November, 2000. Critical reflection of the work of the International Office coincides with the running debate on the renewal of the project structures as a whole. The debate on structures since 1997 is an attempt to gain a greater degree of freedom of action in certain sectors, and to give more competence both to new people as well as those who have been active for longer.

At the General Assembly in November 1999, questions were put forward about the desired new structures in connection with the content. In September 2000, a long list of deficiencies was drawn up by the Co-ordinating Committee in which the structures were seen as too complex, incomprehensible, inefficient, too slow, opaque as far as their role was concerned, and without relevance to a strategy. In October 2000, a Subgroup then drew up proposals to be considered in November at the General Assembly. These were the first steps to bring the association's Board of Directors into the arena, to encourage the membership of individuals, and to assure an encouraging environment for those who were already committed to the cause. In the subsequent discussion, however, it soon became clear that this was not the expected breakthrough.

The Weak Link: The relationship between the Teams and the International Office

The most tense relationships have been developing between the teams and the International Office. The accompaniment of the team members in their practical work does not belong to the tasks of the first co-ordinator. In the case of the successor to the co-ordinator, the personal guidance and care of the teams belongs partly to the prescribed list of duties. Teams and International Office meet one another there, however, as counterparts when it comes to the allocation of duties and decisions about minor matters. In this case, the International Office assumes its demanding role as decision-maker, and sometimes volunteers give vent to their frustration. The relationship becomes critical – regardless of persons in the co-ordination department – at the point where matters turn upon the question of statements and expenses and bank transfers, as well as explanations for this or that amount. In every co-ordination epoch there is stress between the teams and the International Office concerning bookkeeping. And on every occasion, the co-ordinators in the International Office feel left alone in the matter by the Co-ordinating Committee.

With this in mind, then is it a matter of pure co-incidence that the last quarrel to blow up in the Balkan Peace Team started here? Money apparently plays a special role on which it would sensible to reflect. The teams need money for their project and for the freedom to act and negotiate. Booking expenses is an irksome duty whose purpose is not comprehensible to volunteers. Receipts are not always submitted in the completeness demanded. The teams have the right to be supplied with money from their organisation so that they can do their job! If the money is not transferred in time, the job doesn't go forward! One could see the situation this way as the teams struggle with the way money should be handled. They see themselves obliged to carry out their jobs. The organisation owes them better management in this respect.

On the other hand, the International Office sits at the other end of the spectrum when it comes to being responsible for money. It is here that account must be submitted to donors for money spent. To put the matter in a nutshell: the project is a good one when everything balances nicely financially! How otherwise can money be requested if, in spending it, there is no resort to flawless proof of how it has been spent? For this, the International Office is directly responsible to the donors. And, conversely, the teams owe them good management!

These, perhaps, are the two sides of a coin. The breaking point comes when it has to be decided which party has priority. Is it more important, say, to observe events at the next demonstration in Prishtina or somewhere else or to sort through the mounting heap of receipts that have been lying around for the last three months?

Sources

BPT CC minutes 5.-7.9.94; 20.-22.2.98; 4.-6.9.98, 2, 10f., 5; 20.11.98; 19.-21.2.99; 28.-30.5. 99; 12.-14.9.99; 5.-7.5.2000; 8.-10.9.2000; CC/GA minutes 13.-14.6.98, 10; BPT GA minutes 20.-21.11.98, 4, 1; 20.-21.11.99; 12.2.2000; 18.-19.11.2000; BPT IO, 14.10.96; 4.9.97; 25.5.99, IO News 35; Interview Albert P. 2/1998; Charles O. 1997; Claire P. 1998; Friedhelm D. 1/1997; 2/1998; Jacques B. 1998; Monique Z.; Sabine M. 1997; Sebastian K. 1998; Simone V. 1997; Müller, personal records 30.1.98.

(4) All About Volunteers

The Balkan Peace Team is an organisation, which despatches volunteers to crisis areas. A small budget requires that which is concerned with co-ordination be largely self-organised when it comes to finding suitable candidates, organising their selection, preparation, placement and accompaniment to their area of service. The International Office is particularly involved with making first contacts and finding candidates for service. In 1999, there were 250 enquiries from people who had for the most part heard of the work of the Balkan Peace Team via its own websites, and those of the International Peace Brigades, and who wanted to know more. From this number, between 20 and 30 actually apply. The co-ordinator then seeks interviewers to go through a questionnaire. Later, two trainings are organised for successful candidates.

All volunteers must spend an orientation day in the International Office. A similar relationship between enquiry and application has been known since its inception in the first two years, namely, 1994-96. The co-ordinator had contact during this period with approximately 500 people. They are interested in the BPT and some of them are rather frustrated because they cannot travel to their place of duty immediately, or are in possession of false or out-of-date information. About 50 people are crystallized out of these first contacts as being sufficiently suitable and motivated enough so that they can undergo one of the eight training periods of the first two years.

Altogether, about 50 volunteers did service with the Balkan Peace Team between February 1994 and February 2001. The first were only six months at the scene, but there is a tendency later towards extending service. From February 1995, service with the BPT is officially set at a year. This is because volunteers can fully develop their capacities within that time. A year later, service is lengthened to two years.

This is not to say, though, that all volunteers are enrolled for exactly that period. Work with the Balkan Peace Team is very intensive. After one, one-and-a-half or two years, exhaustion is considerable, and the transition thereafter into normal daily life difficult. Quite a number of volunteers quit service before their contract runs out, especially in the Kosovo team where they found themselves subjected to great pressure. There are cases of earlier departure in the Croatian teams, too, but there mainly because of dissension having arisen within the team. There are no regulated means by which personnel can leave before the end of the term assigned to them. This is a matter left to the crisis mechanism of the teams or the Sub-groups.

A large number of volunteers after service remain true to their former commitments, and many carry on working in the region, in this case for organisations such as the OSCE, organisations allied to the UN or others. For these, the Balkan Peace Team is the start of a career, and such a project serves, as one co-ordinator has put it, as a *"career catapult"*.

For local activists, this network of trusted colleagues who move on to responsible positions in powerful organisations is of great advantage, because then *"they are again with us, and we again cooperate with them, although they are a part of other organisations"*.

How do Volunteers Come to Work in the BPT?

There are several ways to become aware of the Balkan Peace Team. There are the specialist homepages, but there is also a widely spread advertisement programme of member organisations. It is in this way that Frances came to the BPT. During her researches in the USA, she came across the info-page of the International Fellowship of Reconciliation, enquired at the International Office for more information, and was later asked to attend an interview. Another possibility is that of direct application via a member organisation. The Austrian Peace Services as an institution, which has an interest in maintaining its own volunteers in the Balkan Peace Team is one such. The Brethren Volunteers Service continually sends volunteers who do two years' service with the Balkan Peace Team. The teams in Croatia advertise themselves among other international volunteers within their own transmission range.

That age group between 25 and 35 is, according to the co-ordinator, particularly open-minded to the work of the Balkan Peace Team. The training is completed, but the choice of a profession not finally determined. At the same time it is clear that, for the person concerned, this is to be a temporary, transitional phase.

The Balkan Peace Team, too, has its own ideas about whom it wants to employ as volunteers. Above all, it wants qualified women. The understanding that women have equal rights plays just as important a role as the organisation's capacity to deploy women in the field. Women's groups are important target groups; many organisations are run by women. The first recruitment campaign for volunteers in autumn, 1994, happily brought in many volunteers; most of them, however, were young men. In the first team there is one woman and the other three are men. On the first training course, there is the situation of one woman and nine men. In the recruitment campaigns it is found that, on average, only a third are women who apply. The co-ordinator, in commenting on this, says: *"And when we've sent out the papers, then from this one third women who ask at all in the first place they, too, in nine out of ten of cases have disappeared!"*

For women who are inclined to the feminist view, the fact that men in the Balkan Peace Team dominate all the committees could well be an unattractive prospect. This is the critical view of one woman on a training course - and once again the only woman in the group - and also that of later volunteers. This is a problem, and the need for female volunteers increases. As much for the team start in Kosovo as for the first team change in Croatia, experienced women were needed. At the turn of the year, in 1994, women were then targeted as potential volunteers. Women are presented prominently in leaflets about BPT and women applicants were favoured, contacted and telephoned. In order to interview women applicants, greater expense in travelling here and there was taken into account. It was made clear to them that places in the team would be left open when they happened not to be occupied by women. This strategy, signalling a serious interest in the recruitment of women, was crowned with success and a development of which the co-ordinator of that time was very proud. The ratio of the sexes during training did an about turn, and at the beginning of 1996, a genuine selection between women applicants was made possible. And at the end of this year, it became necessary to earnestly target men!

By the end of 1996, the main elements of selection comprise four points. In the first place, volunteers must register their motivation, experience and previous knowledge in a questionnaire. Interesting candidates are then invited to interview. After gaining a positive impression this during a talk, invitation to training follows, and finally reference persons indicated in the application forms are also taken into account.

The Decision: From Training to Assessment

In the first place, training serves both the process of selection as well as a preparation for service, and in this it follows the example of the International Peace Brigades. The process has its deceptive aspects, however, as one trainer points out after having trained many people for the Balkan Peace Team. For him, the processes of maturity which are promoted by training do not fit in with a subjectively experienced examination situation in which at least one phase of one's own life is decided upon. One volunteer, on the other hand, for example, found her training of great help to her. This consisted of a 14-day course consisting of teaching units of human rights, dealing with conflict situation involving the playing of roles which, above all, concerned the management of violence. The process of selection has not remained in her memory as something of a problem. According to her, those responsible for decisions on acceptance or non-acceptance from the Co-ordinating Committee made the correct assessments as to who was suitable and who not, even when this was hard to digest for those unable to make the grade.

This process of selection becomes critical when certain applicants do not have to submit themselves to decisions while on training, since they have been selected for other reasons, say, as a result of an arrangement between member organisations. This, too, frequently happens and is cause for irritation among other participants. Added to this is also the eventuality that different people have a different opinion about the status of a volunteer, and when it comes to the training it is not clear any longer who said what about whom. This will be a *"pretty frequent problem for the Balkan Peace team over the next few years"*, says one trainer who is fairly regularly exposed to this problem and is frequently left with its consequences.

For those taking part in training, pre-selection increases the pressure of competition when, for example, of three free places suddenly only two become available, one of which is reserved for a woman and five men compete for one really free place in the team. This situation is aggravated when the eventuality is not clear beforehand, so that someone can consider the possibility of later training when the chances of acceptance are greater. The same happens when a previously selected volunteer fails to leave a very good impression on those on the course with him or her, and the question of quality standards is thrown up.

From the summer, 1996, efforts are made to replace distinction via selection by an assessment, and preparation by training. So it is that by 1997 this then becomes general practice. The new concept envisages a suitability test spread over several days and the assessment is to take place in a training and conference house called 'Expeditie' in Holland. The essence of the course turns upon dealing with stress and the ability to work as a team. There are information units on the Balkan Peace Team and its work, and the test consists of *"long role-playing"*. The inventor of this has remarked that, *"This begins in the evening. The people, i.e. the assessment participants for a Balkan Peace Team, each being part of a group, say, of three and this goes on right* through the night until late the following morning. In this way, one test everything they have learned. How do you introduce yourself? How do you behave at a police razzia? What do you say and not say when you go over the border? What do you take with you and what not?" In games such as this, the characteristics of those interested are shown during teamwork and in tricky situations. Has one here to do with an individualist? Are the people still in control of the situation? Are they in danger of 'burn-out'? Are they paralysed by fear or can they think of something? In the course of time, there develops a clear, inner feeling which those who are judging will have learnt to follow. The decision that a person is not suitable closes a door for that person. With the development of assessment and testing techniques, the Balkan Peace Team reaches its optimum standard of assessment whereby volunteers can be chosen.

Training Courses Responding to Changes in Demand

Training programmes, seen as an element in preparation, provide a good mirror reflecting how large the gaps are between concept and reality, and also show how practice itself changes. The first team later finds fault with the training in that they feel that human rights, dialogue and a sense of cultural sensitivity has fallen short of their expectations. Someone from the region itself was lacking, and so practical matters such as 'How does one introduce oneself?', 'How does one make contact?' and strategical thinking fall short of the mark. As one of the volunteers happens to come across his own training record, he is able to see and compare what has become of many a principle and discerns right away what a gap there is between the 'basic rules' making up the content of the teaching programme, and the reality experienced on the scene. At the turn of the year, 1995-96, the Team has the impression that in the recruitment of volunteers, there is something else suggested than that which volunteers are confronted with, and feel that they would like to see the work presented more honestly.

The Team as training requirements articulates new, up-to-date questions. One of these, for example, is that of sexual harassment. The Kosovo team cannot see its reality reflected hardly at all during training. The examples presented come from what has been experienced in Croatia. In 1997, training programmes are undergone in the region itself, for example, in Ossijek. After 1998, there is co-operation with the Croatian training group, 'Centre for Peace Studies', about which Jacques is very pleased, because *"those working in Yugoslavia have gone through training programmes from all over the world: if there's anyone who knows all about the approaches to training, then it is they!"* In the Autumn of 1998, structural problems demand a fresh look at training programmes.

With little money and few volunteers, BPT training at home is jettisoned in favour of suggesting that volunteers undergo their training on the scene. Training-in-the-field actually begins in the summer of the same year when a meeting of the team is combined with a day of training on mediation. New volunteers are trained by team members on the spot, both before and after the team meeting. The hitherto accepted understanding that two weeks' training is necessary seems now no longer to be valid. One tends more and more to convey the needs of volunteers during training and to thoroughly think out what these essential requirements are so as to re-shape training programmes.

In February 1999, a new training concept embodies an integrated approach covering all aspects of selection, introduction, preparation, qualification during the time with the team and individual accompaniment. However, the diminishing number of teams puts paid to this idea. Since the assessments reliably see to it that sufficient new volunteers are at hand, it seems that home training programmes, seen as indispensable preparation, are beginning to lose their validity.

Pooling, Placing and Tailored Transitions

Training programmes and later assessments are, so to speak, an access to the 'pool' of volunteers. However, the need to adjust to the requirements of the team, the volunteers and the Balkan Peace Team standards is an art in itself. Different expectations have to be taken into account. The Balkan Peace Team needs a pool of trained people from which it can choose a few weeks or months in advance when necessary. Volunteers for their part need scheduled and realistic perspectives in regard to their deployment within a given time. And the teams want to be certain that service periods overlap as well as to be able to make a note of those whom they would prefer from the pool.

In the period between 1994 and 1996, it is decided at the end of training who will be taken into the pool if it has not already been arranged. The flow of information is difficult to organise in such a way that information coming in from training programmes into the Co-ordinating Committee is correct and doesn't clash with other information that might be in circulation. Information coming in frequently does not have the quality required by the Co-ordinating Committee, which could assist it in the process of selection. It is difficult, too, to co-ordinate training and the need for replacement in the teams. The two follow different rules. Training programmes need a minimum number of participants, otherwise they have to be postponed. This causes a difficult situation at the end of 1994, because at that time volunteers need to be replaced urgently, but because the scheduled training programme possessed too few enrolments, there was no pool of potential replacement volunteers. Unexpected withdrawals from already placed volunteers constitute another problem at this time considering the inadequate personnel situation. In such a case, suitable people are sought and, although this is against the rules, there is the thought of sending untrained people to the teams simply to fill an unseemly gap.

The varying demands of the teams, the organisation and potential volunteers is a matter that can hardly be harmonized. Potential volunteers want to know who has been pre-selected when new volunteers are needed and when the next training will take place in order to assess their own chances and plan matters accordingly. This information, however, will not be forthcoming, because the Balkan Peace Team doesn't know in the first place whether all the places in a training programme will be occupied, and in the second, whether the applications made to it correspond with its expectations, and, in the third, because free places can only be allotted when team members inform the BPT long beforehand when they intend to leave – and also keep to their intentions. Finally, it is also possible that the internal dynamics of project development – especially that in Kosovo – could overturn any kind of previous planning.

The effect of this is that the overlap time in the teams no longer exists and, with it, the possibility of introducing training and also the orientation of the new. At the beginning of 1996, it looks as though for the third time a volunteer will be working alone in the Croatian 'team' in Split when a newcomer arrives. From the point of view of the trainers it seems almost as if there is an exceptional provision for every volunteer, and so the impression arises that principles are not adhered to in general. On the other hand, it can be that standardisation is not the answer to the problem either. Every subsequent replacement is apparently something of an adaptation, a tailor-made fit, as it were, that must be implemented to suit every individual and account for all the variable factors.

Very gradually, usable standards begin to become evident for the flow of information issuing from experience with the preparation and invitation to training. The kind of placement is adjusted again and again. At first, members of the personnel group allocate new volunteers to the teams by their written applications without having first having made their acquaintance. This is something which is certainly not uncommon. When the assessments are introduced, Claire, from the personnel group, conducts the selection interviews with a colleague from the Co-ordinating Committee who is also engaged in making assessments.

The question as to which new volunteers will fit into which team will be considered during the interview between each respective Sub-group appointed for Croatia or Kosovo. The teams, too, are involved here, but possess only a fraction of the information available about the person being interviewed. In spring, 1998, this agreement had taken on the character of a declaration of need. The Kosovo team had special demands of its own for its team members, and a kind of priority of choice with regard to those volunteers at disposal. At this point of time, the Kosovo team wanted a woman, preferably a US American, because of their good contacts with the American embassy. The teams from Otvorene Oci at this moment still cannot decide and report their needs immediately afterwards.

The severity of the problem of finding persons at the right time who are suited to the needs of the team seems in later years to moderate in view of the separation of training and assessment. And also in view of the fact that there is direct personal contact between potential volunteers and those who decide on their future. The continuity of personnel probably contributes to this decline, inasmuch as those responsible have developed a sense in the course of time for the necessarily rough-and-ready indications of the teams about their needs, and so bring these requirements into line with the profile of the volunteers in the pool.

What Is To Be Done When Things Fail to Fall into Line? Managing Conflicts within the Team

On one or two occasions, situations arise where team members gain the impression that a new colleague is not suitable for the work. What is to be done here? An initial evaluation is introduced after three months, which completes the probation phase. This could be a means for a genuine, mutual test, but in effect does not come to anything. There is no means of registering a 'formal complaint' in such a situation. The volunteers do not find the Co-ordinating Committee acting as a kind of counterpart to take over responsibility in situations such as these. As a consequence, the problem is somehow resolved internally and the result is private injury and bad feeling.

The presence among the teams of differing quality expectations, incompatible ways of working and also basic attitudes towards work and rest provides enough possibility for irritation and conflict. This kind of thing eats away at the energy of volunteers and is very often reason enough for them to terminate their service prematurely.

Members of the Co-ordinating Committee and those in the Sub-groups certainly see themselves as active in solving such problems. They complain, for instance, that they are often informed of conflict too late, and so cannot intervene in time to assist. Much therefore remains within the team and is regulated there. If it turns out that the matter can't be put right within the team and the Sub-group is requested to step in and negotiate, it is often too late. The volunteers are left with the feeling that in such situations the Balkan Peace Team is irresponsible and hypocritical.

One member of the Sub-group, Charles, has drawn experience his own conclusions about intervention which is not particularly successful and therefore attempts to 'inoculate' new volunteers as soon as possible by saying, *"Right: what I say to all the new recruits is – and that three times – at the beginning, in words and in writing and in general to them all is: 'When you, my friends, don't tell me what's the matter, then of course I don't know what's the matter. So, please, tell me what's the matter!'"* Here, too, of course, it is a case of whether personal acquaintance has provided a basis for trust or not which makes the difference. This is the decisive factor. A volunteer will use this bridge of communication and in this way feel that she is taken seriously, and that in this way the difficult starting phase can be overcome.

Living and Working in the Team - Stress Factors and Personal Accompaniment

There are certain stress factors, which cannot be avoided in working with the Balkan Peace Team. The 'Office' in Prishtina, for example, is in the spring of 1995, also in reality a private room decorated with various things belonging to the host family. While in the Kosovo team in Belgrade, one volunteer, writing at the end of 1996, describes a working day of 17 hours, in incredibly cramped conditions in the apartment. There are no means of withdrawal, since every room is occupied with work. The teams in Croatia experience the same constriction. It is impossible for one to get out somebody else's way, for example, which, in the case where there is emotional tension, demands great self-control. Not only restriction, but also isolation presents a problem.

In many cases, volunteers work alone over several weeks and find themselves submitted to the permanent demands of local activists. The constant need to be on hand over a long period of time is exhausting. The expectation placed upon oneself to be there for their support is also hard on the nerves. In Croatia, after the first team's performance, great expectations were placed on their successors. This was somewhat like a long shadow looming over their work to whose demands the next person was not always willing to conform.

Local activists criticised the Balkan Peace Team for not adequately furnishing volunteers with their material needs. In this, they were thinking of cars and the dangers of accident associated with them. The very fact of not being able to afford enough for working comfort is to put at the door of the Balkan Peace Team, and this in itself provides an element of stress. Here, indeed, we can see where the price is paid when there is not enough money for accommodation, material furnishings and numerically insufficient personnel appropriate to the team's needs.

Other stress factors are to be found in the nature of the work being done, work in a war zone or post-war zone. Devastation and war, the confrontation with dead people are things which are hard to deal with psychologically. It is also extremely hard if not impossible to deal with the acceptance of violence as a means of solving conflict in a society. Feelings of rage, hate and contempt leave deeply rooted impressions on the minds of volunteers. Quite a number of women co-workers in the teams experienced Croatian society as sexist, and male colleagues of partner organisations were not an exception to the rule.

Many of these stress factors are inevitable, but ways to avoid them or to deal with them are nevertheless being sought. How the Balkan Peace Team deals with the deprecatory assessment of women in their own societies and those in which the teams work, is one of those areas that can be properly dealt with inasmuch as women are deliberately sought to serve as volunteers. However, a policy such as this automatically takes into account that the highest level of authority, which foreigners can achieve, will be lacking. A former co-ordinator has briefly listed the attributes needed for this in saying that the 'highest authority' should be male, white, possess a Western passport and be over thirty-five years of age. In order to get to grips with stereotypes, which also, incidentally, determine the relationship between the sexes among the local groups, the teams lay down certain rules on how to behave. In this, the sensibility of the male colleagues in the team is a decisive factor. One woman volunteer has described this in the following way: "When she is in conversation with an activist while the male team colleague is busy with the washing up, is a situation which can be considered as a real support, and one which also undermines male tactics to wait until the woman visits the toilet before talking about relevant matters of strategy".

In order to effectively deal with varying stress factors, it is necessary to cultivate the ability to gain a certain distance between themselves and their circumstances. Again and again, members of the Co-ordinating Committee are obliged to remind volunteers that it is necessary to pursue other interests in life separate from their preoccupation with work, and to maintain these. Free time is recommended in their contract, and volunteers are encouraged to enjoy this. However, this is precisely what they don't do as a rule. In particularly difficult phases such as the conquest of the Krajina region, volunteers seek individual help.

An institutionalised form of getting to know about the emotional position of team members is the column occurring in the 14-day report, 'Hearts and Minds', which goes to the Co-ordinating Committee, but not all team members make friends with this medium. For many, on the other hand, it is a place where they can pour their hearts out and one which they regularly seek. For others, it is a place, which they can use for voicing concrete issues. In a similar way, reports of sexual molestation appearing in the column can serve as a support for volunteers. This, of course, is not in any way a substitute for direct confrontation with the problem. In such cases, volunteers are asked to seek out reliable partners with whom they can speak about such matters.

This can be an acquaintance in the country itself or people concerned with co-ordination in the International Office. This depends on the personal relationship between the volunteer and the co-ordinator, since, strictly speaking, the International Office is not specifically equipped to deal with these issues. The volunteers belonging to the Brethren Volunteer Service who send teams and the Austrian Peace Services both have their own internal mechanisms and specific personnel responsible for the care of volunteers. Regular visits are a part of this care. The same service was once part of the Balkan Peace Team for at least some time, but does not seem to have been adapted as general practice.

Whether the Sub-groups in Croatia and Kosovo can afford this standard of personal accompaniment depends very much on how they understand their job as a member in the Sub-group. In the Sub-group in Croatia, there is a larger need, because the number of volunteers is larger. Moreover, it extends to two offices. The members of the Sub-group see their respective roles in different ways. For the one individual, feedback in reports is a primary concern, and every two weeks is enough to give positive or negative accounts on developments. Another person will feel that the main issue is to develop the contents of the work together with the team. For him, the condition underlying personal accompaniment is that one knows each other personally, and this has only recently been the case. For a time, the only woman in the group who is familiar with personal care takes up the job of accompanying team members, and in so doing, invests a lot of time and energy in mediating a conflict within the team. After she has left and the position remains free for a time, another woman fulfils this function. Seen from the point of view of the Balkan Peace Team, these Sub-groups are the place where personal care is established. This is, however, what the General Assembly at the end of 1998 laid down, prescribing at the same time that there should be one person in these groups who is in particular responsible for the accompaniment of volunteers, and that this person is to be on hand for longer than a year.

The teams also have the opportunity for mutual exchange. One opportunity they use is the so-called 'summit meeting'. These are frequently responsible for many an impulse which can improve the working climate. Suggestions such as these are then passed on to the Co-ordinating Committee. Among these suggestions, too, there is also the earnest request to inform people in both directions of how things stand as far as their feelings and emotions are concerned. The teams go on to work reciprocally. An exchange with the other office channels is made, and this provides backing, if help is not forthcoming from the Co-ordinating Committee. It is an exchange with people who do not need to be acquainted with every detail, since they are themselves intensively concerned with the work of the Balkan Peace Team.

The possibility of re-appraising co-operation together is also at hand within a team. However, when both people are burned out in a team, they are not able to help each other anymore. The theme of 'burn-out' is touched upon in the volunteers' self-evaluation assessment. This, too, is an instrument by which volunteers can reflect from time to time on their situation and give themselves an opportunity to get out of the daily round of routine This is mostly given at summit meetings.

When the situation in Kosovo came to a head, the Kosovo team raised the question as to what the Balkan Peace Team thought it was possible to do in order to help volunteers to deal with their traumatic experiences, and whether they were going to take responsibility for their psychological health. This sets off a typical process of seeking and explaining which, at various stages of the discussion, it is asked how one recognizes the signs of trauma, in what routine of assessment can it be discerned and how, during training, can this theme can be integrated. Enquiries at health insurances is another, further development in this direction, and there is general acknowledgement that the Balkan Peace Team indeed has a responsibility here. It is also ready to take over this responsibility. To this end, a corresponding passage is to be entered into the contract between the parties and the claim for assistance in such a case, formulated in writing.

The Volunteers of the Balkan Peace Team

The former co-ordinator finds the volunteers applying from Croatia to be the most successful. They fulfil *"demands at all levels"* which include such requirements as personality, and the *"secondary virtues of being able to deal with a computer, drive a car, speak the local language, knowing something of the country and so on..."*. Another trainer puts the emphasis elsewhere. He is more concerned about the *"ability to work within a team, possess experience, diplomatic skills, and such matters."* In order for a volunteer to be successful, he should, according to the assessment of this trainer, possess concrete experience in the form of that found in civil society organisations, i.e. clarity about that which awaits and team competency. From the perspective of the Co-ordinating Committee the most important ability is that one is in the position to develop activities, plans and programmes with one or two other people. Those who just drift along are a problem.

And how do volunteers see these required qualities? Looking back, a former volunteer sees it so:

> *"One must be a quick thinker and a something of an actor. You have to be quick, too, in making contact with others, but at the same time exercise a lot of self-discipline and be able to look after yourself. You have to be a good organiser and not be afraid of making mistakes. You have to be able to deal with being entirely on your own and possess the ability to find new*

friends. And you need patience, too, with foreign ways which can sometimes bring you to the brink of desperation when, for example, you have to sit for three to four hours as a non-smoker with folks puffing away around you for most of that time and then, on top, you have to be able to handle a computer, drive a car and have bags of energy."

A catalogue of demands of professional standards which volunteers are expected to live up to and which bring Monique Z. to the edge of sheer desperation, are nevertheless standards which are always looked for in candidates by the BPT. She can only find candidates who are enthusiastic and who also have recognizable development potential, and she must count on the possibility that they will have the chance to further develop this potential. For her, therefore, the test period is important for volunteers in that they can take advantage of this chance.

Qualified personnel who are able to transform a conflict situation in a professional way is something which is virtually non-existent, and certainly not a thing to be had for mere 'pocket money'. There is just no such thing as a pool of qualified personnel from which one can choose and so be able to put their skills into operation where the need arises, regardless of where and when, and then expect this personnel to be active without further guidance. From this point of view, the time of the Balkan Peace Team is a time of qualification.

Local activists notice this and they criticise the BPT for the fact it lets people depart at a time when they have really become good at their work. But the Balkan Peace Team has no other alternative.

However, if one wishes to acquire a adequate picture of the performance of the Balkan Peace Team in Croatia and Kosovo, then it is necessary to consider this aspect as well. The performance of the teams has come to fruition through the work of volunteers who have brought with them certain skills and knowledge into the fray. During their time with the Balkan Peace Team, they have been confronted with unanticipated challenges, have managed them and, as a result, matured from this experience. What would have been possible if basic qualifications in the matter of processing conflict had been further extended? That, again, is one of those questions which must remain open.

Sources

BPT 11.2.2000; 24.5.94; 31.5.94; BPT Belgrade 9.6.97; BPT CC minutes, 2.-4.5.94; 5.-7.9.94; 13.-14.3.95; 5.-8.5.95; 16.-18.7.95; 30.9.-1.10.95; 1.-2.6.96; 20.-22.2.98, 10, 12, 14; 4.-6.9.98, 9-12; 22.11.98, 1; 19.-21.2.99, 2; 28.-30.5.99; 12.-14.9.99; BPT CC/GA minutes, 13.-14.6.98, 13; BPT GA minutes, 15.-16.10.94, 9f.; 20.-21.11.98, 7; 20.-21.11.99; 18.-19.11.2000; BPT, Field BPT 17.2.97; BPT volunteer 13.9.94; BPT volunteer Elisabeth A. 4.1.96; 20.1.96; Erna P. 11.10.94; BPT IO 20.12.94; 5.2.95; 24.2.95; BPT Kosovo/a Biweekly 1.3.95; Büttner, 3.11.97; Interview Albert P. 1/1997; 2/1998; Anselm F. 1997; Charles O. 1997; Chris N. 1997; Claire P. 1998; Daniel M. 1/1997; Diana M. 1998; Frances E. 1998; Friedhelm D. 1/1997; 2/1998; Hanna L. 1997; Hubert P. 1998; Jacques B. 1998; Katrin G. 1/1997; Laura Z. 1998; Mary F. 1997; Monique Z. 1998; Paul C. 1998; Raj S. 1997; Rosa T. 1997; Sara F. 1998; Simone V. 1997; Stefan K. 1998; Susanne S. 2/1998; Valeska 2/1998; Verena J. 2/1998; Xaver A. 1997; OtOc no date, 4.95; 11.-13.12.95; 10.4.96; OtOc Sp Biweekly 16.-30.6.95, Confidential; 16.-31.5.95, Confidential; 1.-15.8.95, Confidential; 1.-15.10.95, Confidential; OtOc Zg Biweekly 1/8.95, Confidential; 1/1.96.

Chapter 5 The Balance of the Balkan Peace Team and Lessons Learned

(1) Looking Back: Decisive Moments in the Life of the Balkan Peace Team

What is there to balance out in the Balkan Peace Team? A short review of the most decisive moments reveals what has been learned during its existence. The survey below makes it clear how compressed these experiences are.

- Western Europe in the spring of 1993; the idea is first formulated. The few pages of text constitute a breakthrough, a daring exploit and a promise. Indeed, something like this could work! Yes, that could be the answer!

- Western Europe in February 1994, the first team drives to Croatia. The concept has undergone an incredible transformation and, on the way into reality, collided against hard facts. The departure of the first team is a milestone in more than one sense. Yes, we can say that this coalition has bitten quite through its internal obstacles, has its ideological and internal organisational interests under control, so much so indeed that it has actually got a team on the way. What in fact the possibilities of non-violent intervention, using teams of volunteers are remains to be experienced and sounded out. Back in peaceful Western Europe, the member organisations wait to learn what they can about the exploit.

- Western Europe, October 1994, the General Assembly discusses and confirms the concept of the Croatian team. The day-to-day life of the team during the summer and autumn of 1994 demonstrates that there are meaningful roles for foreign teams to play and possibilities for action.

- Kosovo, Easter, 1995. The Kosovo team begins with its observation of human rights violations. An interrogation by the police follows, and withdrawal from Kosovo to Belgrade is the result, in order not to endanger the partners. Even the most careful of attempts in the direction of watching the process of human rights observation are called off after this state intervention. It proves to be an important change of course.

- Croatia, May and August 1995: the war returns to Croatia and the Croatian team takes on new tasks in the changed situation. Human rights observation by the team, information platform, the writing of reports and the setting up of networks – these are the roles, which the team has to adopt within the shortest time. Here, the continuity of the teams pays off: it knows the country, its people and the situation.

- Western Europe, November 1995: the General Assembly re-orientates the work of the Belgrade team. The decision that the team should remain in Belgrade for the foreseeable future and direct matters from here for Kosovo is a departure from the assumption that the team should be in Kosovo. The work now orientates itself deliberately to the needs of the Serbian organisations and seeks from there to awaken interest in holding a dialogue on Kosovo.
- Croatia, autumn, 1996: after a big re-shuffle of the team in Croatia, the Zagreb team now transfers its office to Karlovac. This coincides with the end of the concept that one requires an office in the capital in order to implement the work of setting up networks and playing a role in lobbying. Resulting from this is also the realisation that one needs a good deal of prior knowledge and this is no longer to hand.
- Kosovo, winter, 1996: the first functional short-term advisory activity on the part of the Kosovo team.
- Western Europe, spring, 1997: the separation of training and assessment. In this way continuing conflict is finally arrested and selection and preparation are, from now on, separate from one another.
- Kosovo, April 1997: a weekend of encounter takes place in Prishtina. The Belgrade team has brought together those interested parties from both ethnic groups. The practice of patience, developing mutual trust and bridge building leads to dialogue and the Belgrade team can book success.
- Kosovo, October 1997: student dialogue. Intensive 'shuttle' diplomacy exercised in getting the teams together over a distance; the Belgrade team succeeds in bringing together student leaders from both camps, the Albanian and the Serbian, for their first meeting on common ground.
- Kosovo, spring, 1998: the conflict in Kosovo escalates and so makes dialogue impossible. The Belgrade team morally supports its partners and develops a new role in the matter of supplying information and distributing it.
- Croatia, September, 1998: the Croatian team in Split / Knin plays watchdog on hearing the reports of refugees coming home. It keeps an eye on the implementation of freedom for the return of refugees on the spot as they conform to the recommendation from the international community to go back to their homes.

- Croatia, October 1998: regulated withdrawal from Zagreb. After half a year of intensive evaluation, the Zagreb team suggest the dissolution of the office, since there is no longer any need for it.
- Kosovo / Serbia, March-June, 1999: Just before the NATO bombardment of Belgrade, the team leave the city and the country. War and violence dramatically worsen the possibility for reconciliation between Serbs and Albanians. There is no way back, and that which it was intended to avoid has now come about.
- Western Europe, November 1999: the decision taken for an individual project for the construction of a youth centre. This corresponds to a new start with work in Kosovo under completely different conditions. It is the attempt to combine reconstruction with dialogue and also to maintain the traditional network role. At the same time, work in Croatia is called off completely after June 1999, at a time when the team in Split has completely fallen apart and after no great enthusiasm is shown anymore in subsequent exploratory discussions which seek a point of departure for a new programme.
- Western Europe, March 2001. The project in Dragash is handed over to other organisations and the dissolution of the coalition decided upon.
- Western Europe, October 2001: key evaluations and the official suspension of the Balkan Peace Team's activities. Certain 'propositions' are formulated.

In what follows, the effects of the Balkan Peace Team are followed up and the project placed in order. One or two of the 'propositions' and self-evaluations arising from the final meeting of the Balkan Peace Team are included in these assessments, but also a number of assessments proposed by volunteers and partners from the region are integrated into them. It is important to determine from these values what significance the project has had in working on conflict in general and for those participating and for partners.

(2) The Balkan Peace Team as a Non-violent Project and its Functions as a 'Third Party'

What, exactly, has the Balkan Peace Team been, and what functions as a so-called 'third party' has it managed to fulfil? What, in fact, is 'non-violent' about the Balkan Peace Team? Is there any such thing, and if so, where did this principle have its effect and its significance?

Non-violence as an individual value of orientation, especially in this project, has played a prominent role for those taking part, both for volunteers and organisers during their commitment. Interviews have always been testimony of this fact. And more. The founding organisations of the Balkan Peace Team, especially, find the challenge to develop alternatives to violence in exemplary activity a particularly distinct one. Without the effectiveness and intellectual orientation born of a tradition and practice of non-violence, it is probable that the idea would not have found expression. Looked at this way, this particular aspect of non-violence can be seen as having an existential significance for the Balkan Peace Team.

The practice of the project's ideals in Croatia, however, looks quite different. Here, the ideal of non-violence has suffered considerable attrition in the attempt to deliberately distinguish the Balkan Peace Team's approach from other actors such as state and inter-state organisations like the United Nations. As help towards orientation in Kosovo, on the other hand, non-violence has played a prominent role, especially in the employment of the concept, 'chain of non-violence' (see chapter 3,1). *"A number of players in the Kosovo-Albanian society were introduced to the idea of non-violence,"* the self-assessment reads. Whether international organisations such as the OSCE or the European Observation Mission in Croatia, allowed themselves to be convinced of the value of non-violent intervention is not sure. Particular experience with non-violent strategy during the everyday work of the teams cannot be spoken of as playing any kind of role. Much more important here was the general skill to communicate.

Is, then, the Balkan Peace Team 'just another' NGO among the many committed to a cause? Here, too, there are differences. The conflict researcher, NORBERT ROPERS, in his essay written in 1998, quite roughly categorizes NGOs into four groups and, responding to an enquiry, also specially and systematically classified the Balkan Peace Team into his scheme of things. What follows is the result of that assessment:

Group	Type	Activity	Objectives	BPT
1	Movement-NGOs	Bringing human rights infringements to public notice and to intervene politically on behalf of the disadvantaged group	Goal: to internally and externally influence political agendas.	BPT-yes
Group 2	Structurally orientated NGO dealing with conflict	Attempt to influence the system of internal conflict operations in crisis zones in the direction of constructive models, structures, qualifications, and 'players'.	Goal: to change the political and social system from the inside.	BPT-yes
Group 3	Third party-NGO	To be active, even directly, as a third party, organize dialogues, workshops etc. or to support third parties as bridge-builders in implementing concrete measures	Goal: process orientated, initiates dealing with conflict from outside by initiating it itself or by support	BPT-limited
Group 4	Aid-NGO's	Try to offer humanitarian and material help etc. which, in the first place, arise from emergency and development situations, but which is also increasingly made a relevant theme for dealing with conflict.	Goal: to create the material and humanitarian conditions and physical protection which are prerequisites in order to be able to transform the conflict.	BPT-no

In addition, he writes:

"In this grouping, the Balkan Peace Team, in my opinion, falls above all into the first and second category, and fits in well with the philosophy of an NGO. On the one hand, it is a classic example of a human rights NGO interested in the protection and emancipation from violence of especially endangered people under threat and, on the other, a newer, structure orientated NGO dealing with conflict, one which is intent on creating the condi-

tions for constructive reduction of conflict on the spot in that it supports the activities of local people. It also performs the roles listed in the 3rd category (i.e. mediator intervention), but only in a very limited way and at the lower or medium levels."

Ernst V. from the 'Federation for Social Defence' sees the significance of the BPT above all in the 2nd category. *"The importance of the Balkan Peace Team – when we consider it in relation to former Yugoslavia – lies in the fact that it has been able to encourage organisations and people to involve themselves in democratic developments and so set up these for themselves."* Work in Kosovo, on the other hand, fits better into category 3 after the team has found its productive talent. One of the former volunteers is of the opinion that, *"We were not welcome to everyone and on every occasion."* Activists from the region, as, for example, a leading personality in the Council for the 'Protection of Human Rights and Freedom', however, is very positive in the assessment: *"If reconciliation is going to happen, the work of the Balkan Peace Team must continue and be strengthened."* This very significantly confirms the approach to identify people and groups composed of Kosovo-Albanians and Serbs who are ready for dialogue and to support them. The fact that the Balkan Peace Team has only been able to do this in individual cases, and on a temporary basis, is not in itself a decisive factor. It was an exemplary means to show how a 'chain of non-violence' can be set up and what contribution it can make towards reconciliation. Moreover, it shows how small contributions following the right concept can open the way to understanding.

The assignment of the Balkan Peace Team into three of four categories at the same time makes it clear that the BPT as an external, 'third' party has carried out quite different functions. This is actually no small wonder when one takes into consideration that it was exposed to differing conditions and varying possibilities in which it could unfold its activities in several different countries. This broad 'wavelength' is felt by all participants, despite all the limitations imposed upon it, to have been an enormous theoretical and practical achievement. The fact that this 'broadness' could in fact develop perhaps hangs together with another here, the fact that they had a corresponding niche. The 'proposition' arising from the assessment describes this as follows: *"Perhaps peace teams are most useful in situations that are being neglected, or working with groups that are being neglected - with the international saturation of Kosovo, this was in the end very difficult."*

This means that projects such as this are, in fact, in the vanguard from both the theoretical concept and practical point of view. They themselves may not be able to reach society at large, but are capable, nevertheless, of developing concepts towards realistic, workable prototypes.

(3) The Effects ... Tracking Them Down in Croatia

What concrete significance has the Balkan Peace Team had in dealing with conflict? Again, its work in Croatia and also that in Serbia/Kosovo must be reviewed individually. 'The people belonging to minority groups must be treated with respect!' This could well describe the objective, and in this two levels become visible. The one is help given in a concrete case. Thus, when family Sepic is able to return to their former apartment, then this can be considered as a success. The other level is a general one. When laws can be changed or when state executive organs can be persuaded to treat minorities with respect, then that, too, is success. The range of success on this second level is naturally much greater, and the Balkan Peace Team can say with truth that it has had its rightful portion of success in connecting the first, the individual and the second, the structural level, in this connection. Direct categorisation is not possible, since there are still other players in the game who also have their rightful claims. Accordingly, claims to success seem only to be justified when one can point to encounters with other players who admit to having later changed their conduct to conform with the desired direction or conduct themselves in a given situation in a way which is desirable. How, then, do participants see the fruits of their actions?

For participants of the Balkan Peace Team, the individual case counts. The coordinator, interviewed in 1997, stresses this point: *"There are the small successes which I find really great, I mean the dialogue project between Kosovo-Albanians and Serbs. That's what I call success! The individual cases where folks could simply be helped, where one could support them."* She goes on to say that a larger range could not be possible to assess with such a small number of personnel, say, three people in a war zone. *"Unspectacular, minute work"* – this was one description of work-in-the-field given by someone interviewed who belonged to a member organisation. A former volunteer adds: *"And I think that there are probably certain villages out there in Croatia where the authorities treat the minority population with a bit more respect than they might have otherwise done, because we were there and had spoken with the police there or had made reports."* Or wrote about it in a report or whatever.

In 1997 at another place somewhere in the Krajina area in Croatia, the team visits an Orthodox mass attended by refugees having returned to their homes in order to see *"how things are progressing"*. The first mass after three years is celebrated without incident. Valeska, who is also there as a volunteer, remarks: *"Perhaps it was that we were there, despite the fact there were no problems. And I feel it's difficult to judge fully how successful our work is."* This is somewhat different when, for example, a volunteer accompanies a local activist to a demonstration of extremist groups in order to make observations. The participants react pretty aggressively to being watched. Valeska, speaking of such moments, says: *"Then you have a day like the one where we went to this rally, you know, and then you say: 'Oh, yes, now I know what BPT is about'".* These are quick snapshots, so to speak, of certain, concrete situations.

How is it with processes which last longer? Reconciliation, for example? Verena accompanies teams of local organisations when these invite villagers to talk of their experiences. During these conversations she sits and listens to personal histories. They feel that they can talk freely to a foreigner. In this way, such people hear for the first time how it is with the 'opposite number', how it was with the 'others'. How often can Verena be at such interviews? How many conversations must there be before understanding coalesces into reconciliation? *"You can't say that I've contributed to the reconciliation process in Croatia. That's perhaps possible in a year and a half during this project. You can't gather any fruit or experience, any sort of 'harvest'. Everything else is an illusion."* To go for impact...? *"I don't think that's in the nature of the mandate,"* Valeska adds. Perhaps we can describe the task like this: To accompany meaningful processes during to which foreigners can qualitatively contribute? This, too, requires sound knowledge. Which of the processes is the right one? What, precisely, can this qualitative contribution be to which only someone from outside can contribute? Can those who are at hand to make it make this contribution?

Looking for traces and tracks pays off. Every task shows different results. One former volunteer was not so willing to accord the laurels directly to the Balkan Peace Team when villagers are able at least to return to their homes after this opportunity had been previously denied them. What he then writes, however, reaches beyond the help assigned to individual cases. *"What we can do,"* he goes on, *"we can attribute these cases to the people who can exert pressure. And I don't even know if our presence would have made a difference one way or the other but, I think what we can do is, we can put these cases in touch with people that can exert more pressure".* Here, Frances is sure of her point. She organised a visit of the American ambassador for expelled Serbs. At the same time, he met Croatian people who now live in the houses formerly inhabited by Serbs. The dimensions of the dilemma came to light in discussions of people who had been expelled, promised things, but who were nevertheless denied return. Frances describes the consequences: *"And the result of that was pretty hard*

US line foreign policy for Croatia. And the eventual change in the policy. It wasn't only because of that visit, but it certainly helped. And - so I think we can feel pretty proud of that. That was one of the Otoc things last spring which was pretty strong."

The fact that the work of the Balkan Peace Team substantially contributed to a change of climate with regard to the return of refugees is something of which it is firmly convinced in its final assessments. The evaluation describes effects, which the BPT also helped to bring about in that it was able to interest powerful elements at other levels in the problems of localities.

Another example: On being asked about the effects of his work, another former volunteer indicates the work of the Otvorene Oci during evictions in Croatia. *"I think - when you started talking about evictions- and I was thinking about evictions, too, well - the evictions did die down eventually. And I think that one of the reasons they went away is because there was such a movement against evictions and we were part of that movement, a pretty big part. We played a coordinating role. I think that we've given a lot of international exposure to local NGO's which has helped."*

In this connection, the Balkan Peace Team sees matters in its final report as follows: It substantially contributed to a change in the way these were carried out and in changes introduced by law with regard to evictions. It is in this way that it played a significant role within a movement as a whole. Here, we are not concerned with large individual bodies like the US in the form of an ambassador who has been motivated to take part, but rather in bringing about pressure and mobilisation from inside the country itself and taking the matter to the attention of the international public. Here, too, the individual contribution must be distilled from the rest. The same volunteer adds: *"I think that we've always been here - sort of within the stream of things, you know, and I think that we're a part of the overall effect that peace activism and human rights activism in Croatia in general have had on Croatia."* As a part of international publicity on the situation of human rights in Croatia, volunteers are willing to allow themselves a *"very subtle effect"* on the way matters develop when their reports are picked up and cited by international organisations or by the American Foreign Affairs Department.

Are there other effects or provable improvements in the case of large populations perhaps? The Balkan Peace Team feels that there are. As a result of observations of the evictions and the accompaniment of the Balkan Peace Team on these respective occasions, it was certainly a factor which was instrumental in that not more Serbs left the Krajina region or more houses were destroyed and that, sometime later, their papers were restored to them. *"I don't know whether there are more Serbs in Western Slavonia than there otherwise would be, had we not been there. ... Probably that's dubious. And Eastern Slavonia I don't know that we had any big success"*, a former volunteer remarks who had personally experienced refugee movements from these areas, looking back on those times. One sees here, the nearer one approaches, the more self-critical the evaluation.

Of the distance between one's radius of action and the higher levels above, a former volunteer, who had experienced the escalation in Krajina, says: *"I mean you can do stuff at the grassroots level and which is very important and which contributes to change. But at the same time, there has to be some sort of change in the overall structure, which wasn't forthcoming when I was there. It was getting worse, you know"*. Sudden escalations destroy the small, previous successes, *"It was such a bad situation that you just didn't know if you were doing anything worthwhile at all, because no matter what you did, something else came along ...and changed things."*

The Balkan Peace Team could register influence resulting from its activities in reflecting on the change of government in Croatia, which, in the year 2000, brought in a new political era. It might possibly be that its support for opposition groups did in fact bring about a very small contribution to the change. One should think bigger and act. This is the assessment the Balkan Peace Team made of itself in its final assessment. *"Concerted effort for peaceful change (lobbying, political pressure etc.) needs more than one project"*. Here, a new kind of conceptual thinking is required together with an idea of just how such a co-operative scheme could work. If many organisations within the Balkan Peace Team have brought about one single common project, then it is clear that an effect at several levels in the conflict needs the collaboration of many such projects on the part of NGOs, and, presumably, could reach above this to include inter-state players and organisations. Truly, a task that has still to be tackled!

However, is one right in assuming that influence on larger conflicts can at all be expected from the Balkan Peace Team? This volunteer has a clear statement to make on this point: *"The Balkan Peace Team is not there to bring about changes in the country. The BPT is there to support the people, who, for their part, must change the situation. And when the people can do this, then the Balkan Peace Team must withdraw."* This is quite another working level. Here, we are not so much concerned with changing the conduct of those who are in power, but with the certainty of behaviour of those who want to bring about change from within. How far has the encouragement of this capacity on the part of local partners developed? In 1997, one volunteer was asked this question. His response was that, *"Obviously the human rights organisations are not necessarily more professional and excellent - than they were. They're still fighting, so in this sense, we have failed."*

His colleague, on the other hand, takes up a view which employs another yardstick. *"There's still dissension everywhere, but this is simply more integrated in certain structures and processes. It is now normal for local organisations to have meetings with certain UN people. And, moreover, that the activists inform the UN people or the OSCE people about the situation – that they have contact."* The integration in international structures and in autonomous working ability of local groups – these, for the volunteers who were interviewed in 1998, were the original objectives. He feels that these objectives have been reached. Seen thus, *"perhaps it was time for us to go."*

In its closing self-assessment in October 2001, the Balkan Peace Team tries to identify and to assess its effects within the teams' working area in Croatia. According to this, it had opened new vistas for local groups by accompaniments and the division of labour. Even more prominent than this, the teams in Split had tried again and again to advance co-operation, to cultivate the supply of information and co-ordination among local groups. As the result of strong support, one small human rights group in particular had managed to hold on and even expand its sphere of influence. Without the team, it would probably have fallen apart, and, presumably, had less influence on events.

How do those affected see matters? They, too, go through a course of development with the Balkan Peace Team. They have learned how to use the 'internationals' in order to impress their own authorities, and have profited, too, from their qualities of expertise. Many testimonies to this have been alluded to in the chapter on teamwork. While many team members of different generations try persistently, and sometimes with frustration and, frequently in vain, to improve the quality of co-operation of local activists, it is these that will have to assume the role of teachers in initiating those generations of teams coming after them into the professional expertise of the work. In 1998, a volunteer described how he adopted his work of observing trials in court or that of the situation as a whole. *"...and I think I learned almost all that, not from the training we've had here or from BPT training, but from working with the locals who've been doing it for much longer than me - a sort of learning on the job."*

In the course of time, partners in Croatia have developed a very keen sense of what they can expect from different international organisations. In autumn, 1999, that is to say, almost looking back on the history of the Balkan Peace Team, we had the following assessment:

> *"On the one hand, there are organisations which 'monitor' or 'observe'. Then there are others, which possess the 'power to change'. These international 'power' organisations can then be divided into a 'political' and a 'humanitarian' area. An example of a monitoring organisation is the International Committee of the Red Cross. An example of a 'political power' organisation is the OSCE, and a 'power humanitarian' organisation is the United Nations High Commissioner for Refugees. Grassroots organisations like the Balkan Peace Team are categorized as 'observer' organisations and ranked there as 'observer and supporting' and are thought of as standing very close to one's own organisations. Their volunteers represent growth and expansion of their own possibilities in otherwise difficult areas of access. However, no one expects that such organisations or projects can have any direct effect on changing the situation."*

The 'expansion of their own possibilities' – how does one imagine that? A scheme can perhaps clarify things. The diagram below shows the most important players for Croatia to which the Otvorene Oci teams manage to gain access to the local partners. It also shows how successful they are in producing a lasting effect. The players are represented at three levels according to how powerful they are. The number of people increases as one proceeds from the top to the bottom and, proportionately, their proximity to power decreases. To permanently change things, all of them are important. The inventor of this table showing the stages of power, the peace researcher, JOHN PAUL LEDERACH, emphasizes: *"It is not possible to bring about peace or widespread social change at one level alone."* The horizontal line indicates the special region, then the country, other individual states and finally, the international level. All players, from the smallest basis initiative up to the halls of the international community, find their place in this scheme. In this case, it shows how the range of the Croatian partners has enlarged as a result of their co-operation.

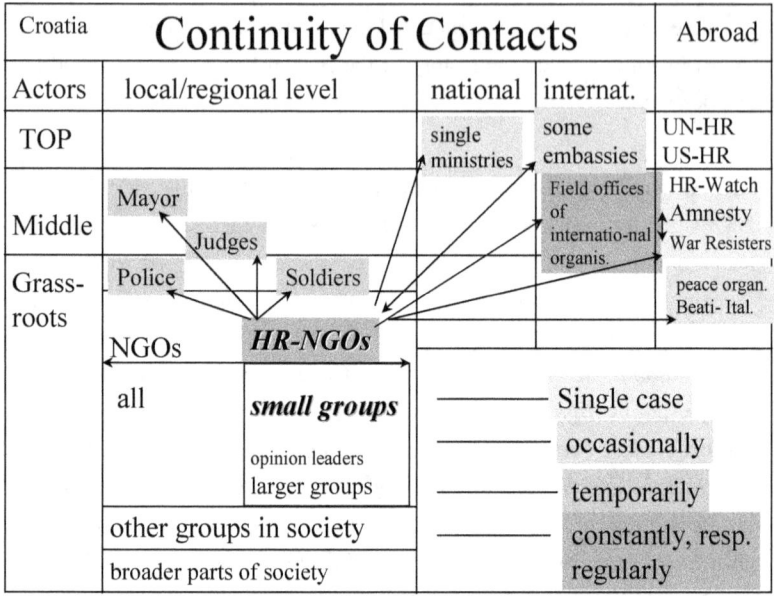

The groups with which the teams in Croatia mainly co-operate belong to those orientated to human rights and non-governmental organisations (MR-NGOs in the table). The arrows express the increase in range as the result of teamwork. They mean that, as a result of team activities, new contacts, currents of information right up to co-operation have developed for the local groups. As far as contact with local authorities is concerned, it is often only a matter of obtaining information feedback from players otherwise inaccessible for local groups. These contacts, on the one hand, reach to the highest state authorities in Croatian society when, for example, the team sends a letter to the ministry. They come into direct contact with the local mayor or with the examining magistrate and legal representatives of law and order at the local level when the team alarms the police. Similarly, when the teams speak to soldiers, they automatically reach their opposite numbers at local level.

As far as international players are concerned in Croatia, there are the embassies on the one hand, and on the other, the staff of offices in international organisations about whose presence teams are informed at local level. From this, a mutual relationship can develop when, for example, embassies support the activities or projects of local groups. Finally, the team establishes contacts and co-operation with international peace organisation networks and foreign peace organisations which, for their part, can become active in the interests of Croatian groups. Here, represented at the arrow for the War Resisters to Amnesty International, they can begin to co-operate with other networks.

This certainly impressive expansion of the action radius is only consistently effective when it is permanent. The question then is: How many influential players can be won over on a permanent contact basis for this purpose? The permanency of the contact is expressed by the intensity of colour in the box: the darker, the more permanent. It is clear that permanent and dependable bridges to international organisations in the country can be established.

(4) Effects ... Looking for Tracks in Serbian und Kosovo

How do things look as far as Kosovo is concerned? An undesirable side effect has been mentioned several times. This was the potential jeopardy local activists were exposed to and the exposure to police interrogation in the case of people renting apartments. In the case of subsequent spying on activists in Prishtina and on looking back, the Balkan Peace Team holds itself partly responsible.

The question of the effect the Balkan Peace Team has had in Kosovo has to be answered in the perspective of different times and in different ways. Mary, who was singularly active in setting up a new start, and looking back on the new positioning of Serbian and Albanian groups within the scene, had the following to say at the end of 1997: *"I think everybody is quite happy with BPT. So, yeah, in that sense - I'm quite happy, too!"*

Is there evidence in the Kosovo team of provable individual assistance? This question can be answered in the affirmative in several instances. In the fact, for example, that individuals were cared for through international contacts, which ensured their 'survival', mentally and physically. A more significant effect can be assumed to have taken place for those young people who were involved in the dialogue project and others for whom the Dragash project was organised. In the latter, it can be assumed that they developed a better understanding for their 'opposite numbers'.

In the immediate vicinity of the project, one can assert that local people were encouraged during the protests in Belgrade in autumn and winter, 1996. The Team also feels partially responsible for the speed with which, in 1997, dialogue developed. More groups received quicker support, because the Team supported the development of groups. Most importantly, the Team has been appraised for its part in bringing Serbian and Kosovo-Albanian activists together, and that this contact remained intact even during the course of the war, and continued thereafter. Another considerable plus point, which can be attributed to the Team, is the encouragement of young women during the Dragash project to develop their capabilities in a strongly patriarchal society. Certainly, without the Balkan Peace Team, there would have been no connections whatever between the Kosovo-Albanian and Serbian activists in individual cases from which, incidentally, permanent relations have since developed.

On the level of conflict between the Federal Republic of Serbia and the Kosovo-Albanians, however, the Balkan Peace Team cannot be said to have brought about any effect, especially during the renewed escalation of hostilities in 1998. Notwithstanding, volunteers managed nevertheless to reach those making critical decisions as a result of their being able to acquire information and pass it on. How their information was subsequently made use of does not affect assessments being made here (cf. assessment in chapter 3.3) The commencement of dialogue as carefully introduced and cultivated by the Balkan Peace Team can in fact be valid for the future.

This is particularly applicable in the case where reconciliation between ethnic groups is to be successful in the future. For this, there is the need to continue to work at it. The fact that the initial approach of the Balkan Peace Team can be so positively evaluated as described above shows that, for the participants, it is appropriate. Perhaps this is the most important contribution made by the Balkan Peace Team.

(5) What Has the Balkan Peace Team Brought to Its Participants?

On what might be called the very individual levels of the Balkan Peace Team, it has been decisively responsible for a number of 'personal enterprises' in that six marriages have taken place between volunteers and local inhabitants. Ernst V. from the Federation for Social Defence is not referring to this aspect exclusively when he maintains that, *"For those people working in the teams, there is an enormous widening of mental horizons and a further development of their personal potential."* This fact can be confirmed by a former volunteer who brings the matter succinctly to the point:

"Definitely, I mean I think if you survive Otoc or BPT, then you are a very much stronger person. And unfortunately you become even more frustrated with the thousands of other internationals working in the region who just don't seem to have a clue about what they are doing. Because you feel like you have a different perspective. And you feel like you've done your time and you've volunteered and you've learned the language and you've been in some tough situations, and that - yeah, you want to be able to use that insight in a way that's productive."

The time spent with the Balkan Peace Team has taught another volunteer, Tobias, *"...what the situation here is actually like."* He is able to judge, *"... regarding the mass movement of populations. How that affects people."* It is not only the Balkans, which people from the West can better get to know, but one comes to learn about *"living in a post-war society, about working in a post war society."* Above all, volunteers learn about the tools of human rights observation, the monitoring of trials and later, above all else, from local activists. After that, they are fit for careers in international organisations. The Balkan Peace Team gave them a start chance and a challenge to test themselves. The organisers, too, can assert that their international co-operation in the Co-ordinating Committee has been a great 'cultural experience of understanding.'

(6) How Has the Idea Progressed in the Meantime?

"It can be done in a different way," the former co-ordinator says. That's what the Balkan Peace Team wants to show. In this, it was not alone. It was a *"contribution to the whole movement, to that which is there to move,"* she underlines. And in this it is a parry to the *"inflated importance of the military,"* as one representative of a member organisation has flatly put it. The 90s was a period, which first submitted the idea of working with conflict. The Balkan Peace Team is one of the first concrete projects in this area. As a pilot project it will not fit into any kind of structured scheme or into any formula, and it follows no developed standards, because there aren't any.

It is at the same time an indication of hope and encouragement that one can be active in promoting peace and do something new in this direction.

However, having said this, the idea of non-violent intervention has only partly become reality for the Balkan Peace Team. Charles O., in an interview taking place in 1997, drew attention to certain open theoretical problems of conception: *"This, for me, is a point about which I'm not too clear. How far can it go? I mean not only from the point of view of the size of the groups or teams, but also how many of these kinds of teams can work on a given conflict? Certainly it's more than there are now in the Balkan Peace Team."*

Peace services establish themselves and the way despatching qualified personnel works

The Balkan Peace Team sees itself as a forerunner of the civil peace service in Germany. The reason for this is that in talks, consultations with governmental bodies and in political circles as well as in publications it is referred to as a concrete example. The organisation that vigorously promotes this concept in Germany, the 'Forum for Civil Peace Service', was founded in 1996. It has become the driving force of the link-up of peace services with many European countries.

At a large European conference at Den Haag, 'The Hague Appeal for Peace', in the spring of 1999, the new 'European Network of Civil Peace Services' is officially started. Its members hail from the Netherlands, France, Switzerland, Russia, Great Britain, Italy, Georgia, Scotland, Norway, Austria, Finland and Germany. At home they are all active in qualifying, pool building and practical project work. Interest in promoting civil peace service in their own countries and in Europe is that which unifies them all. This means co-operation at the European level. One becomes engaged in the work of the 'EPLO', the 'European Peace Building Liaison Office' in Brussels. The first pilot project is to start in 2004 on Cyprus. This is the first crucial test for the network, which desires to show that it can achieve what it demands. The motivation, which led to the Balkan Peace Team is evident here as well, but also the thought of sending teams and organising international co-operation in Europe. The European network has a broad basis, and so the chances increase of finding suitable people to send out. As far as the BPT is concerned, the pool of trained, experienced people, which has yet to be realized, could have the chance to develop here. The number in a team increases. In Cyprus, a team of five to seven people is envisaged which should be experienced in mediation. The period of service is fixed at two years. This is time enough to get used to things and gain intimate knowledge of the situation. Such are the chances of carrying on with the idea of non-violent intervention.

The Balkan Peace Team has taught its members to consider resources. A short questionnaire set up by the author in the year 2000, circulated by German organisations and sent to the 'Austrian Peace Service', revealed that questions as to financing, programme development in the operational areas, relations to local partners, as well as accompaniment and care of volunteers, were all relevant matters. Even if the Balkan Peace Team was unique in its international structure, its problems are apparently not all home-made, but point to as yet unsolved structural challenges, and not only latent in Germany it seems.

What links the members in the European network together is not simply the idea, the concept, but the ubiquitous problem of not having sufficient money. The lessons of the BPT draw attention to the structures. How must the network be modified if, of necessity, it is already further developed into a project organisation? How can it organize the accompaniment of its teams, the guidance of its project, and can organise that which has been learned from experience? How many resources will it be able to mobilize for this transfer? Will the European network be able to find its way out of the trap of poverty, and so be able to care for all the parts of its project so that they are all sufficiently supplied and properly equipped before going on to something new?

Non-violent Peace Force: The Non-violent Army for the Global Village

The conference at Den Haag in May 1999, saw the formation of another initiative, that of the 'Non-violent Peaceforce'. This takes up the question of non-violent intervention again from basic considerations in that it desires to found an international 'peace army' made of civilians, people who are trained in non-violent strategy. In November 2002, the initiative with its beginnings in Delhi has now grown to become an established organisation. Before this, there was a two-year run-up period involving a study of whether such an organisation was viable. The Balkan Peace Team was also investigated so as to ascertain possible lessons to be learned from experience. The separation from training and selection, for example, was integrated into its programme. As far as this is concerned, the Balkan Peace Team sees itself as a forerunner. The fact that experience gained by the BPT has been taken into consideration, guarantees the co-operation of one of the organisers from the Balkan Peace Team in the new organisation. The demands are high. The non-violent peace force will realize what, for the Balkan Peace Team, was an inaccessible utopia: an alternative to military intervention. At the end of 2003, eighty-two organisations from every continent are members of an initiative that, for the first time, spans the world, one that began its first project in Sri Lanka in the same year.

The paths of the Balkan Peace Team and that of the initiator of the Non-violent Peace force had already crossed in Kosovo. In October 1998, the possibility of an intervention involving possibly a thousand volunteers in order to stop the escalation of conflict in Kosovo was tentatively assessed. At that time, the Team saw no chances of success without risking the lives of the volunteers. Was that a timid assessment and a wrong recommendation? This question will remain open.

At that time, there were neither trained volunteers in a corresponding number, nor a supporting structure at hand. Whether the 'Non-violent Peaceforce' will be able to radically change this and whether the question as to the possibilities of non-violent intervention will finally be answered – that, too, will be new history. One thing is clear, however; the search will continue.

Sources

BPT June 1999 Report; Junge, ca 2003; EN.CPS 31.12.2003; Lederach 1997, 46f.; Müller 2000; Müller, Minutes 2001; Müller 2002; Non-violent Peace force 31.12.2003; Non-violent Peaceforce Feasibility Study 2001, 186, 255; Poort - van Eeden 2003; Ropers 24.1.1999; Ropers 1998; Schweitzer, Clark, 2002, 48f.; Interview Anselm F. 1997; Charles O. 1997; Chris N. 1997; Diana M. 1998; Ernst V. 1997; Frances E. 1998; Friedhelm D. 2/1998; Mary F. 1997; Nicole M. 1997; Simone V. 1997; Tobias K. 1/1997; Tobias 2/1998; Valeska B. 1/1997; 2/1998; Verena 2/1998; Xaver A. 1997.

Balkan Peace Team Co-ordinating Committee's meeting in Paris, May 1996

Balkan Peace Team's General Assembly, October 1995

The first team's 'office' and flat in Croatia, 1994

Volunteers' major occupation: A new report has to be written.

The attack on a volunteer in Split makes the headlines

House eviction in Zagreb 1994. A woman is forcibly removed from an apartment

Volunteers investigate the devastation in the Krajina, August 1995 and after

Blown up houses in Cetina, Croatia

Returnees like this old lady live without electricity, windows, and water, because they are refused entry to their own homes.

Human rights activists consult returnees on a camp site, 1998

A volunteer and a local human rights activist investigate damage in Plavno, Krajina

A mine field near Ruzic warns people to keep out

Graveyards are regularly reviewed as to whether new graves without names can be found

Side by side with local human rights activists, the volunteers visit the Krajina to document, investigate, and report

In this Orthodox church in the Plavno Valley, this 300-year-old bible has been vandalized

"Here the war ends. Serbs out. This is Croatia!" This is how returnees are welcomed in Kovacici near Knin in spring 1997

The U.S. ambassador visits human rights activists in Split

A delegation from Germany is informed on the situation of the returnees in Golubic, 1997

Observers from the European Commission Monitoring Mission (ECMM, here the men in white), and a Balkan Peace Team's volunteer document the damage in a hand grenade attack. Vojnic, summer 1997

The report on the return of refugees into Kistanje needs to be finalized

Chapter 6 Appendix

(1) Abbreviations

BG	Belgrade
BPT	Balkan Peace Team
CC	Co-ordinating Committee
CRA	Children's Relief Association
DOS	Dalmatians odbor Solidarnosti (Dalmatian Solidarity Committee)
ECMM	European Commission Monitoring Mission
EPLO	European Peace-building Liaison Office
EPB	Équipes de Paix dans les Balkans
ET	Exploratory Team
EU	European Union
Forum ZFD	Forum Ziviler Friedensdienst (Forum for Civil Peace Service)
FRY	Federal Republic of Yugoslavia
HR-Watch	Human Rights Watch
IO	International Office
KFOR	Kosovo Force
LDK	Ligue démocratique du Kosovo
MAN	Mouvement pour une Alternative Nonviolente
NATO	North Atlantic Treaty Organisation
NGO	Non-Governmental Organisation
MR-NGOs	Menschenschrechts (Human Rights) - NGO
OSZE	Organisation for Security and Co-operation in Europe
Otoc	Otvorene Oci
PPK	Parliamentary Party of Kosovo
SMS	Short Message Service
UNO	United Nations Organisation
UNHCR	United Nations High Commissioner for Refugees
UNTAES	United Nations Transitional Administration in Eastern Slavonia
USA	United States of America
UNICEF	United Nations Children's Fund
UNMIK	United Nations Interim Administration Mission in Kosovo

(2) Sources and Literature

Ages, Ted. Presentation, Appendix D. Report on IFOR Strategy Meeting on former Yugoslavia, 26-28 March 1993, Basel, Switzerland.

Amnesty International. 4.96, Croatia: Continued Violence Used by Uniformed Personnel in Connection with Evictions, External, AI Index: EUR 64/08/96; 4.97, Out of the margins - the right to conscientious objection to military service in Europe, AI-Index: EUR 01/02/97; 8.98, Croatia: Impunity for Killings After "Storm", Report - EUR 64/04/98.

Antiwar Campaign Zagreb. 18. 7.93, letter; 28.5.96, Violic trial.

Böhm, Beata. Hilfe bei Wiederaufbau und Stabilisierung der wirtschaftlichen Strukturen - "Das Pakrac-Projekt", S. 180-207 in: Zivile Konfliktbearbeitung; eine internationale Herausforderung, Münster, agenda 2001, Studien für europäische Friedenspolitik, vol. 8.

Bozicevic, Goran. Friedensinitiativen in Westlawonien und der früheren Krajina, p. 33f. in: Friedensforum 5.95, Bonn, September/Oktober 1995.

BPT. 1.4.93, project proposal: Kosovo Peace Team; 13.5.93, Kosovo Peace Team Meeting Minutes, London; 30.5.-2.6. 93, Kosovo Peace Team: Report of the Visit in Pristina 30th of May - 2nd of June; 7.6. 93, Project proposal: Nonviolent intervention in Kosovo: Sending a Team in international volunteers, update; 15.6.93, Report of Meeting, 15th of June in Paris; 6.7.93, fax Co-ordinator, 1f.; 19.7.93, Report of the meeting of the Executive Group in Verona; 24.8.93, fax Co-ordinator; 14.9.93, Notes Meeting Coordinating Group in Paris; 22.9.93, Minutes Meeting September 15 in Paris; 1.11.93, Defense of human rights - urgent actions and alarms; 1.11.93, What could non-partisanship mean in the Croatian context? Relationship to Antiratne Kampanje; 7.11.93, Precisioning Goals of the Croatia Project; 7.-9.11.93, minutes meeting London; 14.11.93, Letter Co-ordinator; 14.11.93, Letter Co-ordinator to BSV; 14.11.93, fax to Antiratne Kampanje; 23.11.93, Agreement for Service; 23.11.93, minutes telephone conference; 30.11.93, Proposal fundraising; 27.11.93, fax Co-ordinator; 22.12.93, minutes telephone conference; 2.1.94, minutes founding meeting of the 'Förderverein Balkan Peace Team'; 18.1.94, fax Co-ordinator to CC; 24.2.94, Memorandum; 28.2.9420.4.94, Last message from Belgrade; 4.4.94, Balkans Peace Team ET to Kosovo, No 1; 5.4.94, BPT ET Day 2; 6.4.94, bptet3; 7.4.94, Memo for consultation with BPT coord.; BPT no date , 4.94, Day by day account of Kosovo; 15.04.94, e-mail Co-ordinator to Exploratory Team; 21.4.94, Summary from final day of BPT ET to Kosovo; 24.4.94, Ellen´s addendum to Daniel on BPT; 25.4.94, Role of Kosovo Team, next steps; 24.5.94, Letter Co-ordinator to CC; 31.5.94, Letter Co-ordinator to CC; 20.8.94, Letter Balkan Peace Team to the office of the Patriarch of the Serbian Orthodox Church in Belgrade; 6.11.94, Report of the preparatory meeting with the Kosovo-team, Zurich, 3.-4.11.94; 23.11.94, Message from Balkan Peace Team; 3.12.94, Report of a travel to Kosovo and Sandzak from 14 to 24 November 1994; 3.12.94, 3rd weekly report - week 48 (4) - 1994; 5.12.94, 4th weekly report - Week 49 (5) - 1994; 18.12.94, 5th weekly report - Week 50 (6) - 1994 (18.12.94); 21.12.94, Report and State of Affairs as per 21 December 1994; 6.1.95, Balkan Peace Team, Kosovo Project, Project Proposal; BPT no date, ca. 3.95, Project Evaluation 1, Results of the Evaluation of Otoc; no date, ca. 24.4.95, Easter95; 20.7.95, Julycc, Report by the team on activities since the last GA; 31.12.95, Profit and Loss Statement 1.01.1995- 31.12.1995 and balance 31.12.95; 9.6.96, Visit in May-June; 12.96, Profit and Loss Statement 1996. Report 1996; 11.2.97 Summit Minutes; 12.97, Profit and Loss Statement, 1.1. 1997-31.12.1997. Report 1997 new; 31.1.98, Assets of BPT as of Jan. 31, 1998 in DEM, ASS-0198; no date September 98, Funding Report 1998-09; 6.9.98, Report to CC provisional 1998-09; 15.9.98, Calculation of BPT finances rest of 1998, CAL 998.xls; 26.11.98 Draft Budget 1999; BPT 5.99, Evaluation; BPT June 1999 Report; 9.12.99, Provisional Financial Report for 1998 (not for distribution); 17.1.2000, Budget 2000 Provisional, 1999-11; 25.1.2000, Income 1999; 11.2.2000 Ex-volunteers list. 30.4.2000, Project for setting up a 'Balkan Peace Team' in Mitrovica. Statues of the 'Équipes de paix dans les Balkans'; 9.6.2000, Budget 2000-2001 DYC summary; 19.1.01, Invitation to the GA; 10.2.01, Copy of 2000-2001 Preliminary Overview; 3.01, Exploration Mission Report.

BPT Belgrade / FRY / K(osovo). 6.2.96, Hearts and Minds; 15.2.96, Belgrade analysis; 5.96, Post Dayton Serbia and Kosov@; 12.96, Report 1996. The First Ten Months; 4.97, Kosov@ Political Update; 5.97, Report on the first step of a dialogue project between people from Nis and from Prishtina facilitated by Balkan Peace Team; 9.6.97, Halfyearly Report, January to June 1997; 7.97, Kosov@ current update July 1-15.97; 1.10.97, Student Protest in Prishtina; 12.97, Halfyear Field Report, June-November 1997; 5.98, Daily Reports on the Events in Kosovo from March until May 1998; 12.98, Half Year Report, June - November 1998; BPT-K: 10.99, CC Confidential Report; 12.99, CC Confidential Report – Not for Distribution; 2.3.2000, From the Team; 2.3.2000, The website; 7.3.2000, Draft 6 Month Report; BPT-K 13.3.2000, Team's Suggestions RE: 6 Mo. Report; 3.7.2000, June Confidential Report; 26.9.2000, Periodic Report, 3.99 – 4.2000; 17.11.2000, Report on the work of the BPT-Kosovo/a Team; 3.2001, Dragash/s Team Report to GA, Bonn, 23-25 March 2001; 9.1.01, e-mail team to CC-Plus; 10.1.01. e-mail team member regarding agreement with UNICEF; 11.1.01, e-mail team to CC-Plus; 12.1.01, e-mail team to CC-Plus.

BPT (Team in Kosovo and/or Belgrade:) Biweekly. Monthly Report Kosovo/a, 8.2.95, Report 1995/01, 26.1.-1.2.95; 15.2.95, Report 1995/02, 2.-15.2.95; 1.3.95, 3rd bi weekly report 15.-28.2.95; 24.3.95, 4th Bi Weekly Report, 1.-15.3.95; BG/Kosovo, 11.-18.6.95, weekly update; BG, 2.7.95, 1st biweekly report BG team, 15.6.- 1.7.95; 16.8.95, No. 10, 4.-15.8.95; 6.9.95, No. 11, 15.-31.8.95; Belgrade, 5.3.96, 11.- 25.2.96; 11.3.96, 26.2.-10.3.96; 27.5.96, No. 6, Confidential; 13.8.96, Number 7. and 8; 4.9.96, No. 10, 16.- 31.8.96; 10/2.96, No. 14, 16.-30.10.96.; 11/1.96, No. 15, 1.11.-16.11.96; 11/2.96, No. 16, 16.-30.11.96; 12/1.96, No. 17, 1.-15.12.96; 12/2.96, No. 18, 16.-31.12.96; FRY, 1/1.97, No. 19, 1.-15.1.97; 2/1.97, No. 20a, 15.-.31.1.97; 1/2.97, No. 21a, 1.-15.2.97; 2/2.97, No. 22a, 15. - 28.2.97; 1/3.97, No. 23a, 1.-15.3.97; 2/3.97, No. 24, 15.-31.3.97; 1/4.97, No. 25, April 1.-15.4.97; 2/4.97, No. 26, 15.-30.4.97; 1/5.97, No. 27, 1.-15.5.97, Confidential; 2/5.97, No. 28, 16.-31.5.97; 1/6.97, No. 29, 1.-15.6.97; 2/6.97, No. 30, 15.-30.6.97; 1/7.97, No. 31,1.-12.7.97, Confidential; 2/7.97, No. 32, 14.-31.7.97, Confidential; 2/8.97, No. 34, 15.-30.8.97; 1/9.97, No. 35, 1.-15.9.97; 2/9.97, No. 36, 15.-30.9.97, Confidential; 1/10.97, No. 37, 1.- 15.10.97; 2/10.97, No. 38, 15.- 31.10.97, Confidential; 1/11.97, No. 39, 1.-15.11.97; 2/2.98, No. 46, 15.-28.2.98; 2/9.98, No. 53, 15.-30.9.98; 1/10.98, No. 54, 1.-15.10.98; 2/10.98, No. 55, 16.-31.10.98; Monthly Report, No. 1, 12.98-12.2.99; No. 2, 12.2.-10.3.99; No. 3, 10.-31.3.99; No. 4, 4-5.99; No. 5, 15.6.-15.7.99.

BPT CC. Daniel M., 2.10.95: Vojnic Proposal, 10.1.96, Response to interviews, biweekly, phone call; 3.3.2000, Re: From the Team; Edgar E., 15.11.99, Complete OtOc evaluation; 6.3.2000, Re: From the Team; Mary F., 20.4.99, Subject: some input on current situation + contact details; Sabine M., 1.8.95, War Situation;

1.8.95, Western Slavonia; 26.8.95, Knin office DOS; 18.2.96, Your recommendations/analysis; Martin K. 12.1.01, e-mail to Team, Saturday Meeting; Sebastian K., 4.3.2000, Re: The website.

BPT CC minutes. 1.2.94; 2.-4.5.94; 5.-7.9.94; 14.u.17.10.94; 12.-14.1.95.; 13.-14.3.95; 5.-8.5.95; 16.-18.7.95; Kosovo-Day, 16.7.95; 30.9.-1.10.95; 14.-15.9.96; 1.-2.6.96; 1.-2.3.97; 20.-22.2.98; 13.-14.6.98; 4.-6.9.98; 20.11.98; 22.11.98; 19.-21.2.99; 28.-30.5.99; 10.-12.9.99; 19.11.99; 11.-12.2.2000, 13.2.2000; 2.-5.5.2000; 8.-10.9.2000; 19.11.2000; 9.-11.2.01.

BPT France Newsletter. A bridge over the Ibar, No. 4, 2002.

BPT GA minutes. 2.2.94, 15.-16.10.94; 4.-5.11.95; 14.-16.11.97; 13.-14.6.98; 20.-21.11.98; 20.-21.11.99; 12.2.2000; 18.-19.11.2000; 23.-25.3.01; 12.10.01.

BPT IO. No date 1994; Profit and loss statement 1994; 20.12.94, Letter IO to Austrian trainer; 5.2.95, fax Co-Ordinator to volunteer; 24.2.95, fax IO to the Coordinator for the training programme; 8.9.95, Re: Urgent! Please respond quickly!; 22.9.95, Letter to CC; 14.10.96 IO News 23; 4.9.97, IO News 33; 25.5.99, IO NEWS 35; 20.1.2000, Note to CC and supporters about the successful training and the start of the team; 4.3.2000, Re: From the Team; 13.3.2000, RE: ...letter re 6 month report; 21.3.2000, Comments CC minutes; 12.1.01, e-mail to CC-Plus.

BPT Newsletter. 1.3.94, No. 01; 1.5.94.

BPT volunteers. 13.9.94, Letter of participants in training to the CC; Erna P. 11.10.94 Letter to the CC; Frances E. 30.5.97, Letter to the CC; Field BPT 17.2.97, CC - evaluation "our hearts and minds to you".

Broken Rifle. Special on WRI Seminar, 8.8.-10.8.99: The Changing Face of the Military, International Seminar, Steinkimmen, Germany, compiled by Ellen Elster, March 2000, No. 45.

BSV 8.1.93, Invitation, "Verhinderung... Kriegsausweitung"; Nov. 1993, Circular BPT Co-ordinator regarding alarm network and structure; Tamara P. 2.2.01, e-mail to BPT.

BSV-intern. No. 1, 1991, 4.

Büttner, Christian. 3.11.97, e-mail from Split during research travel.

Bulletin d´information du Mouvement International de la Réconciliation. No. 13, septembre 1992; No. 15, novembre 1992; No. 23, septembre 1993.

Calic, Marie Janine. Kosovo vor der Katastrophe? SWP-aktuell, No. 20, March 1998.

Calic, Marie-Janine. Krieg und Frieden in Bosnien-Herzegowina. Erweiterte Neuausgabe, Frankfurt 1996

Circular BSV. No. 3, 3rd quarter 1993.

Clark Howard. Civil Resistance in Kosovo, Pluto Press 2000.

EPB. 9.4.2000. Minutes Meeting EPB-BPT.

EN.CPS. European Network for Civil Peace Service, Cyprus Project, www.en.cps.org, date 31.12.2003.

Ferizi, Abdullah. Nansen Dialogue Mitrovica, p. 2. in: A bridge over the Ibar, BPT France, Newsletter, No. 3, September 2003.

Der trügerische Frieden. Bericht der Internationalen Balkan-Kommission, Reinbek 1997.

Filip Pavlovic, Franklin de Vrieze. Federal Republic of Yugoslavia, p. 283-289, in: Searching for Peace in Europe and Eurasia, edited by Paul van Tongeren et al., Lynne Rienners Publ. 2002.

Fitz-Report. Assessing Nongovernmental Organisations in Croatia. Needs, Development and Networks of Local NGOs, parts 1-3: Fitz-Report,1997.

Forum Ziviler Friedensdienst. Website: www.friedenbrauchtfachleute.de, date 31.12.03.

Frankfurter Rundschau. "Pazifisten in Sarajewo freundlich empfangen", 15.12.92, article daily.

de Vrieze, Franklin. Kosovo, p. 289-309, in: Searching for Peace in Europe and Eurasia, edited by Paul van Tongeren et al., Lynne Rienners Publ. 2002.

Friedenszeitung. Friedensinstitut Ljubljana: "Konferenz zur albanischen Frage", No. 131-132, 1992, p. 10; November 1994, p. 10.

Giersch, Carsten. Konfliktregulierung in Jugoslawien 1991-1995. Die Rolle von OSZE, EU, UNO und NATO, Baden-Baden 1998.

Hämmerle, Pete. No date 2000, Report on Balkan Peace Team (BPT) 1996-2000 for IFOR-Council 2000 in the Netherlands.

Hren, Marko. "Yugoslavia: after the Party, a climate of fear." WRI XX triennial background paper, reprint from Peace News, April 1991.

Hren, Marko. An essay on borders, p. 1f., in: The broken biscuit 2. Daily bulletin of the XXth WRI Triennial, La Marlagne, 29 July 1991.

Hren, Marko. Yugoslavia: Peace Upheaval, p. 4 in: The broken Biscuit 5. Daily Bulletin of the XXth WRI Triennial, La Marlagne, 1 August 1991.

HRW, Human Rights Watch. World Report 1998.

ICG, International Crisis Group. 17.2.1998, Kosovo Briefing.

International Helsinki Federation for Human Rights. Press release 12.2.98 to Bronislav Geremek, OSCE Chairman-in-Office.

IFOR. 12.7. 93, circular Balkan Peace Team update 1; 7.8.93, letter to Co-ordinator BPT; 9.8. 93, letter to Co-ordinator BPT.

IFOR Steering Committee. Minutes January 1993, September 1993, January 1994.

Informations Charles O., 23.4.98, 7.2003; Oskar K. 8.5.2003; Peter D. 22.4.97; Sabine M. 5.1.03, April 2003; Martin K., 4.2003; Jens K., 19.8.2003.

Interviews with Volunteers. Albert P. 1/1997, 2/1998; Anselm F. 1997; Anton K. 1997; Chris N. 1997; Diana M. 1998; Felix P. 1998; Frauke L. 1997; Frances E. 1998; Hanna L. 1997, Hubert P. 1998; Katrin G. 1/1997, 2/1998; Laura Z. 1998; Mary F. 1997; Rosa T. 1997; Sara F. 1998; Stefan K. 1998; Susanne S. 1/1997, 2/1998; Tobias K. 1/1997, 2/1998; Valeska C., 1/1997, Verena J. 1/1997, 2/1998; 2/1998; Vincent P. 1997; Volker Q. 1997; Xaver A. 1997.

Interviews with member organisations, Co-ordinating Committee, International Office, partners in Germany. Charles O. 1997; Claire P. 1998; Daniel M. 1/1997, 2/1998; Ernst V. 1997; Eugene D. 1998; Friedhelm D. 1/1997, 2/1998; Jacques B. 1998; Jens K. 1998; John M. 1998; Monique Z.1998; Nadine O. 1997; Nicole M. 1997; Paul C. 1998; Sebastian K. 1998; Simone V. 1997.

Interviews with activists, partners in Croatia, Serbia and Kosovo. Andrea Z. 1997; Anna D. 1998; Horst T. 1997; Helena P. 1998; Ivan J. 1997; Raj S. 1997; Ruth S. 1997.

Interview international organisations: Sybille M. 1998; Umberto U.1997.

Junge, Mareike. A Real Nonviolent Alternative in the Resolution of Conflicts, www.en.cps.org, Stand 31.12.03.

Kat, Wam. Information Portfolio for the Slavonian Network of NGO's, compiled by Wam Kat, June 1995: Balkan Peace Team Western Slavonia Office.

Kruhonja, Katarina et al. Croatia, p. 248-264, in: Searching for Peace in Europe and Eurasia, edited by Paul van Tongeren et al., Lynne Rienners Publ. 2002.

Large, Judith. The war next door. A study of second-track intervention during the war in ex-Yugoslavia, Lansdown 1997.

Lederach, John Paul. Der Beitrag Dritter beim Aufbau des Friedens. Eine Perspektive des 'Friedens von unten', p. 45-56 in: Die Wahrheit der Absicht ist die Tat. Friedensfachdienste für den Norden und den Süden. Eds. Josef Freise and Eckehard Fricke, Idstein, 1997.

Loquai, Heinz. Der Kosovo-Konflikt - Wege in einen vermeidbaren Krieg. Die Zeit von Ende November 1997 bis März 1999, Demokratie, Sicherheit, Frieden, ed. Dieter S. Lutz, vol. 129, Nomos Baden-Baden 2000.

MAN 31.1.2000, e-mail Thomas und Nicolas MAN / French CPS.

Mahony, Liam und Luis Enrique Eguren. Unarmed Bodyguards: International Accompaniment for the Protection of Human Rights, West Hartford 1997.

Malmsten Anders Final Report PBI Exploration Team to Croatia January 1993.

Meder, Gerhard and Michael Reimann. Chronik des Bosnien-Konfliktes. Diskussionsbeiträge No. 33/1996 der Projektgruppe Friedensforschung, Universität Konstanz, Juli 1996.

Mindener Tageblatt. 18.9.1991, article daily.

Müller, Barbara. Möglichkeiten der Förderung von Friedensallianzen in Konfliktregionen durch externe Basisorganisationen. Bericht über ein Aktionsforschungsprojekt in Kroatien, IFGK Working paper No. 17, January 2002.

Müller, Barbara. Minutes BPT Debriefing meeting, Oct.12-14-01, page6of7, 2001.

Müller, Barbara. Chancen einer transnationalen Zusammenarbeit? Das Balkan Peace Team und andere Projekte der zivilen Konfliktbearbeitung, p. 39-43 in: Wissenschaft & Frieden, Jg. 43, 4/2000.

Müller, Barbara. Personal records, participation at CC meeting in Split 20.-22.2.98; participation at BPT-NL meeting 30.1.98.

Müller, Barbara, Büttner, Christian. Optimierungschancen von Peacekeeping, Peacemaking und Peacbuilding durch gewaltfreie Interventionen? IFGK Working paper No. 4, October 1996.

Müller, Barbara, Büttner, Christian, Gleichmann, Peter R. Der Beitrag des Balkan Peace Team zur konstruktiven Konfliktbearbeitung in Kroatien und Serbien/ Kosovo. Unpublished project report, February 1999.

Nasa Borba. 15.6.98.

Münchner Friedensrunde. 11.8.93, letter.

Neue Westfälische. 19.2.94, No. 42, article daily.

Nonviolent Peaceforce. E-News June 2003; member organisations; faq; www.nonviolentpeaceforce.org. Stand 31.12.2003.

Nonviolent Peaceforce Feasibility Study. By Donna Howard, Mareike Junge, Corey Levine, Christine Schweitzer, Carl Stieren, Tim Wallis. Co-ordination: Christine Schweitzer, www.nonviolentpeaceforce.org, Hamburg, St. Paul, 2001.

OtOc. no date, summer 94, Handbook for Otvorene Oci volunteers; ca 10.94, "Complicated half month....", 10.94, House Evictions Background; no date, ca 7.98.

OtOc. 29.3.94, Dalmatian Action trial postponed; 31.3.94, Overview of Trial - Dalmatian Action; 5.1994, The Meta-Project; 13.-14.8.94, Minutes summit retreat; 24.8.94, Apartments the floor for human rights Struggle;10.1994, Evaluation of the first six months of the project, Appendix - Local input on Otvorene Oci; 12.94, Appendix to the Field Report December 1994; no date, 4.95, Volunteer Evaluation; ca 2.5.95, Croatian 'Anti-Terrorist-Action' Escalates Conflict. Report mostly for internal use; 7.5.95, Otvorene Oci and the Western Slavonia Conflict. An Internal Report; 8.5.95, Update on Current Work and Situation; 9.5.95, The Situation and Our Work - Update # 4;13.5.95, Report; 25.5.1995, Evictions: Sepic Family finally returns; 27.5.95, Comprehensive Report. Western Slavonia; 6.6.95, The Last Evacuation Convoy to Bosnia?; 15.6.95, A Visit to the Okucani Region; 26.7.95, First eviction based on alleged "enemy activity"; 28.7.95, Update on situation; 4.8.95, War; 11.8.95, Our future; 27.8.95, Re: Knin office DOS; 14.9.95, Minutes of the Rab Summit; 25.9.95, Proposal: Community Center, Vojnic; 11.10.95: Report Vojnic Project; 20.10.95, Update on Kupljensko Camp; 1.11.95: The Reintegration of the Serb-held Areas of Sector West, Six Months After. A Comprehensive Report; 29.12.95, Otoc Summit Dec 95; 11.-13.12.95, Minutes of the Ciovo Summit; 10.4.96, Mins of Rab and personal evaluations; 5.96, Otvorene Oci Bi-Annual Field Report; 18.7.96, Numbers in Western Slavonia; 8.1996, Operation Storm - One Year After. Report; 6.98, Bi-Annual Field Report; 8.98, A Year of Return? An analysis of the current prospects for return in Northern Dalmatia, three years after Operation Storm; 11.12.98, Situational Report; 9.4.98, Draft minutes summit 20.-22.3.98; 11.98, 6 months report.

OtOc Weekly report. 1.-7.3.94, No. 1; 8.-12.3.94, No. 2; 13.-20.3.94, No. 3; 21.- 27.3.94, No. 4; 28.3.-3.4.94, No. 5; 4.-10.4.94, No. 6; 11.-18.4.94, No. 7; 17.- 24.4.94, No. 8.

OtOc Zg. 28.11.94, Registration; 3.8.95, Confidential - Only for immediate CC; 18. 8.95, Follow-Up Report on Krajina Exploration; 22.9.95, A Visit to Kupljensko Refugee Camp; 9.95, Kupljensko refugee camp situational reports (based on HRAT and other UN sources); 7. 9.95, Extremely Important and Urgent Feedback required!; 16.5.96, On the Continuation of Illegal Evictions in the Republic of Croatia; 16.6.98, North Croatia Office Discussion on our role and direction; 8.98, What we do; 8.98, Centre for Peace Studies; 8.98, Antiwar Campaign; 8.98, Zagreb Team.

OtOc Zg Biweekly. 2/8.94; 1/9.94; 2/10.94; 2/11.94; 2/5.95; 1/6.95; 2/6.95, Confidential; 1/7.95; 2/7.95; 1/8.95, Confidential; 2/8.95; 1/9.95; 2/9.95; 1/10.95; 2/10.95; 1/11.95; 2/11.95; 1/1.96; 2.96; 1/3.96; 2/3.96.; 2/5.96; 2/7.96; 2/9.96; 16.-30.9.98.

OtOc Sp. 25.9.94, Some thoughts on registration; 16.8.95, Atmo; 17.8.95, Initial visit to former sector south; 19. 8.95, NGO visit to Knin; 26.8.95 Benk; 14.10.95, Krajina Killings; 8.12.95, Struggling With Attempted Illegal Evictions; 17.12.95, Military Organizes Illegal Eviction Campaign; 19.12.95, Eviction Campaign Continues; 14.6.96, Violic; 14.6.96, The Changing Atmosphere of Dalmatia; 19.7.96, The Trial For the Killing of 18 Serb Civilians; 26.2.97, Legal Eviction Attempt in Split Fails.

OtOc Sp Biweekly. 15.-30.8.94; 1.-15.9.94; 16.-31.10.94; 1.-15.11.94; 1.-15.12.94; 15.12.94 - 15.1.95; 16.-31.5.95, Confidential; 16. -30.6.95, Confidential; 15.- 31.7.95; 1.-15.8.95, Confidential; 15.-31.8.95; 1.-15.9.95; 1.-15.10.95, Confidential; 16. - 31.10.95; 1.-15.11.95, Confidential; 15.-30.11.95, Confidential; 1.- 15.12.95; 2/12.95, Internal; 2.-22.1.96, Confidential; 1.96, Hearts and Minds; 23.5.-7.6.96; 19.8.- 7.9.96; 8. - 22.10.96.; 23.10. - 7.11.96, Confidential; 8.- 22.12.96; 23.12.97-22.1.98; 23.1.-7.2.98; 23.4.- 7.5.98; 8.-22.5.98; 8.- 22.6.98; 8.-22.7.98; 22.8.- 7.9.98.

PBI. 28.11.92. IC281192. Papers for PBI Interim Council; 5.8.93, fax to BPT- Coordinator; 1.9.93, Circular PBI-BPT AHEC to PBI-groups; 20.8.93, International Council Conference Call; 30.10.93, fax to BPT-Co-ordinator; 17.11.93, Intl. Office: Draft Policy on Joint Projects; 19.11.93, IO-Mailing: Update on PBI Involvement in Balkans; 5.12. 94, Balkans Peace Team AHEC: Proposal for official participation of PBI in the Joint Balkans Peace Team Project; 4.-10.1.94, Draft Minutes International Council.

Peace News. 8.1992; 9.94 "An open letter to peace movements"; 7.96, Croatia: Objector beaten into coma by police.

Poort - van Eeden, Janne. Das European Network for Civil Peace Services EN.CPS, www.en.cps.org. date 31.12.03.

Preparation papers WRI Triennial 1991. Introduction to (some of) the Theme Groups.

Press releases of the Federation for Social Defence. Minden 17.7.91, Ljubljana 19.7.91; 21.7.91; 27.9.1991; 6.1993.

Pyronnet, Josef. Mir-Sada Lai paix maintenant, p. 38f. in: M.I.R., Cahiers de la Réconciliation, No. 3, 1993.

Reuters Agency Zagreb. 1.5.95, Croatian Army Attacks Serbs to Unblock Motorway.

Ronnefeldt, Clemens. Die Neue NATO, Irak und Jugoslawien, Internationaler Versöhnungsbund - Deutscher Zweig (Hg.), Knotenpunkt Offsetdruck, Buch/Hunsrück, 2001.

Ropers, Norbert. Die Bearbeitung von Mehrheiten-Minderheiten-Konflikten in der Zivilgesellschaft, p. 83-113 in: Hans-Joachim Heintze (ed.), Moderner Minderheitenschutz: Rechtliche oder politische Absicherung? Bonn 1998.

Ropers, Norbert. Information 24.1.1999.

Rußmann Paul. "Resümee der Tagung Krisenintervention: Blau, oliv oder gewaltfrei", in: Circular BSV, No. 3, 3rd quarter 1992, 3. Jahrgang.

Schmid, Thomas. Ed., Krieg im Kosovo, Rowohlt, Hamburg 1999.

Schmitz, Achim. Gewaltfreie Interventionen im ehemaligen Jugoslawien durch Organisationen der europäischen Friedensbewegung, IFGK, Working paper No. 9, Wahlenau, December 1998.

Schmitz, Hans Peter. Nichtregierungsorganisationen (NRO) und internationale Menschenrechtspolitik, S. 27-67 in: comparativ, H. 4, 1997.

Schweitzer, Christine. "Krieg und Frieden in Jugoslawien", S. 2 in: Circular Bund für Soziale Verteidigung. No. 3, 3rd quarter 1991, 2. Jahrgang. (1991).

Schweitzer, Christine. Mir Sada, S. 3 in: Spinnrad, No. 3, September 1993.

Schweitzer, Christine. Jugoslawien, eine kleine Chronik der Ereignisse, in: Ohne uns 6/95-1/96. (1996).

Schweitzer Christine, Howard Clark. Balkan Peace Team. Eine abschließende interne Bewertung seines Funktionierens und seiner Aktivitäten. Hintergrund- und Diskussionspapier No. 11 des Bund für Soziale Verteidigung, Minden, September 2002.

UN. 4.11.94, Human Rights Situations and Reports of Special Rapporteurs and Representatives. Situation of human rights in the former Yugoslavia. Note by the Secretary-General; 14.3.96, Situation of human rights in the territory of the former Yugoslavia: report of the Special Rapporteur : Bosnia and Herzegovina, Croatia, Yugoslavia, Slovenia, The Former Yugoslav Republic of Macedonia. 14/03/96. E/CN.4/1996/63; 29.1.97, Commission on Human Rights. 53. meeting, Situation of human rights in the territory of the former Yugoslavia. Regular Report by Ms Elisabeth Rehn, Special Rapporteur of the Commission on Human Rights v. 29.1.97 ; 17.10.97, Human Rights Questions: Human Rights Situations and Reports of Special Rapporteurs and Representatives. Situation of human rights in the former Yugoslavia. Note by the Secretary-General.

U.S. Department of State. 31.1.94, Croatia Human Rights Practices 1993; 2.95, Croatia Human Rights Practices, 1994; 3.96, Croatia Human Rights Practices, 1995; 30.1.97, Croatia Country Report on Human Rights Practices for 1996; 30.1.98, Croatia Country Report on Human Rights Practices for 1997.

WRI 23.5.96, Croatian military police beat objector into coma.

WRI Execmins. 029, 7.-9.2.92, 032, 2.- 4.10.92; 033, 15-17. 1.93; 17.-19.12.93; 1.- 2.10.94, 19.-21.5.2000.

WRI Office Report. 1994-1998.

WRI Das Zerbrochene Gewehr. 9.1994, No. 30

ibidem-Verlag
Melchiorstr. 15
D-70439 Stuttgart

info@ibidem-verlag.de

www.ibidem-verlag.de
www.edition-noema.de
www.autorenbetreuung.de

www.ingramcontent.com/pod-product-compliance
Lightning Source LLC
Chambersburg PA
CBHW051805230426
43672CB00012B/2639